Online Roots

*How to Discover Your Family's History
and Heritage with the Power of
the Internet*

Pamela Boyer Porter, CGRS, CGL
Amy Johnson Crow, CG

Amy Johnson Crow, CG
Series Editor

Rutledge Hill Press™
Nashville, Tennessee

A Division of Thomas Nelson, Inc.
www.ThomasNelson.com

For my maternal grandmother, Ollie Kathryn Wilcox Westmoreland, and the babies—they deserve to be remembered

—*Pamela Boyer Porter*

To my paternal grandmother, Adah Young Johnson, who first told me the family stories and to my maternal grandmother, Della Starkey Ramsey, who inspired my first search

—*Amy Johnson Crow*

Published by Rutledge Hill Press, a division of Thomas Nelson, Inc., P.O. Box 141000, Nashville, Tennessee 37214.

The following items mentioned in this book are registered trademarks or service marks: About.com, Ah-ha, Ancestry.com, AniMap Plus, Ask Jeeves, CanadaGenWeb, Certified Genealogical Instructor, Certified Genealogical Lecturer, Certified Genealogical Records Specialist, Certified Genealogist, CG, CGI, CGL, CGRS, Church of Jesus Christ of Latter-day Saints, Classmates.com, Cyndi's List, Dogpile, Family History Center, Family History Library, Family Tree Maker, FamilySearch, Fast, FindWhat, FirstSearch, Genealogy.com, GenWeb, GNIS, HeritageQuest Online, HeritageQuest.com, Immigrant Ships Transcribers Guild (ISTG), Internet Explorer, KBYU's Capturing the Past, Legacy Family Tree, LISTSERV, LookSmart, Lycos, The Master Genealogist, MS Excel, MS Windows, MS Word, National Union Catalog of Manuscript Collections, Netscape Navigator, NUCMC, OCLC, Open Directory, Overture, Periodical Source Index, PERSI, Research Outlines (FamilySearch), Reunion.com, RootsWeb, SearchHippo, Sprinks, The Statue of Liberty–Ellis Island Foundation, USGenWeb, USGS, WorldCat, WorldGenWeb, and Yahoo.

Library of Congress Cataloging-in-Publication Data

Porter, Pamela Boyer, 1954–
   Online roots: how to discover your family's history and heritage with the power of the Internet / Pamela Boyer Porter, Amy Johnson Crow.
      p. cm. — (National Genealogial Society guides)
   ISBN 1-4016-0021-2 (pbk.)
   1. Genealogy—Computer network resources—Handbooks, manuals, etc. 2. Internet—Handbooks, manuals, etc. I. Crow, Amy Johnson, 1966– II. Title. III. Series.
CS14.P66 2003
929' .1'02854678—dc21   2002156153

Printed in the United States of America

04 05 06 07 — 5 4 3 2

Contents

Acknowledgments

MANY FRIENDS, FAMILY MEMBERS, AND COLLEAGUES CONTRIBUTED TO the creation of this book, whether they realized it or not. My husband, Jerry Porter, was always supportive and patient and was willing to help research, edit, proofread, offer ideas, photocopy pages, prepare meals, or clean house—whatever it took. My parents, Charles and Wilma Boyer, always told me I could do whatever I set my mind to. My "genie" colleagues—Paul Milner; Elizabeth Shown Mills, CG, CGL, FASG, FNGS, FUGA; Craig Scott, CGRS; Ann Fleming, CG, CGL; J. Mark Lowe, CG; and others—listened, cooperated, shared information, read the manuscript, or offered advice and encouragement. Ron Taylor, who has shared my passion for history and genealogy for many years, read the draft of the book and asked good, relevant questions. Michael Francis, who taught me about investigation and evidence analysis in another profession, "loaned" me his interesting immigrant families for examples in the book. And of course, a big thank you goes to Nicholas Smith and Andrea Pedolsky of Altair Literary Agency for making it all happen.

—PAMELA BOYER PORTER

There are many people to whom I owe a tremendous debt of gratitude. To my parents Gerald and Claudene Johnson, thank you for your love and for teaching me that a job worth doing is worth doing well. To my colleagues Donn Devine, CG, CGI, and Curt B. Witcher, MLS, FUGA, thank you for the review of my work and for the kind words. To my friends Rhonda R. McClure and Karen S. Smith, thank you for your encouragement and for being there for me. And last, but by no means least, to my family—Terry, Daniel, and Rachel—what can I say? "Thank you" seems inadequate for the encouragement, love, and support that you gave me during this project. None of this would have been possible, nor would it have been worth it, without you.

—AMY JOHNSON CROW

INTRODUCTION

Who Should Read This Book?

IF YOU'RE JUST BEGINNING YOUR FAMILY HISTORY QUEST, WELCOME! This book introduces you to a fascinating hobby that millions of people enjoy throughout their lives. I hope that you find enough here to hook you on Internet genealogical research. If you need more background and instruction about how to research your family history, you should read Barbara Renick's *Genealogy 101: How to Trace Your Family's History and Heritage.*

So you're interested in finding out about your family tree or learning interesting details about your ancestors? *Online Roots* is intended to help you if

- You're new to genealogy, but you're a seasoned computer and Internet user
- You're an experienced genealogist, but you don't know much about genealogical or historical resources on the Web
- You're new to genealogy and to exploring the Internet

To get the most out of the help and suggestions in this guide, you should have a few basic computer skills. You should

- Have access to a computer that can connect to the Internet, either at home or at a local library or school
- Know how to get onto the Internet from your computer

1

🌿 Know how to use a Web browser such as Internet Explorer or Netscape Navigator and how to navigate using the keyboard and a mouse

🌿 Know how to use Windows or your computer's operating system well enough to open, print, and save files

Just what can you expect to find out about your family history online? A good friend who hasn't touched his genealogy for several years recently asked me, "Is it all online now, or do you still have to go to the LDS Family History Centers?" The easy answer to that question is a resounding, "No, it's not all online yet." Every day new digitized versions of original records are placed on Internet sites by the governments of many nations, by commercial companies, and by individuals. But these postings on the Web represent only a fraction of the actual paper documents in existence at archives, historical societies, courthouses, and homes around the world. Yes, you'll still have to make those genealogy field trips to your local Family History Center or library, to dusty courthouse vaults, to sometimes-intimidating university manuscript collections, and to your ancestral homeland.

But so much wonderful information is on the Web today that you'll be continually amazed at what you *can* learn online. A vast array of sources awaits you on the Internet—everything from other people's versions of your family tree to actual digitized land grants from the eighteenth century to descriptions of historical events that affected your ancestors' lives. The thing that excites me most about the Internet is that I can find answers to so many questions—or at least a place to look for the answer. If my research reveals a new ancestor who was involved in the U.S. war with Mexico in 1846, I can quickly find a number of Web sites that provide historical background or listings of soldiers in that war and suggestions for further reading. If I need a costume for reenacting a past event, I can find patterns and pictures on the Web or businesses that sell ready-made historical clothing. I have a high-speed Internet connection and cannot imagine being without it. I've found e-mail addresses for old friends I haven't heard from in years; read the text of an 1836 Power of Attorney written by my fourth great-grandfather in Christian County, Kentucky, and recorded in Cumberland County, Virginia; and located a photograph of my third great-grandfather's first cousin at a Civil War reunion—all in just a few minutes on the Internet. (By the way, although this book is written by two authors, the word *I* has been used for simplicity. The personal examples in this book have been drawn from the experiences of both authors.) You may be surprised to learn that there is probably even a picture of your house on the Web (you'll have to read the rest of the book to find out where).

Another great value of the Web is that you can locate books or original sources in library and archival collections all over the country. Sitting at your own computer in your comfy clothes, you can search indexes online to locate diaries, artifacts, maps, and other materials for an area or family you are researching. Once you know where the items are, you can visit the collection or facility housing them or arrange for someone to extract or copy the information for you. Even though many documents may never be digitized and placed on the Web, indexes to manuscript collections or original materials make it easier than ever for researchers to locate relevant materials.

Some people have asked, "Have the Mormons put their records on the Internet yet?" The Church of Jesus Christ of Latter-day Saints, also known as LDS or Mormons, maintains the Family History Library in Salt Lake City, Utah, the largest genealogical collection in the world. LDS volunteers work around the world microfilming local records and religious records of all kinds—from county land deeds to parish registers to Catholic Church records. These microfilmed records are available at the Family History Library in Salt Lake City, at your local Family History Center, and at select public libraries. The filmed records are not available online, but the LDS FamilySearch Web site does offer access to the Family History Library Catalog. From your own home, you can search the catalog to see whether the records for your research locale or topic are available and print out a list of the microfilms you need. Then just take the list to your local Family History Center to order the microfilms.

You won't be able to construct your entire family history on the Web. You'll need to supplement the wonderful Internet clues and digitized documents with other facts gleaned from research in libraries, archives, and courthouses. Think of yourself as a modern-day Sherlock Holmes investigating very old, cold cases. You'll use a combination of modern computer-age techniques and good old-fashioned gumshoe footwork to find out all you can about your ancestors. And don't forget—a trip to an old rural cemetery with its poison ivy and crawly-critters often results in a serious bite by the genealogy bug!

This book will help you use the vast resources of the Internet for your personal ancestral quest—to locate distant cousins who are researching your family lines, to find a library with just the reference book you need, to look at a digitized copy of a centuries-old land record that your ancestor signed, or to discover the next step in breaking through a proverbial brick wall. If you're new to genealogy, I'll try to steer you in the direction of conducting good, sound research. If you're an avid genealogist who's new to computers, I'll guide your online experience. The chapters progress logically through the genealogical research process. If you're an experienced genealogist, just find the chapter that describes the kind of record you want to look for online.

This guide is not intended to provide a laundry list of all genealogical sites on the Web. That would not be possible in one volume, and some of the links would be out of date before this book even reached the shelf. However, I will tell you about a great number of wonderful sites. Even better, I'll show you how to search effectively for Web sites, for original records, and for other resources that will help you find the clues you need to track down your elusive ancestors. As a Chinese philosopher said, "Give a man a fish and you feed him for a day. Teach him how to fish and you feed him for a lifetime." This guide should provide you with instruction enough to feed what may become a lifelong pursuit of your ancestors.

CHAPTER 1

Getting Your Feet Wet

WHAT DO YOU WANT TO KNOW ABOUT YOUR ANCESTORS? PERHAPS YOU wonder who you look like or why your family is the way it is. Every family has a unique personality. Some are outgoing and friendly, hugging one another every time they meet. Others are reserved and undemonstrative, though nonetheless loving. Some families have secrets they just don't discuss. As individuals, we don't exist in a vacuum—we are very much a product of the immediate family we grew up in and of a larger extended family.

Genealogy is about discovering the individuals and the family groups who all contributed to making you who you are. Building your family history is a lifelong pursuit for most people, but don't let that discourage you if you're a beginner. The thrill of discovery and the fun of sharing what you learn will only feed your hunger to learn more about your ancestors.

Finding Your Way in the Big Wide World

How do you find your ancestors and their real stories on the World Wide Web? This chapter will help you get off on the right foot with genealogy and the Internet. Think of the genealogical research process in terms of building a family home. A good house has a solid foundation that supports the upper floors, just as a real genealogy is built on solid facts that support your conclusions. You must have quality building materials and know how to use the proper tools for constructing a house, just as using reliable records and knowing where to find them is crucial for building your family history. But just having all those resources doesn't guarantee that you can build that house. You need a plan, a blueprint, a definitive idea of how big you want your house to be or how much you can afford to invest in it, whether money or time. And to make the house a real home, you need a family inside the building—not just skeletons or silent names and dates, but real people with exciting stories about their lives, their trials and tribulations, and their triumphs of the spirit.

You Gotta Have a Plan

Experienced homebuilders figure out how much lumber, paint, wallboard, and other materials they need before beginning a project, and they arrange for delivery of various materials as they need them. Similarly, smart genealogists plan their research and search for a few facts at a time online, analyzing and organizing what they learn before downloading more. Going online and gathering all your family history building materials at one time can overwhelm and confuse you. It is better to look at your blueprint and figure out what materials you need for the first phase of your research project, obtain that information, and then analyze and organize it in your genealogy database program or in paper files before going online to download more materials. Otherwise, your project and your workspace will become so cluttered with random facts that you can't see how any of them fit together to form a pattern and provide answers.

Because planning is so important to the success of your research on the Internet, I'm going to start with a simple plan that you can follow in all your explorations. Good genealogical research, traditional and Web-based, begins with the known and works backward to the unknown. That's why you need to start with yourself and work backward, gathering all the information you can about each generation, gradually moving to earlier generations.

In this chapter, you'll learn how to follow a plan for finding online information about a specific person and family, moving logically from one step to the next. If you follow such a design from day one of your Internet search, you'll never become overwhelmed or confused and tempted to give up the hunt.

You Need Good Tools

Besides having a blueprint for your explorations on the World Wide Web, you need specific tools for building your family history—censuses, land records, immigration and naturalization files, vital records, and many more—and you'll need to develop some skill in using them. Later chapters of this book focus on the specific tools you'll need and how to use them effectively. If you already know how to build a good foundation and draw your own blueprint or plan, forge ahead to the tools chapters. If you've already ventured out onto the Internet and quickly became mired in swampland, continue working through this chapter to learn how to mark your trail and move through the process of building your family history.

Planning Your Research

You may want to learn all you can about your mother's grandparents or whether a great-uncle really filed a patent for an invention he allegedly sold to the railroad. Many families have stories handed down about a Native American great-great-grandmother, and your major focus may be to find out about her. Whatever your purpose in tracing your family tree, it's a good idea to start by writing down your overall general goals. Then spend some time thinking about the individual sources of information that might be combined to accomplish your objectives.

For example, to learn about that great-uncle's invention, you may want to search the U.S. Patent Office's online database to see if you can find information about it or even a drawing of the device. But first, you have to know his name. To narrow your search sufficiently, you probably need some more identifying information, such as the area where he lived when he filed for the patent and an approximate time frame. To find your Native American great-great-grandmother, you first have to establish your relationship to her by working backward systematically from yourself to your parent, grandparent, great-grandparent and then to the Native American ancestor. You also need to know her tribal affiliation so you can search the appropriate records. Was she Cherokee or Choctaw, Pueblo or Potawatomi? You may want to search the Internet for historical background about the Indian nations that resided in the area where your ancestor lived to help you understand the context of her life or to help determine her tribal affiliation.

Are you beginning to get the picture? Internet research is not as simple as finding *the* database that contains all your ancestors and downloading it tonight. It's much more exciting than that! Planning your family history work actually opens your eyes to the circumstances of your ancestors' lives and forces you to think about actions they may have taken and records that may have resulted. The Web is jam-packed with tools you can use to find facts and dates and then to go beyond those and explore as much as you choose of the time periods of your ancestors' lives.

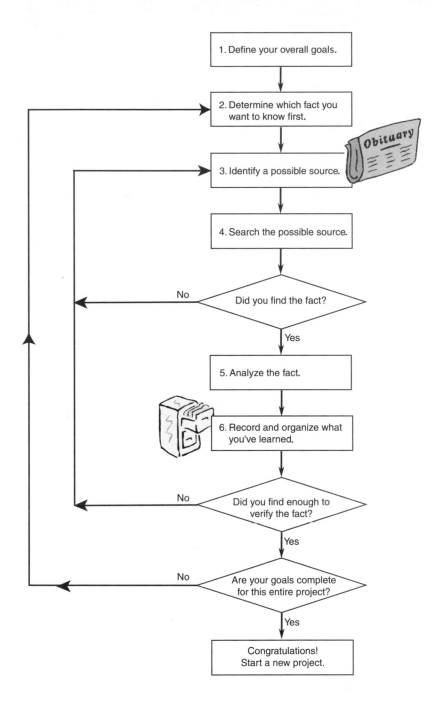

Figure 1.1 Research strategy steps and decisions

The research strategy steps and decisions involved in genealogical research are illustrated in Figure 1.1. Following these steps will help you make the most of your research, so let's explore them in detail.

Step 1: Define Your Overall Goals

Take some time to decide what you want to know first about your family's history, and then write it down. Okay, you want to know all your ancestors back to Moses, and you want them all printed out in a full-color wall chart tomorrow. Be a little more specific here—choose either your mother's or your father's side of the family and write down some of the things you want to know about them.

Step 2: Determine Which Fact You Want to Know First

What one fact do you want to know first, and where will that fact lead you? Start with a simple fact or single piece of information that may be easy to find on the Internet. Each fact is a mini-goal that leads to accomplishing your overall plan.

Step 3: Identify a Possible Source of the Information

Once you decide on your first mini-goal, you need to figure out where the information might be found. Just as practice with plastering and painting provides more attractive results on a house, so research on the Internet becomes easier and more useful as you learn the ropes through practice. Use logic in this step. If you want to locate a birth date, for example, think of the traditional documents that might provide it—

Search engines allow you to perform keyword searches. Most Internet users are familiar with search engines such as Yahoo, Dogpile, Google, and Alta Vista. Users enter a word or phrase, and the search engine scours the Internet to find documents, URLs, or text that contain those keywords. Users then click on any link in the list of results to view the source. For more details about search engines, see Chapter 3, "Wading in Deeper."

Genealogy springboards provide links to online genealogy sources. They are found on a number of Web sites. One of the most comprehensive and well-known genealogy springboards is Cyndi's List of Genealogy Sites on the Internet, with over 175,000 links to everything from Acadian to Writing Your Family's History. Chapter 3 covers several springboards in detail.

a birth certificate, Social Security card application, tombstone inscription, family Bible record, or a school record. Now, where might some form of these records be located online? Use search engines or genealogy springboards to help you find online indexes to records or digitized versions of the documents themselves.

Step 4: Search the Possible Source

Look at the Internet resource you've identified for the name or date you want. For instance, can you find a birth date in the Social Security Death Index or in a genealogical society's local cemetery transcription project that's posted on its Web site? Be sure to read the search instructions for Internet resources that you use; even general search engines work differently. Some are case sensitive, requiring you to enter a name with capital letters. A search field on one site may require that you enter a last name followed by a comma, and then the first name. If you enter a first name followed by a space and then the last name, you may retrieve no matching records, even if there really is a record for your ancestor. So read the instructions and try the same search several different ways. Throughout this book, I suggest search techniques that may work in one or more search engines.

Decision: Did You Find the Fact(s) You Wanted?

If you did find the fact(s), move on to the next step. If you did not, return to Step 3 and try to identify another possible source for the information, performing another search on the Internet in Step 4.

Step 5: Analyze the Fact(s)

Analyzing what you find on the Internet is as important as searching for more information. "Some is good; more is better" doesn't always hold true with genealogy. Good researchers learn to spend more time evaluating the information they find and recording their conclusions than doing the actual research. Analysis involves reading an item very carefully and absorbing all the information it provides, considering other possible sources that may be identified or implied, and formulating the next phase of the research plan.

Step 6: Record and Organize What You've Learned

Organizing your family history is another critical step in the process. It's easy to accumulate a one-inch stack of printed papers in a couple of hours on the Internet. If you—as many genealogists do—place this on the corner of a desk or table, you'll soon find yourself inundated by paper. Like coat hangers in a closet, paper seems to multiply until it fills your entire desk or workspace. And the clutter isn't the only problem. Eventually, you'll visit a Web site looking for a fact and it will seem vaguely familiar. Have you already seen this tidbit on this particular Web site, or did you find it somewhere else? Good genealogists keep a research log to record sources they have checked and the results of their searches; this is essential for Internet research (see Figure 1.2). It's easy to create a simple spreadsheet or word-processing document where you can keep a list of Internet sites you've checked, the date you visited them, and what you learned. It's important that you also note these sources even if you did not find anything about your ancestor. This keeps you from wasting time by checking the same source again in the future. If you take the time to organize your papers and findings as you work, you'll be a far more efficient researcher in the long run.

In addition to keeping a research log, you should record your overall findings and conclusions. Many genealogists enter facts and sources in a genealogy database program, such as Legacy Family Tree, Family Tree Maker, or The Master Genealogist, that provides easy access, search capabilities, and printed reports. Others use a word

Internet Research Log

Ancestor's Name: William TWIDWELL, 1823-1909   **Locale:** Wayne County, Missouri

Source	URL	Date of Search	Results
USGenWeb Missouri Civil War Veterans County Listing	http://www.rootsweb.com/~mocivwar/countyW.html#Wayne	2-13-2002	William TWIDWELL is listed as being in Co. K, 68th Enrolled Missouri Militia. See notes and printout in William TWIDWELL file.
Fort Davidson State Historic Site (Missouri Parks)	http://www.mostateparks.com/ftdavidson/militia.htm	2-13-2002	Article by Jack F. Mays about the service of the 68th Enrolled Missouri Militia in the Civil War, including Company K, of which William TWIDWELL was a member. See notes and copy of article in Military—Civil War (Missouri) file.
Sedricks' Genealogy Research Center—George W. Twidwell Cemetery Transcription	http://www.sedricks.com/wayne/twidwell_cem.htm	5-19-2002	Two William TWIDWELLs buried here, but both are too young to be the William I am looking for. See notes in TWIDWELL family file.
Ancestry's Compiled Military Service Records (Civil War)	http://www.ancestry.com/search/rectype/inddbs/4284.htm	5-20-2002	No records found for William TWIDWELL
Johnson County, Tennessee, Genealogy Page—Johnson County, Tennessee, 1850 Agricultural Schedule, 3rd District, Shouns Cross Roads (later Forge Creek) Transcription	http://jctcuzins.com/census/1850agr3.html	6-15-2002	Transcription provides agricultural census schedule information for William TWIDWELL in Johnson County, Tennessee, for year ending June 1, 1850, enumerated on 3 September 1850. See notes and printout in William TWIDWELL family file. Note: Levi HEATH, William TWIDWELL's father-in-law is listed on the same page. See notes and printout in Levi HEATH family file.

Figure 1.2 Internet research log

processor or spreadsheet to write up their facts and conclusions in a freeform report. The tried-and-true method of manually filling out family group sheets and ancestor charts still works, too. Whatever method you use, Step 6, recording and organizing your information, involves writing down your research findings and conclusions, then saving copies of printouts in categorized files where you'll be able to find them in the future. For more information about organizing your research, refer to Chapter 6, "Document the Drama," in Barbara Renick's *Genealogy 101*.

Free Genealogy Forms on the Web

You can download free genealogy forms, such as family group sheets, ancestor charts (also called pedigree charts), census extraction forms, and correspondence logs from the Internet for your personal use. Forms may be formatted as word-processing documents, spreadsheet files, Adobe Acrobat Portable Document Format (.pdf), or other files, depending on where you download them. Here are a few Web sites that offer free and easy genealogy form downloads. To find more forms with a search engine, try using a phrase like *genealogy forms* or something more specific, such as *genealogy forms Canada*.

- Easy Genealogy Forms *(www.io.com/~jhaller/forms/forms.html)*
- Ancestor Charts and Records *(broadcasting.byu.edu/ancestors/charts/)*
- Ancestry.com various forms *(www.ancestry.com/save/charts/census.htm)*
- *Family Tree Magazine* forms *(www.familytreemagazine.com/forms/download.html)*
- Everton Publishers Free Charts *(www.everton.com/learn/showcontent.php?id=1385)*
- Census Tools Spreadsheets *(censustools.com/)*
- FamilySearch Online Research Helps *(www.familysearch.org):* Click the Search tab, click the Research Helps link, and then click the letter of the area for which you want help. For example, to find the downloadable 1851 Canadian census form, click C, scroll down to the Canada Research Helps, and click the PDF link for the 1851 Canada Census Worksheet.
- Genealogy.com Multi-Language Inquiry Form Letters *(www.genealogy.com/00000023.html)*
- Genealogy Forum's Printable Genealogy Forms *(www.genealogyforum.rootsweb.com/gfaol/beginners/forms.htm)*
- MALKA Jewish Genealogy Research Planner *(www.orthohelp.com/geneal/planner.htm)*
- MALKA Genealogy Research Log *(www.orthohelp.com/geneal/log.htm)*

Sometimes you don't find what you're looking for, but you do find other potentially useful facts. This often happens as I research the Missouri county where five generations of my mother's, my father's, and my adoptive father's families lived. I may be searching on the Web for land records of my mother's family when I run across some early abstracts of land purchases made by my father's ancestors. Of course, I record these purchases and the site where I found them so I can research this further at another time, but I stay focused on my original search goal.

Decision: Did You Find Enough Information to Verify the Fact(s)?

If your Internet search turns up adequate information for your purposes, you're ready to continue with your research project by going back to Step 2 and determining the next fact(s) you want to know. But if you are not satisfied with the results you found, or if you want more verification, you may need to return to Step 3 to identify another possible source of the information.

As you can see, the research process is really a giant loop or circle. You continue through the steps until you've found all the information you need for an individual or a specific branch of your family. Then you begin the process all over with a different line of ancestors.

A Sample Research Project

I recently offered to help my friend Mike learn a little more about his interesting pioneer New Mexico family. The simple steps in this research project demonstrate the kind of genealogical information that is available about this family on the Internet. Chances are good that at least some of the same kinds of sources are available for *your* family, too.

Step 1: Define Your Overall Goals

Good genealogists work from the known to the unknown, beginning with what they know about themselves, their parents, and their grandparents and filling in missing pieces along the way. One possible starting point for your "genie" journey is to search for relatively recent information on the Internet. Since Mike's grandmother, Naphie Francis-Baca, passed away within the past few years, I hope to learn something about her on the Internet—perhaps her age when she died, her ethnic background, and whether family members survived her. Probably no one item on the Web will provide all this information, so I need to break this research project into a multistep plan for

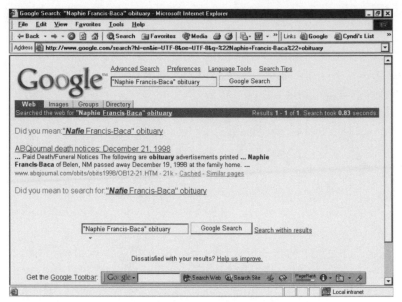

Figure 1.3 Google search for Naphie Francis-Baca obituary

learning about Mrs. Francis-Baca. I'll complete one step and see what can be learned, then go on to the next step for more information.

Step 2: Determine Which Fact You Want to Know First

Although I want to know as much as possible about Mrs. Francis-Baca and her background, I'll start simply with finding where and when she died.

Step 3: Identify a Possible Source of the Information

Several possibilities come quickly to mind as a source of death date and place, including a death certificate, the Social Security Death Index, or an obituary, some of the last records created about a person. An obituary might reveal what I call "Genesis" information—birth date, death date, parents' or siblings' names, begats—just like the book of Genesis in the Bible.

Step 4: Search the Possible Source

I decide to search first for an obituary using Google, a powerful Internet search engine. I enter the query phrase *"Naphie Francis-Baca" obituary*, and Google finds one result: "ABQjournal death notices December 21, 1998" with the phrase "Naphie

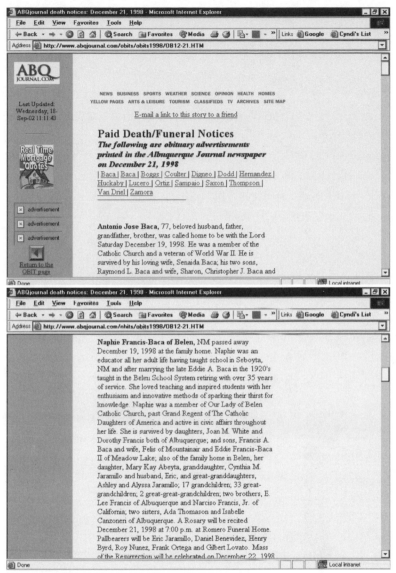

Figure 1.4 Francis-Baca online obituary in the *Albuquerque Journal*

Francis-Baca of Belen" (see Figure 1.3). Clicking on the underlined link calls up an online version of obituary advertisements printed in the *Albuquerque Journal* newspaper, including one for a Naphie Francis-Baca of Belen, New Mexico, who passed away December 19, 1998. A quick read confirms that this is the obituary of my friend's grandmother (see Figure 1.4).

Decision: Did You Find the Fact(s) You Wanted?

The online obituary does provide information about where and when my subject died, so I'm ready to continue to the next step.

Step 5: Analyze the Facts

What can be learned from the obituary of Mrs. Francis-Baca? This short online item is chock-full of important facts—her death date and place, and details about her career, marriage, religion, burial, and surviving family. I use a simple table (see Figure 1.5) to record all the facts and conclusions that can be determined from this one record, milking it for all it's worth. This forces me to read very carefully and analyze what each statement establishes or implies.

Step 6: Record and Organize What You've Learned

While researching the Web for facts about the Francis family, I keep an Internet research log of all the searches and results, whether I discover important facts or nothing at all. The log includes an entry for the search for Mrs. Francis-Baca's obituary. Next, I print a copy of the obituary and include a citation for the *Albuquerque Journal* Web site where I located it. But Mrs. Francis-Baca's is the second obituary in a series of fifteen on the Web page, and it seems wasteful to print all eight pages of the obituaries for that day just for a copy of hers. I use a trick that may help you: To print only a portion of any Web page, select the text you want by clicking and holding down the left mouse button while dragging the mouse over the text to select it. Then click File and click Print from the browser menu. In the Print Range area, choose Selection and click OK to print only the text and graphics you have selected. Besides limiting your printout to the text that you want, the hard copy lists the source at the top of the page and the URL at the bottom; you'll have your source citation printed right on the page (see Figure 1.6).

I find it easiest to organize research results by using a genealogy program to record the facts and sources. The program keeps track of relationships, makes it easy to search for a specific person or piece of information, and

A **URL,** or **Uniform Resource Locator,** specifies the location of a Web site. Just think of it as the address of a Web site.

Fact	Conclusions or Implications
Her name was Naphie Francis-Baca.	Francis may have been her maiden name and Baca her married name.
She died December 19, 1998. She lived in Belen, New Mexico, at the time of her death, and passed away "at the family home."	Armed with these facts, a copy of her death certificate should be available to family members from the New Mexico Vital Records office. There may be records in Belen, Valencia County, New Mexico, with more information about her.
She was "an educator all her adult life having taught school in Seboyta [sic], NM and after marrying . . . taught in the Belen School System retiring with over 35 years of service."	Perhaps there are New Mexico school board records or retirement records for Mrs. Francis-Baca.
She taught in Seboyeta before her marriage.	This is implied by the statement, "having taught school in Seboyta [sic], NM and after marrying the late Eddie A. Baca in the 1920's taught in the Belen School System . . ." Seboyeta may be her childhood residence. It provides a place to start the search for her parents and siblings, and a place to look for her marriage record (since many couples are married in the bride's hometown).
She married the late Eddie A. Baca in the 1920s.	Baca was her married name. Although her age or birth date are not provided, she was probably in her eighties or nineties when she died, based on the fact that she married in the 1920s. Her husband died before she did (he is referred to as the *late* Eddie A. Baca). There may be a marriage record in the 1920s in the area of Seboyeta, where she taught, or Belen, where she lived and taught after her marriage.

Figure 1.5 Analysis table *(continued on next page)*

Fact	Conclusions or Implications
Mrs. Francis-Baca was Catholic, and she was a member of Our Lady of Belen Catholic Church.	This opens up a whole realm of possible church records to search: baptismal, confirmation, marriage, and burial records for Mrs. Francis-Baca and her husband, their children, her parents and siblings, and her husband's family, assuming that he was Catholic, too. Their marriage record should confirm or disprove that assumption.
She was survived by three daughters and two sons, seventeen grandchildren, thirty-three great-grandchildren, and two great-great-grandchildren. Her surviving children's names and cities of residence are listed in the 1998 obituary.	It may be assumed that she had only five children, since none are mentioned as having predeceased her. If I want to contact any of Mrs. Francis-Baca's children for more information, their addresses and telephone numbers can probably be located by using an Internet telephone directory. (See Chapter 4, "Finding People in the Modern Era," for more information.)
She was survived by two brothers, E. Lee Francis of Albuquerque, and Narciso Francis Jr. of California; and two sisters, Ada Thomason and Isabelle Canzoneri of Albuquerque.	Her maiden name evidently was Francis, since that is the surname of her two surviving brothers. Given the assumption that Mrs. Francis-Baca was in her eighties or nineties, her surviving brothers and sisters were probably of comparable ages in 1998 when she died. It might be helpful to search for their names on the Web. Since one brother's name was Narciso Francis Jr., it can be assumed that their father's name was Narciso Francis Sr.
She was buried at the Catholic Cemetery, and Romero Funeral Home, 609 N. Main St., Belen, N. M., was in charge of arrangements.	I may be able to contact the funeral home via e-mail to see if they can provide additional information about Mrs. Francis-Baca. An Internet search should reveal whether any records from Belen's Catholic Cemetery are posted online.

Figure 1.5 Analysis table *(continued)*

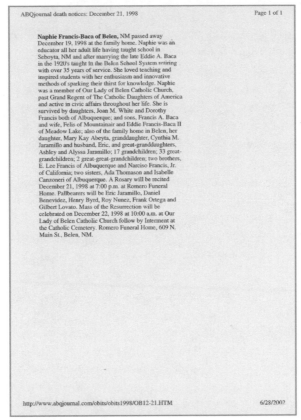

Figure 1.6 Printout of online obituary

provides a variety of printed reports, such as family group sheets, ancestor charts (sometimes called pedigree charts), and ancestor or descendant reports. For this project, I enter every bit of information gleaned from Mrs. Francis-Baca's obituary into my genealogy program, citing the obituary as the source of each fact.

For most projects, I go one step further in the recording and organizing stage and write a research report, adding to it as new information is located. This report contains a written analysis of the project goals and an overview of the findings and conclusions. It provides results of all Internet and traditional research on the project, both positive and negative, and includes copies of any relevant printouts. Finally, it defines suggestions for further research on the family history project. This may sound like a lot of work, but it actually saves time in the long run. If you have set aside a project for several months, reading the research report brings you up to

Genealogy Programs

A frequently asked question among new genealogists is, "Which genealogy program should I use?" The answer is complicated because the question is somewhat like asking, "What kind of car should I buy?" I like my small SUV for visiting rural cemeteries and hauling files and genealogy paraphernalia, but my husband prefers his sporty sedan for speed and comfort. Similarly, genealogists have differing needs in a database program. My advice is, "Try before you buy." Trial versions are available for many of the major genealogy databases, and quite a few are free or inexpensive. These may suit your needs fine if you're just starting to store your family facts in a program. Other programs offer features such as the ability to include photographs or scanned images, complex source-citation templates, customization of data-entry screens, and user-defined searches or reports.

You needn't make a lifetime commitment to your first genealogy program, and your data entry won't be wasted effort if you use a GEDCOM-compatible program. GEDCOM stands for GEnealogical Data COMmunication, which simply means that users of one program can transfer their data to another genealogy program if both are GEDCOM-compatible. There may be problems with the data transfer between programs, but at least you should not have to reenter the three thousand individuals' names and vital statistics.

You can find quite a few genealogy programs in your local software or discount store, but you may want to download some free or trial versions from the Web first. A search for *"genealogy software"* in a major search engine turns up more than sixteen thousand results, enough to keep you occupied for a while. Here are some helpful sites:

- Cyndi's List—Software & Computers *(www.cyndislist.com/software.htm).* This is the most comprehensive list of links to all kinds of information about genealogy software and computers.
- Genealogical Software Report Card *(www.mumford.ca/reportcard/)*
- Ancestral Quest *(www.ancquest.com/)*
- Brother's Keeper *(ourworld.compuserve.com/homepages/Brothers_Keeper/)*
- DoroTree: The Jewish Genealogy Software *(www.jewishstore.com/Software/Ilanot.htm)*
- Family Origins *(www.formalsoft.com/)*
- Family Tree Maker *(familytreemaker.genealogy.com/)*
- Legacy Family Tree *(www.legacyfamilytree.com/)*
- The Master Genealogist *(www.whollygenes.com/tmg.htm)*
- Personal Ancestral File *(www.familysearch.org).* At the FamilySearch.org Home Page, click on the Order/Download Products link, click on the Software Downloads—Free link, and then click on the version you want to download.
- Reunion (for Macintosh) *(www.leisterpro.com/)*

speed on exactly where you are in the process, enabling you to easily pick up your research again.

For the sample research task, I write up my initial findings and recommendations for further research in a simple report for my friend Mike, placing the report and a copy of Mrs. Francis-Baca's online obituary in a file folder. Now I'm ready to move on to the next step.

Easy Source Citations

Good source citations should enable anyone looking at your work in the future to find the same facts and sources. I keep a supply of minisheet 1 x 4-inch printer labels and Elizabeth Shown Mills's book, *Evidence! Citation & Analysis for the Family Historian* (Baltimore: Genealogical Publishing Co., 1997), close at hand. Then, when I print something from a Web site, it's easy to pop up my word processor, refer to *Evidence!* for the proper citation format, and create a label with a full citation. Printing the label and immediately placing it on the face of the document ensures that anyone looking at it knows where the information was obtained. Always place the citation on the face of a document so that subsequent photocopies also contain the source.

To summarize Step 6, record and organize what you've learned (see Figure 1.7). It's simply a matter of keeping a research log as you search the Web, printing copies of the information you want to keep, entering the information in a genealogy program or on paper forms, and writing a research report to keep track of your findings.

Decision: Did You Find Enough Information to Verify the Fact(s)?

The initial goal was to determine where and when Naphie Francis-Baca died, and her obituary is a reliable Internet source for that information. A wise genealogist would also order a copy of a death certificate from the State of New Mexico or try to obtain funeral home or cemetery records since they might contain more information about the subject's family. You'll learn more about these sources in Chapter 6, "Acquiring Vital Records."

I have verified the first fact in the research project, but there's more work ahead. I'm ready to find out more about the Francis family, so I return to the top of the

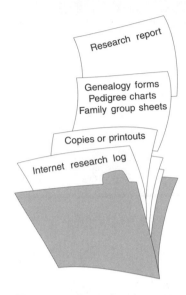

Figure 1.7 Record and organize what you find (or don't find)

Research Strategy diagram and start again with Step 2. As you continue through this book, you'll find more project examples to help you understand how to apply these techniques to your own Internet research.

You've made it through the "bare bones" chapter on planning and starting your family-history-building project. If you continue to practice what you've learned here, you'll be well on your way to constructing an accurate, lasting genealogy. In the following chapters, you'll learn more about the abundance of tools and resources just waiting for you on the Internet and how you can use them to find your ancestors and their families.

CHAPTER 2

Doing the Right Thing

THE INTERNET IS LIKE A HUGE LIBRARY. JUST AS A LIBRARY IS FILLED with books containing text and images, catalogs to help you find things, and people talking to each other, the Internet has Web sites filled with text and images, catalogs and search engines to help you find things, and people talking to each other. The Internet offers many opportunities to make your research exciting and fruitful, but these opportunities come with a challenge: how to differentiate the good from the bad sources.

Same Message, Different Medium

Few of us believe that if something is in print, it must be true. Reading the tabloid headlines of three-headed alien babies, Elvis sightings, and get-rich-quick-while-losing-150-pounds-in-a-month schemes has taught us to question the accuracy of what appears in published sources.

Unfortunately, the critical analysis that we bring to the printed word often does not carry over into the virtual world. Many people who routinely question things in newspapers fall into the trap of believing, "If it is on the Internet, it must be true."

Genealogy is the study of something very personal—your family and, by extension, you. You want to make certain that those people you're adding to your family tree really belong there. To help you in that goal, the National Genealogical Society has published a series of genealogical standards to keep in mind while doing your research.

The last point of the NGS "Standards for Use of Technology in Genealogical **23**

> Technology has not changed the principles of genealogical research, only some of the procedures.

Research" is perhaps the most important—that genealogists "accept that technology has not changed the principles of genealogical research, only some of the procedures." When looking at any source on the Internet—whether it is a Web site, a database, a message board, or a family data file—you have to evaluate it in the same way you would a printed source.

Sources

Whether researching online or off, you should evaluate both the data (information) and where it came from (the source). A source is the place you obtain information about your ancestor—whether it is a person, a book, a Web site, a death certificate, or a note scribbled on a napkin at the family reunion. A source can be described in two ways:

- **Original:** The first or earliest source that presents particular items of information is the original source. When information is captured in some physical form, such as a document, audiotape, picture, or disk, the source is called a record, and the first one made is an original record—even though the information really came from another, more fleeting, source, such as someone's memory or spoken account. Marriage records at the county courthouse and baptism records at the church are examples of original records.

- **Derivative:** Any source that is not original is derivative, one in which the information was derived—copied, compiled, abstracted, transcribed—from another source. Examples include a published book of marriage records, a database of death records, and a transcript of an obituary. A facsimile, photocopy, or scanned image is a derivative record but can serve in place of an original if you're reasonably sure it reflects the original, even when you know how easy it is to alter scanned images.

Whenever possible, it is best to view the original source. The reason for this is obvious if you think back to the children's game Telephone. I remember playing it once with a group of about thirty children. One of the parents started the message, "My

Additional Resources for Evaluation and Source Citations

Barbara Renick's book in the NGS Guides series, *Genealogy 101* (Nashville: Rutledge Hill Press, 2003), takes you step by step through collecting information, evaluating it, and how (or if) to place it in your research.

Elizabeth Shown Mills's book *Evidence! Citation and Analysis for the Family Historian* (Baltimore: Genealogical Publishing Co., 1997), covers evidence analysis and provides the format to use for numerous types of sources.

The National Genealogical Society has published several genealogical standards, including the following guidelines for genealogical research. Other standards appear later in this chapter, in Chapter 16, and in the Appendix; you can also find them at *www.ngsgenealogy.org/comstandards.htm*.

Standards for Use of Technology in Genealogical Research
Recommended by the National Genealogical Society

Mindful that computers are tools, genealogists take full responsibility for their work, and therefore they

- Learn the capabilities and limits of their equipment and software, and use them only when they are the most appropriate tools for a purpose

- Do not accept uncritically the ability of software to format, number, import, modify, check, chart or report their data, and therefore carefully evaluate any resulting product

- Treat compiled information from online sources or digital databases in the same way as other published sources—useful primarily as a guide to locating original records, but not as evidence for a conclusion or assertion

- Accept digital images or enhancements of an original record as a satisfactory substitute for the original only when there is reasonable assurance that the image accurately reproduces the unaltered original

- Cite sources for data obtained online or from digital media with the same care that is appropriate for sources on paper and other traditional media, and enter data into a digital database only when its source can remain associated with it

- Always cite the sources for information or data posted online or sent to others, naming the author of a digital file as its immediate source, while crediting original sources cited within the file

- Preserve the integrity of their own databases by evaluating the reliability of downloaded data before incorporating it into their own files

- Provide, whenever they alter data received in digital form, a description of the change that will accompany the altered data whenever it is shared with others

- Actively oppose the proliferation of error, rumor, and fraud by personally verifying or correcting information, or noting it as unverified, before passing it on to others

- Treat people online as courteously and civilly as they would treat them face-to-face, not separated by networks and anonymity

- Accept that technology has not changed the principles of genealogical research, only some of the procedures

mother went to the store," and whispered it to the girl sitting next to her. Each child, in turn, whispered to the next person what she thought she had heard. By the time those thirty people had heard and passed along the message, it changed from "My mother went to the store" to "The chicken was on the train."

The material you work with in your genealogical research may not go through thirty layers of change, but it is very important to remember that every time a record is copied, transcribed, abstracted, or published in any way, there is a chance for an error to creep in. People can make typographical errors, misread handwriting, or leave out information they don't think is important (but which turns out to be the vital piece of information that you were looking for).

Let's take a look at what you might find on the Internet. Figure 2.1 shows a Web page with abstracted marriage records taken from a local newspaper. Figure 2.2 shows a different page on that same Web site—a page with a scanned image of one of the marriages. Which of these is an original source?

The answer is "neither one." Both are derivative sources. The abstracted marriages are obviously not the original source. They are at least two generations removed—original marriage record to newspaper article to Web site (with possibly more copies in between). The scanned image is also a derivative source, though a generation closer to the original—the marriage record was scanned and posted on the Web site. The scanned image,

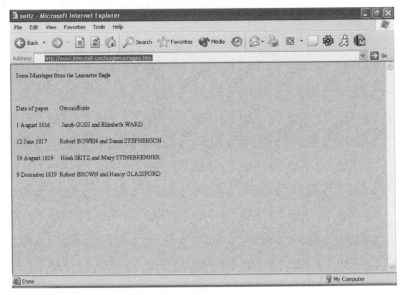

Figure 2.1 Abstracted marriages

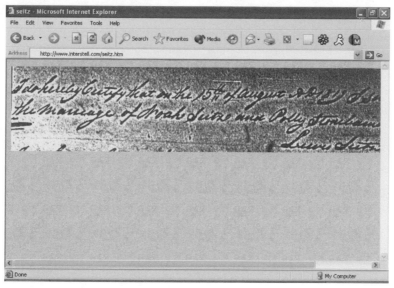

Figure 2.2 Scanned marriage record

though not the original source, is the better of the two sources. Not only is it closer to the original in terms of the number of changes it has gone through, but it is also an actual picture of the original (presuming that the image hasn't been altered).

The majority of the records you deal with on the Internet are like the marriage records from the newspaper—lists and databases compiled from other records. Does that mean that you shouldn't use the Internet? Of course not! You just need to remember that every step away from the original means another possible error in what you are seeing—and that you need to question everything.

As you wind your way around the Internet, you find Web sites with entire families shown on charts or in files called GEDCOM files, which you can download. When you find a site that purports to take your ancestry back seventeen generations, it is sorely tempting to download these files, put them in your own database, and smile at your great find.

> **Use a derivative source as a clue, not as a fact.**

Think for a moment what you would be doing if you did that. You would be assuming that everything in that file is correct and that all of those people are really your ancestors. The sobering thought is that if just one generation in that file is incorrect, you don't have your ancestors, and you've just filled your own database with wishful thinking.

The Internet has been a great boon to genealogists in that it has made it easier to publish research and share it with the world. The down side of this is that too often the research is not documented in any way, so a visitor to that site has no idea how valid the information is. Treat these sites as you would any other derivative source: as a clue for further research. If there are source citations, read and evaluate them. If they cite a book or a document, find a copy of it so you can evaluate that source for yourself. If the citation is to another researcher's file, try to track it down and see if that file has any source citations attached to it.

Even if there are no source citations listed at the site you're visiting, all is not lost. Most sites give contact information, usually an e-mail address, for the person who compiled the information. It can be worthwhile to contact that person. Perhaps he can tell you where he got his information and why he reached the conclusions he did. Also, you never know when you might be contacting the person who inherited the family Bible or the collection of Civil War letters kept by the ancestor that you share.

When making contact with the person who compiled the file you're interested in, try to frame your questions and requests as specifically as possible. Instead of saying, "Send me everything you have on the Skinner family" (which can be seen as an attempt to get all your research done for you), say something like, "I saw your Skinner family Web site and I think I tie into the family. Could you tell me how you know that William is George's father?"

Information

To be as accurate as possible in your research, you need to consider the information, as well as the source. Information falls into one of two categories:

- **Primary:** Information provided by someone with knowledge of the event. A minister who performed a wedding could provide primary information about the wedding date and place.

- **Secondary:** Information given by someone who doesn't have personal knowledge. A child born ten years after his parents' wedding would have secondary information about the date and place of the wedding because he would be relying on what others told him.

When reviewing information, consider the circumstances surrounding it. Just as you don't (or shouldn't) believe everything you read in the newspaper, some genealogical information simply isn't reliable and you should take that into account so the conclusions you reach in your research are accurate. The first thing to think about is time. That very minister who performed the wedding may not actually remember the exact date, especially a few months or a few years afterward. Since time can play tricks with our memories, you need to learn how soon after an event the information was recorded. Generally, the closer to the event, the more likely the information is to be correct.

You must also consider who the informant was. Was he or she a participant or an observer—how deeply involved was the informant with the circumstances of the event? It is natural to believe people when they tell about the circumstances around their births ("It was a dark and stormy night . . ."), but of course, everything you know about your birth, including the date and place, was told to you by someone else.

Certainly, all of us like to think of our ancestors as fine, upstanding people. But circumstances can affect how we represent ourselves—and others. Personal biases, embarrassment, shame, and greed can color the information a person gives. Did a boy lie about his age so he could join the army? Did a man lie about his age to avoid being drafted? Did a mother and father record their marriage date in the family Bible as two months before it really occurred so it wouldn't be apparent that the first child was born only seven months after marriage?

Citing Your Sources—Not Just for Professionals

Source citations do not belong exclusively to the realm of professional genealogists and those who are publishing books about their family histories. They are an essential part of the research process. The purpose of a source citation is to let you and those who read your work know where you got the information. When you begin researching your family history, it is easy to think that you'll remember where you found everything. The nature of genealogy, however, is that information increases at an exponential rate. The number of ancestors doubles with every generation—two parents, four grandparents, eight great-grandparents, sixteen great-great-grandparents, and so on. When you include the information for all the collateral relatives—the brothers and sisters of all your ancestors—you quickly have an amount of data that stretches beyond anyone's capacity to recall.

By taking the time to record your Internet sources, you are creating a ready reference that you can go back to again and again, whether it is to remember where your information came from or to determine how reliable that information may be. For example, was your great-grandmother's death date from a death certificate or from the memory of a descendant eight years after the fact? If a question arises about the reliability of a particular source, the citation contains enough information to allow you, or anyone else who reads it, to go back and locate the source.

The source citation also acts as a guide to your research. If you look at a family group sheet and wonder where you found the death date for your great-grandmother, all you need to do is look at the source citation that you have listed. True, you could go looking through your files and notes, but that takes time and can be frustrating.

When you consistently use source citations, you can more easily evaluate your findings and plan for future research. Recently, I was planning a research trip and decided to work on a line that I hadn't actively researched for several years. In reviewing my source citations, I found that most of my information about the collateral relatives came from a county history written in 1976—not exactly primary information about this family that lived in the mid-1800s. By reviewing my source citations, I quickly determined that this line needed more extensive research.

Finally, having accurate source citations also helps you avoid frustration when working on a common line with other researchers. If they question how you know that Henry was the father of Noah, you can easily provide your proof. Collaborating with distant, and sometimes not-so-distant, cousins is one of the joys of genealogy. When both of you can easily share information and each of you can tell how the other reached her conclusions, your joint efforts are much more productive and enjoyable.

Elements of a Good Citation

Author, title, publishing information, and page number—these are the four basic components of a print citation. When you are citing a source from the Internet, the elements are similar. You should record the following:

- **Author:** This is the person or agency that sponsors the Web site or the author of an e-mail (including both the e-mail address and the person's name, if known).

- **Name:** When dealing with a Web site, this is the name of that site. If the source is an e-mail, this is the subject line.

🍃 **URL:** Include the Web site address (the URL).

🍃 **Date:** If your source is a Web site, this is the date you found the information. If the source is an e-mail, it is the date of the e-mail.

Here is an example of a simple source citation for a listing of one couple's marriage found on a Web site:

Fairfield County Marriages 1800–1811, Fairfield County Chapter of the Ohio Genealogical Society, online *<www.fairfieldgenealogy.org/research/marr00-11.html>*, Saml. Henderson and Betsey Ramsey marriage accessed 1 July 2002.

The name of the specific page is Fairfield County Marriages 1800–1811. The author is the Fairfield County Chapter of the Ohio Genealogical Society. The URL of the site is listed. The specific information (the Saml. Henderson and Betsey Ramsey marriage) is recorded, so there is no confusion about what was viewed. Because Web

Finding Web Sites after They Disappear

The Internet can be ethereal. Sites that are here today may be gone tomorrow (or even later today). If you looked at a site that was helpful, but it doesn't exist anymore, there are a couple of ways that you might still be able to view it.

Google *(www.google.com)* is not only a very powerful search engine, but also an archive of sorts. If the site you are looking for is no longer online, Google may have a copy in its cache. When you search on Google and the link on the results list is no longer valid, click on the word Cached after the URL listing. You may not find a fully functional Web site, but you should get at least most of the text.

The Wayback Machine *(www.archive.org)* is a collection of more than 10 billion Web pages, taking up more than one hundred terabytes of storage. Searching on the Wayback Machine is easy enough—simply plug in the URL (yet another reason to cite your sources). Not all Web sites are included, as it does not archive password-protected sites, and it removes sites when requested to do so by the site's author.

Remember to question the accuracy of these vanished sites. Further research may have been done after the site disappeared that invalidated the conclusions.

sites change so often, it is important to record the date you visited the site so you can say, "As of this date, this is what the site said."

Here is a sample source citation if that marriage information had come in an e-mail from a cousin:

> Cleo Clodhopper, "Granny Great's marriage," e-mail from <cclodhopper8@hotmail.com> to author, 15 November 2001.

The citation includes the name of the person who sent the e-mail, as well as the subject line. Although it is not always possible to get a postal address for the person, you should include it if you have it. A postal address is less likely to change than an e-mail address. The date listed is the date of the e-mail.

Cite What You See

If you ever took a creative writing class, you probably know the expression, "Write what you know." A related concept in the world of genealogy is "Cite what you see," meaning that you need to be careful about what you are citing and how you do it.

In the example of a marriage listed on a Web site, we cited the source (the Web site) instead of the information (the marriage). So in citing the marriage of Samuel Henderson and Betsey Ramsey, I cite the Fairfield County Chapter of the Ohio Genealogical Society's Web site, not Samuel and Betsey's marriage record itself. That's because I didn't see the marriage record; I saw only an abstract of the marriage record on a Web site.

What if Cousin Cleo Clodhopper's e-mail told you the exact volume and page where Samuel and Betsey's marriage record can be found in the Probate Court? Would that change the citation? No. You still cite her e-mail, since that is what you saw. When you get a copy of the record from the Probate Court, you can add a citation to the marriage record itself.

Doing Right by Others: The Internet Is a Form of Publishing

Doing the right thing means more than doing your research the right way. It also means that you conduct yourself ethically. When you think of the word *publication*, you probably think of books, newspapers, and magazines—something that involves paper and ink. While putting material on the Internet doesn't require these tools, the very act of placing information on the Internet *is* a form of publishing. So material published on the Internet is protected by the copyright laws of the United States. Perhaps because it is so easy to do, many people who would never think of taking pages or chapters from a book and reprinting them, will download large files or copy large blocks of text from someone else's Web site and put them on their own. But as the old saying goes, "Just because you can doesn't mean you should." It is simply wrong to take someone else's work and present it as your own. Bottom line: this is not only wrong—it is illegal.

Sources for Finding Information about Copyright

The most authoritative source for copyright information is the U.S. Copyright Office (*lcweb.loc.gov/copyright*). This site also contains the circular "Copyright Basics" (see *www.copyright.gov/circs/circ1.html*).

Two other sources of useful information are the articles "When Works Pass into the Public Domain" (Lolly Gasaway, University of North Carolina, *www.unc.edu/~unclng/public-d.htm*) and "Copyright and Fair Use" (Stanford University Libraries, *fairuse.stanford.edu/*).

Some people make the case that facts cannot be copyrighted. This is true. But a compilation of facts *is* covered under copyright. When someone has done the research and, through that research, come to a series of conclusions, that work is covered. The fact that Samuel and Betsey were married in Fairfield County, Ohio, is not copyrighted, but the compilation of their family data and stories is.

When you publish your research, whether in a book, on your Web site, or on family group sheets you distribute at the family reunion, make sure that you acknowledge where you found the information. Your source citations are a natural way to do this. Give credit where credit is due.

Doing the right thing—whether it is how you evaluate your information, how you cite your sources, or how you treat the information that you find—makes your efforts to find your ancestors more efficient, less frustrating, and ultimately, more enjoyable.

Standards for Sound Genealogical Research
Recommended by the National Genealogical Society

Remembering always that they are engaged in a quest for truth, family history researchers consistently

- Record the source for each item of information they collect

- Test every hypothesis or theory against credible evidence, and reject those that are not supported by the evidence

- Seek original records, or reproduced images of them when there is reasonable assurance they have not been altered, as the basis for their research conclusions

- Use compilations, communications, and published works, whether paper or electronic, primarily for their value as guides to locating the original records or as contributions to the critical analysis of the evidence discussed in them

- State something as a fact only when it is supported by convincing evidence, and identify the evidence when communicating the fact to others

- Limit with words like "probable" or "possible" any statement that is based on less than convincing evidence, and state the reasons for concluding that it is probable or possible

- Avoid misleading other researchers by either intentionally or carelessly distributing or publishing inaccurate information

- State carefully and honestly the results of their own research, and acknowledge all use of other researchers' work

- Recognize the collegial nature of genealogical research by making their work available to others through publication, or by placing copies in appropriate libraries or repositories, and by welcoming critical comment

- Consider with open minds new evidence or the comments of others on their work and the conclusions they have reached

CHAPTER **3**

Wading in Deeper

How do you find an online obituary, your ancestor's land purchases, the historical background of an area your ancestors settled, or your old friend's current e-mail address? The secret to finding anything on the Web lies in knowing how and where to look. This chapter delves into using various search engines and genealogy springboards to find sites of interest. It also introduces you to two essential genealogy resources—GenWeb and RootsWeb.

Effectively Searching on the Internet

Unless you're brand new to computers, you've probably heard of some of the more popular search engines. In this section, you'll learn how to query several to retrieve the results you want. With the hundreds of millions of pages of information available on the Web, how can you ever find what you need? The key is in knowing how to search efficiently and effectively with several different search engines. Simplistically, a search engine is a Web site and software that scours the Internet looking for information stored on other sites, based on query words or phrases that you enter. If you want a more in-depth, yet easy-to-understand explanation, look at "How Internet Search Engines Work" by Curt Franklin at *www.howstuffworks.com/search-engine.htm.*

A Few Words about Boolean Logic

If your eyes glaze over and your heart starts pounding when you hear computer terminology like *Boolean logic*, take heart. What you need to know is really very simple. Even if you don't remember a thing about Venn diagrams from junior high math class, you're familiar with the terms *and, or,* and *not.* Using most Internet search engines is as simple as thinking about what you want to find.

An example: I want to find all the information in cyberspace about an ancestor, Jesse Westmoreland. I need to search for *Jesse **and** Westmoreland* to find only references to a person by the name of Jesse Westmoreland. A search for *Jesse **or** Westmoreland* would result in references to any Jesse or any Westmoreland, including towns or counties by that name or a same-named glassware from England.

And/or differences are readily apparent, but where does the *not* come in? Suppose I want to search for the surname Westmoreland, eliminating any references to a Westmoreland County or the glassware in the results. The query entry should be *Westmoreland not county not glass.* The search engine then combs the Web looking for any mention of Westmoreland where it is not in close proximity to the words *county* or *glass.* Look at Figure 3.1 to see the difference in the number of Google search results or "hits" based on which particular query phrase was used on a given date.

All search engines work a bit differently. Some ignore common words like *the* or *a* and assume an *and* between words. Some require that you enclose a phrase in quotes to search specifically for that phrase, such as *"Jesse Westmoreland."* Some search engines allow you to use a plus sign (+) for *and* or a minus sign (-) for *not.* Many even help you by providing an advanced search form with blanks you can fill

Search Term	Number of Google Search Results
Westmoreland	351,000
Westmoreland -glass	189,000
Westmoreland -glass -county	120,000
Westmoreland -county	118,000
Jesse Westmoreland	15,600
"Jesse Westmoreland"	58

Figure 3.1 Results based on search phrase used

Finding Your Query Phrase Text in Search Engine Results

Your search for an ancestor's name in a search engine may find dozens of references and links to Web sites, but just what does that mean? It means that the name you entered appears somewhere on each of those Web sites. You eagerly click on the first link in the list of hits and move to a Web site that contains the text of a four-hundred-page book. How will you ever find your ancestor's name without reading each page until you spot the name?

It's simple—use the Find feature of your Internet browser. In Internet Explorer, click Edit and then click Find on This Page, or use the keyboard shortcut Control F (hold down the Ctrl key and press the F key). A small window pops up where you can enter the name you searched for, similar to the screen shown in the accompanying figure. Your browser software then moves directly to the first occurrence of that name in the Web site you're viewing, whether it's on page 1 or page 399.

The name or phrase you searched for may appear more than once in the Web page, so don't stop with the first one. Keep clicking Find Next in the Find window until no more instances of the phrase are found.

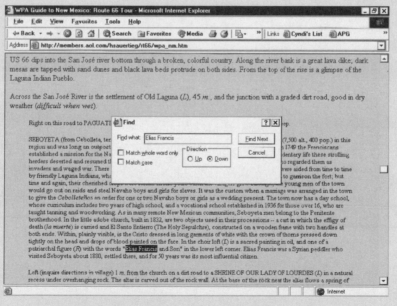

Find feature in Internet Explorer

in to make your query easier. Make it a habit to read the Help or the Frequently Asked Questions (FAQs) pages on the search engines you use. If you don't enter your search terms correctly for that particular search engine, you'll get fewer or inaccurate results.

Not all search engines are created equal. Some search only the titles of Web pages, while others seek out every word of text on the pages. Some explore billions of sites, while others search only millions. Some, called metasearch tools, look within other search engines and provide results from several sources. You may ask, "Which one should a genealogist use?" That question is much like "Which genealogy program should I try?" or "What kind of car should I buy?" The answers to all these questions depend on your needs. You may want to use different search engines depending upon what you hope to find, or try the same query in different search engines. Let's return to our query for Jesse Westmoreland and see how several search engines work and produce varying results.

Google Search Engine

Google *(www.google.com)* is one of the new kids on the block of search engines, but it is widely recognized as a powerful tool. Its index contains more than two billion URLs, meaning you're more likely to find a match for your query. Google returns results that match all your search terms, either in the text of a Web page or in links pointing to it. An excerpt of the text that matches your search term is displayed with each result, so you have a good idea whether it is relevant and, therefore, a site that you want to visit. Google also offers a link to a cached, or saved, version of the Web page just in case the original page is unavailable.

I use Google regularly and even installed the Google toolbar in my browser so it's always present in the Internet Explorer window. That way, I can conveniently search right from the toolbar, rather than having to move to the Google home page. If you want to install the toolbar in your browser, just visit *toolbar.google.com/*, download the file, and follow the instructions for installing it to your Internet browser.

Translation Help

If your search turns up Web pages in a language other than English, Google can translate those in Italian, French, Spanish, German, or Portuguese (see Figure 3.2). Click on the Translate This Page link to the right of the Web site's URL. The program translates the original Web page in Spanish to an English version (see Figure 3.3).

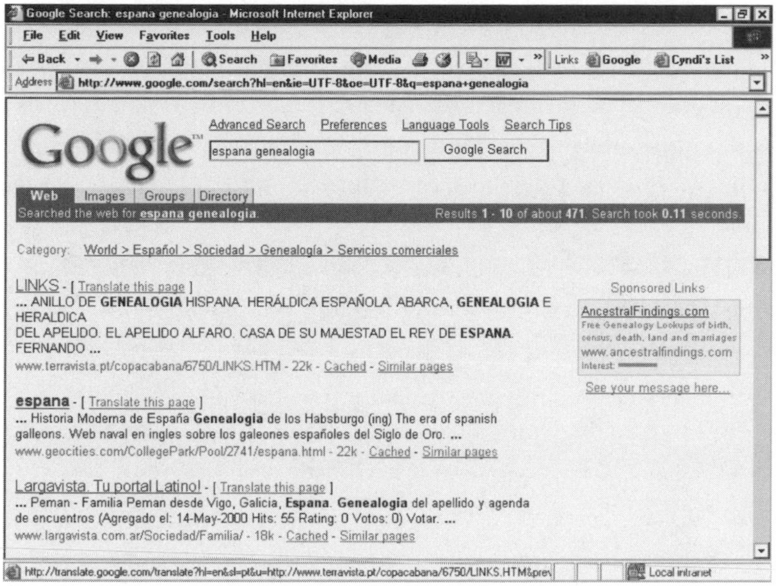

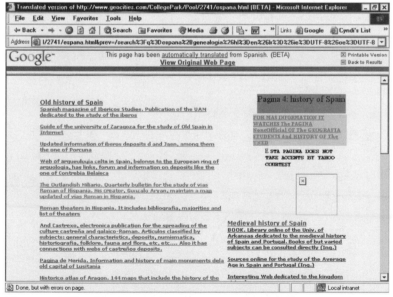

Figure 3.2 Translation help

Figure 3.3 Translated Spanish page

Quick Telephone and Address Search

You can use Google's search screen to quickly find a phone number and address for a person. In the Google search box, type a last name, city, and state. You can further narrow your search by adding a first initial or name, too. If Google finds a publicly listed phone number and address that matches your search, the person's name, address, and phone number appear at the top of the Google search results screen, as shown in Figure 3.4.

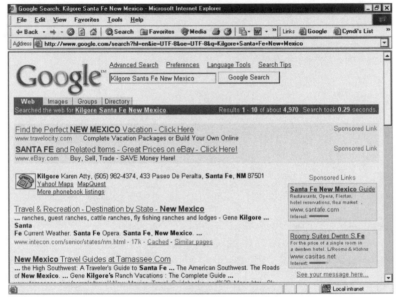

Figure 3.4 Telephone and address search

Other Special Google Searches

Google also searches for the definition of a word in your search phrase, a stock quote for tracking your investments, an image or photograph, Usenet discussion forums such as *soc.genealogy.Hispanic,* and the Google directory of categorized topics. To learn more about Google's advanced features and comprehensive search capabilities, see *www.google.com/help/.*

Google Search Results

Searching for *"Jesse Westmoreland"* in Google returns fifty-eight results (see Figure 3.5), including mention of that name in online Virginia and Tennessee marriage records; 1790 Virginia tax lists; Lanier and Wilson family histories and genealogies; an Arizona cemetery;

the 1999 alumni directory of a Charleston, West Virginia high school; and queries on RootsWeb mail lists. The hits also include references to individuals with names like John Jesse Westmoreland Brookes because they contain the phrase *Jesse Westmoreland*. Obviously, not all these search results are relevant to research of a Virginia ancestor in the 1800s, but the Google excerpts of the text around the search phrase and the Web site URLs themselves help determine which are likely to yield genealogical goodies.

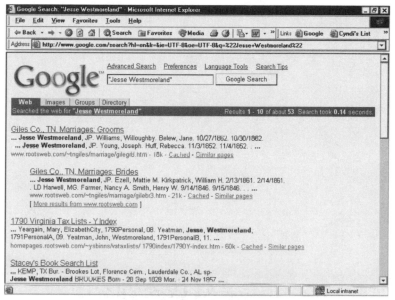

Figure 3.5 Google search results for *"Jesse Westmoreland"*

Yahoo Search Results

The same search for *"Jesse Westmoreland"* in Yahoo *(www.yahoo.com)* results in only nineteen Web page matches. But some of the individual matches also contain a link to more results from the referenced Web site. For example, Result 1 in Figure 3.6 provides a link to more results from *www.rootsweb.com*.

Yahoo also offers a search of news stories and photos, audio/video, and the *New York Times*. Since these sources are of recent vintage, they don't offer much for your genealogical search, but they may help you find the article about your cousin in Seattle who was in the news last week. You can even search Yahoo for over 70 million full-text research documents in journals and magazines, newspapers, wires, and transcripts. Results provide a summary of each article that matches your search query, and

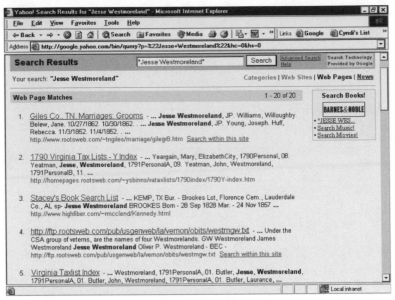

Figure 3.6 *Yahoo! search results for "Jesse Westmoreland"*

you can purchase an online copy of the article. Be sure to click the Advanced Help or Search links right beside the search button in Yahoo for detailed help about all these searches.

Lycos Search Results

One of the earliest search engines, Lycos *(www.lycos.com)* offers searches of the Web, news, and shopping sites. The Lycos search screen does include advertising banners like the one you see in Figure 3.7, but they're easy to ignore. Lycos helpfully provides links to other search engines at the bottom of each page with its Need a Second Opinion? feature. You can even save time when exploring Lycos search results by clicking Fast Forward to the right of the title link. This splits the Lycos window, with the search result links on the left side and the Web site or document that contains your search phrase on the right side, like the results in Figure 3.8. To view the next relevant Web site text, click on the next numbered link in the left-most window.

Dogpile Metasearch Results

Dogpile *(www.dogpile.com)* is a metasearch engine that combs multiple search engines at the same time, giving you results from several different sources, including About,

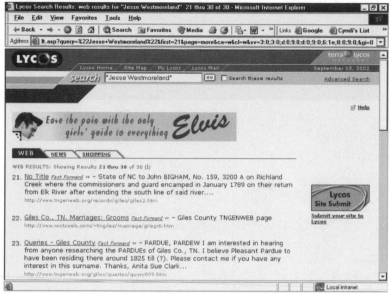

Figure 3.7 Lycos search results for *"Jesse Westmoreland"*

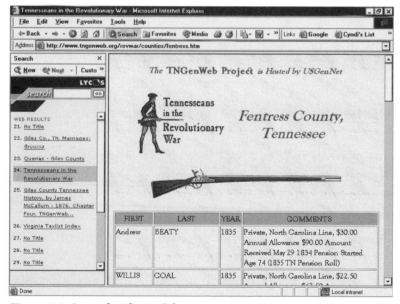

Figure 3.8 Lycos fast-forward feature

Ah-ha, Ask Jeeves, Dogpile Web Catalog, Fast, FindWhat, LookSmart, Open Directory, Overture, SearchHippo, and Sprinks. Dogpile searches four search engines at a time until all are searched or until ten matches are found for your query phrase. Dogpile also enables you to search images, audio, files, news, multimedia, shopping, or message boards, and it provides sections for yellow pages, white pages, and classifieds.

For the search phrase *"Jesse Westmoreland,"* Dogpile returned matches from these search engines: nine results from Overture, ten from Fast, ten from Ask Jeeves, and ten from SearchHippo.

Using Multiple Search Engines

When searching for a name, location, or topic on the Internet, it's best to try several search engines. You retrieve different results depending on which ones you use. Try the same search periodically, too—just because your ancestor's name isn't found on the Web today doesn't mean it won't be there buried in a newly transcribed document two months from now.

Here are a few of the better known search engines and their URLs:

- Alta Vista *(www.altavista.com)*
- Ask Jeeves *(www.aj.com)*
- Dogpile *(www.dogpile.com)*
- Google *(www.google.com)*
- HotBot *(www.hotbot.com)*
- Lycos *(www.lycos.com)*
- MSN Search *(search.msn.com)*
- Webcrawler *(webcrawler.com)*
- Yahoo *(www.yahoo.com)*

To learn more about search engines and how to search the Internet, visit Southern Oregon University's Internet Searching Tools site *(www.sou.edu/library/searchtools/)*, Windweaver's Search Guide *(www.windweaver.com/searchguide.htm)*, or J. Marcus Ziegler's The Search Page *(www.accesscom.com/~ziegler/search.html)*.

Different Search Engines, Different Results

I performed exactly the same search for *"Jesse Westmoreland"* using Google, Yahoo, Lycos, and Dogpile. However, the results varied greatly. All the search engines returned hits that obviously were not relevant to my Revolutionary War ancestor or his family, although these hits all contained the words *Jesse* and *Westmoreland*. A few important Internet Web sites were found by *all* the search engines. But a quick look at a few of the results reveals that only one of the search engines turned up some items. Six relevant articles mentioning Jesse Westmoreland are listed in Figure 3.9, along with the search engines that found these results. This exercise should convince you that Internet search engines are valuable tools for genealogical research, but that it pays to use more than one for the same search.

Internet Item of Interest Containing "Jesse Westmoreland"	Found by Search Engine(s)
Giles County, Tennessee, Marriages	Google, Lycos, Yahoo, Dogpile (Overture)
Virginia Tax List Index	Google, Lycos, Yahoo
Confederate States of America Veterans	Google, Yahoo
Family History of Joseph Westmoreland	Google
Tennessee Pension Roll of 1835	Dogpile (Overture)
Tennesseans in the Revolutionary War	Lycos, Google (found by Google only when repeating the search with omitted results included)

Figure 3.9 Different search results with different search engines

Springboards to Genealogy Sites

Many Web sites contain links to other Internet sites of interest to those researching a particular topic. These springboards can launch you on your genealogy search in a fast, efficient manner.

Cyndi's List

Cyndi's List of Genealogy Sites on the Internet *(www.cyndislist.com)* is one of the most comprehensive springboards to myriad genealogical resources (see Figure 3.10). Cyndi Howells is a real live person who started a Web site a few years back with a few genealogy links to help her local Washington State genealogical society. Her project mushroomed, and today Cyndi's List contains more than 150 categories and more than 175,000 links to other sites of interest to genealogists. If you don't know where to look for a Web resource, think first of Cyndi's List.

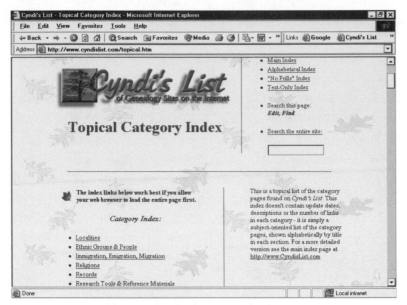

Figure 3.10 Cyndi's List of Genealogy Sites on the Internet

Do you wonder how much your ancestor's 1848 estate was worth in today's dollars? Cyndi's List contains a money category with links to sites that provide information about foreign currency, the value of U.S. dollars from 1789 to the present, articles and book reviews about money, and at least three dozen other links to money-related sites.

Genealogy springboards help launch you to Web sites that can provide information about the topic you're researching. A few springboard sites of general interest include:

- Access Genealogy *(www.accessgenealogy.com/)*
- Cyndi's List *(www.cyndislist.com)*
- RootsWeb *(www.rootsweb.com)*
- Surname Springboard *(www.allenlacy.com/spring.htm)*
- USGenWeb *(www.usgenweb.org)*
- WorldGenWeb *(www.worldgenweb.org)*

Would you like to find a newspaper in the area where your ancestor lived? Check out the newspaper category on Cyndi's List for links from Australian newspapers on the Internet to Yukon news online. You can find a link to just about any topic of genealogical or historical interest from Cyndi's List. This is another Web site I use so frequently that I have added a Cyndi's List link to the toolbar of my Internet browser.

Topical or Local Springboards

The Web sites of most historical or genealogical societies contain links or springboards to other Web sites of interest to someone researching in the area. For example, New England Historic Genealogical Society *(www.newenglandancestors.org/links/)* provides research and general links, government links, and historical and genealogical society links to organizations in Massachusetts and surrounding states. Try searching on the Web for a phrase similar to *history genealogy Oklahoma* to find a historical or genealogical society or archives in the area you're researching. Additionally, search the Federation of Genealogical Societies Society Hall *(www.familyhistory.com/societyhall/)* for a genealogical society.

USGenWeb

USGenWeb *(www.usgenweb.com)* is a nonprofit all-volunteer organization dedicated to providing genealogical research Web sites for every county and state in the United States. It has its roots in Kentucky, where the Kentucky Comprehensive Database Project evolved into the KYGenWeb Project in 1996. That same year, volunteers decided to create a set of pages like Kentucky's for all states, and USGenWeb was the result (see Figure 3.11). WorldGenWeb was established soon after.

The USGenWeb Project has several components:

- **State Pages Project:** As starting points for your research, state pages provide information about the area and its resources. Each state page also provides links to its county USGenWeb pages.

- **Archives Project:** Here you find transcriptions of public records, such as marriage bonds, wills, military records, tax lists, and burials. The USGenWeb Archives Project also encompasses the Digital Map Library, the Pension Project, and the Special Collections Project.

🍃 **Census Projects:** The USGenWeb Census Projects feature transcriptions of census records by volunteers and proofreaders. Read more about these records in Chapter 7, "Finding Ancestors in the Census or Other Lists."

🍃 **Tombstone Project:** Volunteers have recorded tombstone information in cemeteries around the United States, and you'll find links to them here. Read more about cemetery research in Chapter 6, "Acquiring Vital Records."

🍃 **Other Projects:** USGenWeb also sponsors the Kidz Project, with the goal of helping children learn about genealogical research; the Lineage Project, which provides a list of researchers seeking descendants of a particular ancestor; and the Genealogical Events Project, which provides a list of genealogical events across the country.

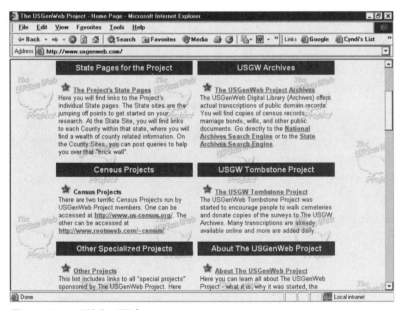

Figure 3.11 USGenWeb site

All database records available from USGenWeb are free, and all have been transcribed by volunteers. Be sure to read any explanatory text within the transcripts, and use these transcribed sources as clues to help you find the original. A copy of the original record can usually be ordered for a fee from the appropriate courthouse, state archives, or National Archives branch.

Help for Researchers

The Help section of USGenWeb *(www.usgenweb.com/researchers/researcher.html)* is a good place to start your genealogical quest since it supplies information about a wide variety of topics, including varying calendar systems, naming patterns, genealogy vocabulary, wars, genealogy software programs, early laws, and photographic preservation.

USGenWeb Project State Pages

USGenWeb State Pages are structured by state and then by county. Most state Web sites contain a map of the state's counties, information about its history and geography, genealogical and historical societies and libraries, procedures for obtaining vital records, special projects, mailing lists and message boards, links to other relevant sites, and a host of other helpful information. Each state Web site contains links to the counties within the state, and counties are the core of the USGenWeb Project State Pages.

USGenWeb county pages usually contain a history and description of the county, addresses for the county courthouse, libraries, genealogical and historical societies, links to sites of interest for the county, researchers in the area, and indexed or abstracted records of interest to genealogists. A typical county USGenWeb site, the Christian County, Kentucky site shown in Figure 3.12, contains

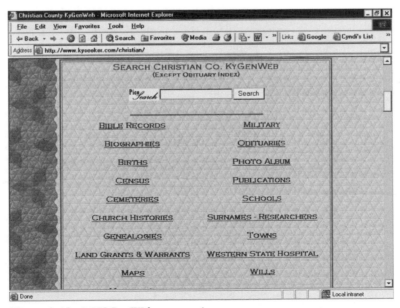

Figure 3.12 A USGenWeb county site

a great deal of helpful information for any researcher with ancestors in that county. It includes a link to the Christian County Message Board, where anyone with a question or information to share can post a message. It allows searches of a wide variety of transcribed records or resources, including Bible records, biographies, births, census records, cemeteries, church histories, genealogies, land grants and warrants, maps, marriages, military, obituaries, researchers, and institutions in the area.

County Web sites may provide links to other helpful sites, such as state death record indexes, and they usually offer information about local histories or publications relevant to the area. Most county Web sites also contain links that make it easy to subscribe to the genealogy mail list for the county or to visit another USGenWeb page for a bordering county. If you are a new genealogist or an experienced researcher beginning work in a new county, a stop at the county's USGenWeb site will help point you in the right direction.

CanadaGenWeb

The Canadian GenWeb Project *(www.rootsweb.com/~canwgw)* is available in both English and French versions. CanadaGenWeb is modeled after the USGenWeb Project and was established in 1996 with the same goals—to collect and distribute free genealogical data on the Internet. Its major projects at the national level include CanadaGenWeb for Kids, a Project Archives, and a Family Bible Transcription Project. Each province has its own GenWeb site, and many provinces sponsor additional projects at the regional level. The organization and content of CanadaGenWeb is very similar to the USGenWeb Project.

WorldGenWeb

WorldGenWeb *(www.worldgenweb.org)* is also a nonprofit organization composed of volunteers who provide free genealogical information on Web sites around the world. These volunteers work countless hours to provide genealogical resource and reference information for specific countries and regions in the WorldGenWeb Project, including country- or county-specific free e-mail lists.

Generally, there is a Web site for each geographic location, such as a country or county. Most GenWeb sites contain cemetery locations, maps, a brief area history, and contact information for local public record offices, libraries, archives, and associations. Each area Web site may also include query pages or message boards, indexes or transcripts of census records, cemetery records, biographies, surname registration lists, or other resources for genealogical research.

Worldwide Resources

If you're new to genealogy or just beginning your research in a new country, visit the WorldGenWeb link for How to Start Your Research at *www.worldgenweb.org/howtostart.html*. It explains what information you need to get started and how to use the resources of WorldGenWeb.

Researching in a New Country

Access the WorldGenWeb list of countries at *www.worldgenweb.org/countryindex.html*, and click on the country you want to research. For example, clicking on the link for Germany directs a user to the CenEuroGenWeb (Central Europe GenWeb) site. As you see in Figure 3.13, Germany has a resource page, and there are additional pages for regions within Germany, from Baden-Wurttemberg to Thuringen. Clicking on one of these locations brings up the WorldGenWeb site for that area, and clicking on

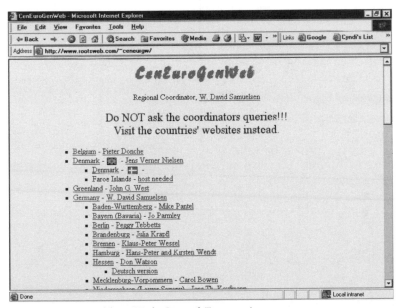

Figure 3.13 WorldGenWeb Central Europe site

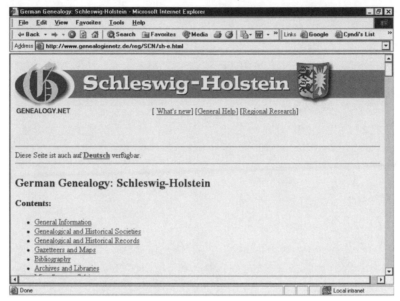

Figure 3.14 WorldGenWeb Schleswig-Holstein (Germany) site

a name to the right of a location enables you to send an e-mail to the Web site's coordinator for that area.

Using Schleswig-Holstein in Germany as an example, Figure 3.14 shows just a few of the resources available to someone researching that area:

- **General Information:** Describes the state of Schleswig-Holstein, bordering areas, counties and independent towns and religious divisions within the state, maps of the counties, and settlement maps of the twelfth and thirteenth centuries.

- **Genealogical and Historical Societies:** Provides a list of German and United States organizations relevant to the area.

- **Genealogical and Historical Records:** Describes records available for the region, including church, civil registration, census, address books, citizenship, education, immigration and emigration, tax, and military records.

- **Bibliography:** Lists history and genealogy books for the area.

- **Archives and Libraries:** Provides the names and address of facilities in Schleswig-Holstein.

- **Miscellaneous Subjects:** Links to volunteers and professional researchers who help with Schleswig-Holstein research and to publishers and booksellers.
- **Other Resources:** Links to mailing lists for Schleswig-Holstein and to personal or family Web sites of others researching this area.

With resource pages for many countries of the world, WorldGenWeb is a valuable starting point for genealogical research outside the United States.

RootsWeb

RootsWeb *(www.rootsweb.com)* is the oldest and largest free genealogy site on the Internet (see Figure 3.15). It includes everything from an online class for the new genealogist, to search engines and databases, to free Web space for your genealogical or family association, to message boards and mailing lists and surname lists. Not only does RootsWeb have an enormous number of tools for any genealogist, but it also provides links to many other sites of interest.

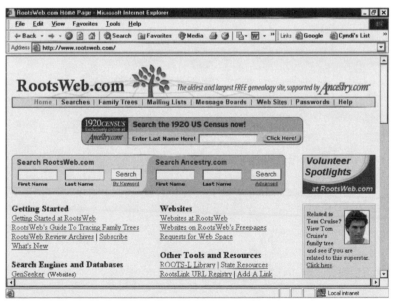

Figure 3.15 RootsWeb

If you don't know how to begin a new research project or you need help getting started, look first at RootsWeb. If you're looking for an ancestor, try the WorldConnect Project with its more than 200 million names, check the RootsWeb Surname List with its more than a million surnames, or search RootsWeb's more than 25,000 mailing lists or 175,000 message boards. Many of the resources and tools discussed in this book are hosted by RootsWeb, so you'll hear more about this Web site in later chapters.

By now, you may be feeling just a bit overwhelmed by all the information that's available on the Internet. Remember to take it slow and use your research plan to ferret out the specific information you want. Using one resource at a time to find the fact you are looking for simplifies your search. After a while, you will have learned to use many new resources. The search engines and genealogy springboards can help you find a great deal of information, but it's up to you to analyze what you find in order to reach solid conclusions. Don't forget to record your search results in a research log and your conclusions in a report or genealogy program. In the following chapters, you'll learn how to use specific tools to continue building your family history.

CHAPTER **4**

Finding People in the Modern Era

SURPRISINGLY, GENEALOGY ISN'T JUST ABOUT FINDING PEOPLE WHO have been dead for hundreds of years. You can use twentieth- or twenty-first-century resources to find a recently deceased family member or a living person. Once you trace living relatives from common ancestors, you can share your research or even plan a family reunion. This chapter points out a few Internet tools that may help you.

Social Security Records

Do you remember getting your Social Security card when you first went to work at the local drive-in restaurant? You had to fill out an application that included your name, birth date, place of birth, sex, race, and parents' names (including your mother's maiden name). You also affixed your own signature to the application. Think about that. Wouldn't that very information solve a lot of family mysteries in your search? The Social Security Act was passed in 1935, and 30 million U.S. residents applied for and received Social Security numbers between November 1936 and June 1937. Social Security Administration (SSA) applications dating as early as 1936 can be helpful to the genealogist seeking facts about an ancestor. While Social Security card applications are not available online, some online research aids can help you order the applications.

Social Security Death Index

The Social Security Death Index (SSDI), made up of more than 68.5 million deaths reported to the SSA, is widely available free of charge and can provide important information for researchers. Most of the people in the SSDI died after 1962, but a few deaths go back as far as 1937. All information in the SSDI originates from the same source, the SSA's Social Security Death Master File. Companies like Ancestry.com or Genealogy.com purchase the file from the SSA and create their own versions of the SSDI. Some Internet versions contain more information than others, so it's good to search for the same name in several versions. The SSA's electronic file provides the following data:

- **Social Security Number:** The first three digits in a Social Security number comprise the area number. Before 1972, this number identified the state in which the applicant's original Social Security card was issued. Since 1972, all Social Security numbers have been assigned and issued from one office in Baltimore, and the area number identifies the zip code of the applicant's mailing address. An applicant's mailing address, either before or after 1972, may not be the same as his or her residence, but the area number is an indicator that an applicant resided in or used an address in a particular state at the time the Social Security card was originally issued. A list of area numbers and corresponding states is available on the SSA's Web site at *www.ssa.gov/foia/stateweb.html.*

- **Last Name, First Name, and Middle Name:** The SSA database allows twenty letters for last names and fifteen letters for first and middle names. (Very few middle names are included in the Death Master File.) If a name is longer, final letters may be truncated.

- **V or P Code:** This code indicates whether the death has been verified with a family member or someone acting on behalf of the family (V) or whether a death certificate proved the death (P).

- **Date of Death and Date of Birth:** If a death occurred before 1988, the date of death may contain only a month and year, but that should be enough to help you find a death certificate, obituary, or other type of death record for the person.

🍃 **State or Country Code of Residence:** This code indicates the decedent's last residence. No new information is available in this field after February 1988.

🍃 **Zip Code of Last Residence:** This represents the zip code where benefits or correspondence were last sent. Bear in mind that someone else, such as an attorney or family member in another state, may have been administering the person's financial affairs, so this may not be the zip code where the person last lived. Nor is this zip code necessarily where the person died—the benefits and correspondence may have gone to the home address, but the person may have died in a distant hospital, perhaps even in another state. While the SSA records show only the zip code in this field, some SSDI Internet versions convert that zip code to a city, state, and zip code. This may not accurately reflect a decedent's last residence, since some zip codes represent multiple rural areas and other zip codes have changed over time.

🍃 **Zip Code of Lump Sum Payment Recipient:** This field contains the zip code where the last benefit or the lump-sum burial benefit was sent. SSA records show only the zip code, but some SSDI versions convert that to a city, state, and zip code.

Social Security Death Index

Use the Social Security Death Index (SSDI) to find recently deceased relatives or anyone whose death has been reported to the Social Security Administration (SSA) since about 1962. Here are some of the free versions of SSDI available on the Internet:

- Ancestry (*www.ancestry.com/search/rectype/vital/ssdi/main.htm*)
- FamilySearch (*www.familysearch.org*). Click Search and then click U.S. Social Security Death Index.
- Family Tree Maker (*www.familytreemaker.com/fto_ssdisearch.html*)
- Kindred Konnections (*www.kindredkonnections.com/*)
- Lineages, Inc. (*www.lineages.com/vault/SSDI.asp*)
- RootsWeb (*ssdi.genealogy.rootsweb.com/*)

You can use different versions of the SSDI online to solve some of your family history mysteries. It's often difficult to find women who married and changed their names. For example, from census and family records, I learned that my grandmother's sister, Lillie Wilcox, was born 20 September 1900 in Missouri, but I was certain she had married and bore a different, unknown, surname when she died. I decided to try an SSDI search for a woman named Lillie born on that date.

The FamilySearch version of SSDI allowed a query using just Lillie's first name, but allowed entry of only a birth year of 1900, not the exact date. Therefore, FamilySearch's SSDI returned more than 200 Lillies born in 1900, too many to sort through.

Family Tree Maker's SSDI did allow entry of just a first name and exact date of birth, and resulted in six Lillies born 20 September 1900. This is a reasonable number to sort through.

Kindred Konnections' and Lineages' versions of SSDI required that a last name be entered, so they were not helpful for trying to find someone whose last name is not known.

At first glance, the RootsWeb query screen for the SSDI does not seem comprehensive enough to help in this search. In Figure 4.1, you can see that it contains fields only for last, first, and middle names and a Social Security number. But look carefully, and you'll see an Advanced Search button. When you click that, a detailed search form displays, like the one in Figure 4.2. There, entering a first name and an exact date of birth provides a list of only seven women named Lillie who were born on 20 September 1900. A quick scan of the results, shown in Figure 4.3, reveals that the last one, Lillie McClary, is the likely candidate for my grandmother's sister. Her Social Security number was issued in Missouri, and her last residence was Piedmont, Wayne County, Missouri, only a few miles from my Lillie Wilcox's birthplace. See how a little detective work using a modern resource can provide a woman's married name and a death date?

What about the relatives who "got away"? You can use the SSDI to track down those elusive collateral lines who left the area. All five of my late grandmother's brothers left Wayne County, Missouri, and our branch of the family long ago lost touch with them. Are they still living? If not, where are their families?

A search of the RootsWeb version of SSDI turns up four men matching the names and birth dates of my grandmother's brothers: Bert Wilcox, died in November 1976, last residence St. Louis, Missouri; Robert L. Wilcox, died 25 May 1992, last residence Bernie, Missouri; Louis W. Wilcox, died 14 June 1993, last residence Bland, Missouri; and Clyde Wilcox, died 6 November 1997, last residence Parsons, Kansas. Grandmother's brother

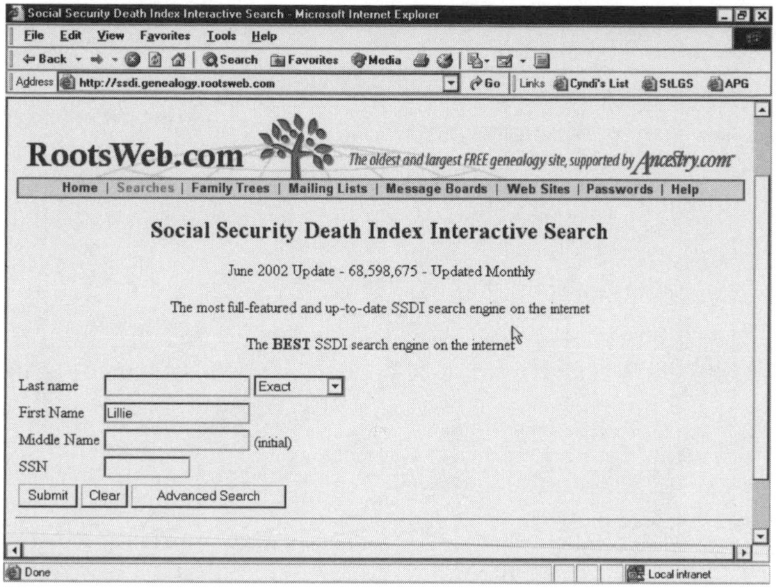

Figure 4.1 RootsWeb SSDI Basic Search query

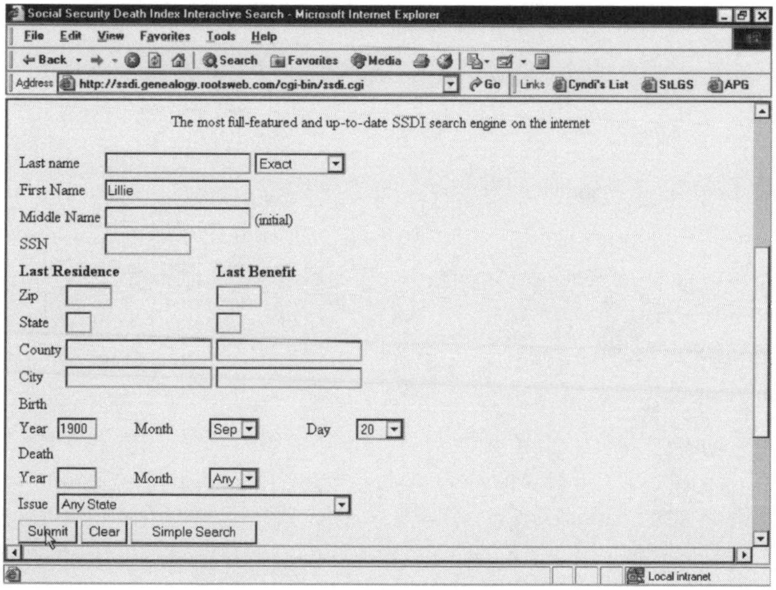

Figure 4.2 RootsWeb SSDI Advanced Search query

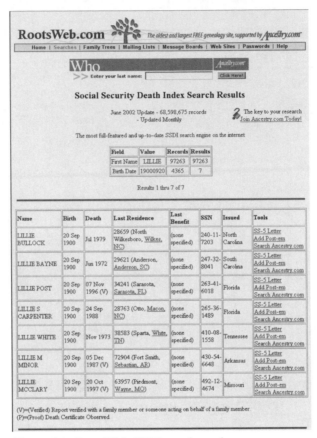

Figure 4.3 RootsWeb SSDI search results

Elmer Wilcox, born in 1915, was not found in the SSDI; he may still be living or his death may not have been reported to the Social Security Administration.

The SSDI contains enough information to help verify that the four hits are, in fact, my grandmother's brothers, but this is not proof positive. The names and birth dates match those provided by my grandmother's sister, and the last residences generally reflect the last information our family had about the uncles' locations. Using the death dates and locations in the SSDI, a prudent researcher should also obtain death certificates or obituaries for each of the men to verify their parents and siblings. Since the SSDI provides Social Security numbers for deceased persons in the database, it might also be helpful to order copies of the original Social Security card applications, which provide an applicant's birthplace, original signature, and parents' names.

Ordering Social Security Number Applications

Under the Freedom of Information Act (FOIA), the Social Security Administration fulfills requests for copies of original SS-5 Social Security Number Applications of deceased persons for a fee (currently $27), if you provide the Social Security number. If you do not know the Social Security number, the search fee is a few dollars more (currently $29). Be sure to include the person's Social Security number, full name (including maiden and name at death), sex, date and place of birth, date of death, and parents' names. Provide proof of death, or state that the person is listed in the SSA Death Master File. Include the following statement: "Microprint required—Printout not sufficient." A computer extract of a Social Security Number Application can be obtained for a fee (currently $16), if you provide the Social Security number. If you do not know the Social Security number, a computer extract is a few dollars more (currently $18). Mail SS-5 and Claim File Requests and payment to Social Security Administration, Office of Central Records Operations, FOIA Workgroup, P.O. Box 17772, Baltimore, MD 21290.

Most answers to questions about the Social Security Death Master File or about ordering original applications or files are found on the SSA Web site (ssa.custhelp.com). Select the Miscellaneous category and the Death Records (Death Index) subcategory; click the Search button to display the most common questions. Click on the subject question for a detailed answer.

Your Relative Isn't in the Social Security Death Index?

People included in the SSDI are those who have died since 1962 (with a few exceptions), who received Social Security benefits, and whose deaths have been reported to the Social Security Administration by someone, usually a family member, estate administrator, or funeral home. If you don't find a name in the SSDI, it probably means the person died before 1962 or never received Social Security benefits, or the death was never reported to the SSA. Take the case of a woman who paid Social Security taxes most of her life, but died in 1964 at age fifty-nine before ever collecting benefits; her name is not in the SSDI because there was no reason to notify the SSA of her death. Another example is the young man who died in an automobile accident at age twenty-five in 1953; his minor daughter collected Social Security survivor benefits until she was eighteen. Neither the man's nor his daughter's name is in the SSDI. Why not? He died in 1953, before the computer database was in use, and he never collected any benefits. His daughter did collect survivor benefits, but she is still living, so she should not appear in the SSDI.

Not everyone was eligible for Social Security benefits in the past. For instance, railroad employees and some public employees participated in their own retirement programs. When the Social Security program began, occupations such as farmers, attorneys, and physicians were not included. Refer to the Social Security Administration's Web site at www.ssa.gov for answers to questions about coverage and dates of benefits for various occupations.

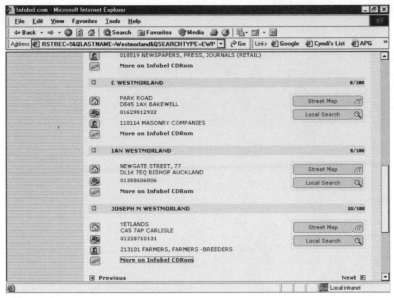

Figure 4.4 Infobel United Kingdom People Finder

Telephone Directories

A huge number of address and telephone listings are available on the Internet. You may be able to find the number of your long-lost cousin in Norway or a library in Newfoundland. But be creative—what other uses can you find for phone listings? A search for all listings of a unique surname may define an area where the name is most prevalent in a country, providing a possible place for your research. For example, a search for the surname Westmoreland at Infobel's United Kingdom Web site *(www.infobel.com/uk/)* provides 237 listings, plus an additional 100 listings for the spelling variant Westmorland. Look at Figure 4.4 for sample listings. If the locations within Great Britain for this surname were plotted, there would most likely be a cluster area where the majority reside, indicating a possible locale in which to begin research on that surname.

City or County Directories

From the mid-nineteenth century forward, many cities, towns, or counties published annual or sporadic directories that provide information about each adult resident,

Online Telephone Directories

How can you find telephone and address listings for individuals and businesses on the Internet? Many major search engines, such as Yahoo and Google, offer U.S. street address and phone number lookups within their advanced search features; read the search engine's help or search tips for instructions.

To find some of the myriad directories available on the Internet, enter a phrase such as *"telephone directory"* in Google or another search engine. To narrow the scope further, try *"international telephone directory"* or *"Germany telephone directory."* Here is a sampling of the many online directories:

- AnyWho *(www.anywho.com)*
- Australia White Pages OnLine *(www.whitepages.com.au/wp/)*
- British Telecom *(www.bt.com)*
- Canada411 *(canada411.sympatico.ca/)*
- Germany Telefonbuch (available in English) *(www.teleauskunft.de/)*
- Infobel (includes Belgium, Canada, Denmark, France, Italy, Luxembourg, Netherlands, Spain, United Kingdom, United States) *(www.infobel.com/world/default.asp)*
- Switchboard *(www.switchboard.com)*
- Teldir.com (worldwide telephone directories on the Web) *(www.teldir.com/)*
- Telefonski imenik Slovenija (Slovenia telephone directory) *(tis.telekom.si/)*
- WhitePages.com *(www.whitepages.com/)*
- WhoWhere International Directories *(www.whowhere.lycos.com/wwphone/world.html)*
- Worldwide Directories *(www.phonenumbers.net/)*
- Yahoo! People Search *(people.yahoo.com/)*

including a street address, occupation or employer, spouse's name, marital status, home ownership, names of adult relatives living in the household, and even the name of a widow's late husband. City directories also contain listings for businesses, schools, organizations, cemeteries, hospitals, and newspapers in a classified business section.

Some city directories include a section or a separate volume sometimes referred to as a crisscross or reverse directory. This index provides a list of streets alphabetically and numerically, allowing users to look up an address and determine the resident or business at that address.

City or county directories can be a boon to genealogical research, but where can you find them? The Library of Congress has a vast collection of U.S. city directories available on microfilm. Although these directories are not available for interlibrary loan, viewing the list at the Library of Congress Web site *(www.loc.gov/rr/ microform/uscity/)* clues you in to the cities and years for which they were published. Figure 4.5 illustrates a few of the Michigan city directories available at the Library of Congress. The National Archives and Records Administration in Washington, D.C., also maintains a large collection of microfilmed city directories for many locations in the United States. To see which cities are available, view the NARA Web site *(www.archives.gov/research_room/genealogy/census/city_directories_1930.html.)*

What if you can't go to Washington to look at these city directories? Most local libraries have a collection of directories for their areas. Search the online catalog of a major library in the area you're researching to see whether it has local city directories. You may be able to e-mail a request to the reference desk at the library requesting a lookup in a particular directory. Some transcribed or scanned city directories have been placed on Web sites by individuals or organizations. For more help on finding a specific directory, refer to the sidebar "Online Telephone Directories" on page 63. The

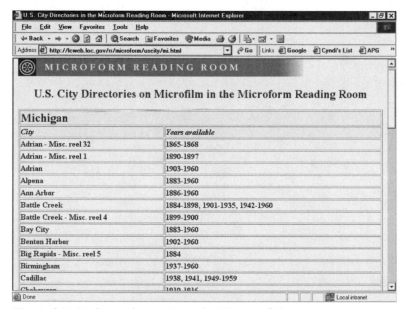

Figure 4.5 Michigan directories at the Library of Congress

City Directories category of Cyndi's List *(www.cyndislist.com/citydir.htm)* also points you to quite a few Web sites that may be helpful.

School Records

School records may include student censuses, grades, enrollment, information about teachers and administrators, budgets, curricula, and other facts. These records are usually retained by local schools or school boards, but they may have been removed to county or state archives or other facilities. If the school had a religious affiliation, records may be found at the archives of that denomination. To locate school records for a region, try a Google search of a term such as *"school records" + Colorado*. Figure 4.6 shows a sample search result for Colorado, listing the location of school census records for each Colorado county. Although the school censuses are not available on the Internet, this information points to the exact repository holding the original records.

The Internet offers great resources for finding old school friends and classmates. Try using a search engine to find Web sites associated with your school, or register with and search Web sites like Classmates.com *(www.classmates.com)* or Reunion.com *(www.highschoolalumni.com)*.

County	Location of Records	County	Location of Records
Adams	County Clerk & Recorder	Kit Carson	School Dist. R-1 thru R-6
Alamosa	School Dist. RE-11	Lake	Archives 1880 - 1961
Arapahoe	Archives 1870 – 1964	La Plata	School Dist. R-9
Archuleta	Archives 1889 – 1964	Larimer	Archives 1879 – 1920
Baca	School Dist. R-4	Las Animas	Archives 1878 – 1964
Bent	Archives 1903 – 1960	Lincoln	Archives 1936 – 1942
Boulder	Archives 1877 – 1965	Logan	Archives 1911 – 1959
Chaffee	Archives 1884 – 1926	Mesa	Archives 1914 – 1964
Cheyenne	Archives 1951 – 1959	Mineral	Archives 1901 – 1964
Clear Creek	Archives 1874 -	Moffat	School Dist. RE-1
Conejos	Archives 1953 – 1967	Montezuma	Archives 1926 – 1963
Costilla	Archives 1920 – 1959	Montrose	County Clerk & Recorder
Crowley	School Dist. RE-1	Morgan	Archives 1899 – 1907
Custer	Archives 1891 – 1944	Otero	County Clerk & Recorder
Delta	Archives 1954 – 1967	Ouray	County Clerk & Recorder
Denver (1 district)	School Dist. 1	Park	School Dist. RE-2

Figure 4.6 Colorado State Archives school census records

Real Estate Records

Real estate records can help you locate individuals or the present owners of a historic property. Since real estate and property tax transactions are public record in many states, some counties provide a searchable database that includes an owner's name and address and the property's description, value, and date of purchase. To look for such a database, use a search phrase similar to *"real estate tax"* + *"Dona Ana County"*. For a partial list of links to county Web sites with assessment information, go to *arl.kevino.com/* and scroll down to Municipal and County Assessment Data on the Web or visit *www.lawresearch.com/investigate/inv-pr-county-city.htm*.

Voter Registration

Voter registration lists often contain information such as name, address, place of birth, length of residence, and even the date and court of record for naturalization. To find these lists, do a Google search similar to *"voter registration records"* + *Boston*. Results might turn up a searchable database of current voters or a transcribed list of voters in previous centuries. More likely, you'll find a site describing microfilmed or original voter registration lists and their locations within the area you're searching. You can then contact the appropriate agency to request a search for specific names.

Businesses and Licenses

Most states require registration of businesses and corporations, and quite a few offer online searchable databases of corporate information, including a business's startup date, its current status, and the name and address of its registered agent. To find a business entity database, use a search phrase like *"Missouri corporation registration"*. A list of links to free public record sites, including trademarks, corporations, or businesses, can be found at *www.peoplefindernow.com/freelink.htm*.

You can see how the Internet helps you find information about living or recently deceased relatives—information that may enable you to bridge the gap to your common long-ago ancestors. The next chapter offers tips for uncovering family sources from living individuals and from a world of Internet resources.

CHAPTER 5

Revealing Family Sources

THE FIRST PLACE YOU SHOULD BEGIN YOUR FAMILY HISTORY PURSUIT is with your own family. The golden rule in genealogy is to begin with yourself and work backward, proving each link to a new generation in the past. You will learn far more from an interview if you have a plan. This chapter points you to resources that help you plan and carry out effective interviews with relatives, share information with others, and identify and locate sources of personal papers such as Bibles, diaries, or letters.

Interviewing Living Sources

An African proverb reminds us that when an old person dies, a library burns. Many genealogists rue the fact that they did not begin their research sooner, while grandparents or great-grandparents were still living and could provide rich details about earlier times. One of the first and most important steps in your research should be to interview the oldest living members of your family while they are still able to provide reliable facts and family stories.

The Internet offers a large assortment of aids and suggestions for interviewing living sources, from questions that will draw out the answers you want to exercises that teachers can integrate into a history curriculum. Questions such as, "How did your family celebrate Christmas?" or "Where were you and what did you think when you learned about the bombing of Pearl Harbor during World War II?" move your interview in a direction that provides you with valuable family information.

The Association of Personal Historians helps others preserve their personal histories and life stories. Its Web site *(www.personalhistorians.org/)* provides tips for writing life stories, memory sparks to help ignite recollections, and links to beneficial resources for personal historians.

The Oral History & Interviews category at Cyndi's List *(www.cyndislist.com/oral.htm)* provides links to guides for interviewing family members, analyzing the credibility of family legends, preparing an oral history, and conducting video or audio interviews. Cyndi's List also contains links to libraries or institutions with oral history programs or collections; links to books, software, or supply sources that aid in oral history collection; and links to societies that specialize in oral or personal history.

Prepare for your interview by assembling the proper equipment and scheduling an appointment with your subject. It's also important that you make your subjects comfortable and ask them open-ended questions that they can fully answer. Web sites like the one shown in Figure 5.1, KBYU's Capturing the Past: How to Prepare and Conduct an Oral History Interview, help you prepare for and develop questions for your meeting.

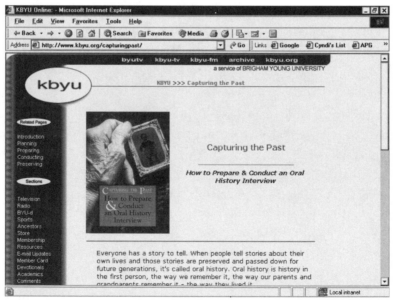

Figure 5.1 KBYU's Capturing the Past

Oral History Interviews

Oral history interviews should draw out facts and vivid memories from the person you're inter-viewing. To find resources on the Internet, try a Google search of a phrase similar to *"oral his-tory interview."* If you're stumped when it comes to the kinds of questions to ask a family member, check out a few of these Web sites for suggestions:

- Genealogy.About.Com's Oral History—Interviewing Relatives
  (genealogy.about.com/cs/oralhistory/)

- Get Nosy with Aunt Rosie: How to Conduct an Oral History Interview—Genealogy.com's Learning Center *(www.genealogy.com/genealogy/70_tipsoral.html)*

- KBYU's Capturing the Past *(www.kbyu.org/capturingpast/)*

- Oral History Interview, Questions and Topics—JewishGen Infofile
  (www.jewishgen.org/infofiles/quest.txt)

KBYU's Web site guides you through the four stages of planning, preparing for, conducting, and preserving your interview. It provides helpful tips, such as getting the tapes ready and labeling them before the interview to avoid interruptions, and including the questions when transcribing an interview to provide context for future listeners.

Locating Personal Papers

Wouldn't it be great to find a family Bible recording the bare bones of your ancestors' lives—their names and the important milestones and places they occurred? Beyond that, wouldn't you like to flesh out those names and dates with details about their overland journey on the westward trail, their experiences while serving in the military, or the details of businesses in which they were engaged? Diaries, letters, business account books, and other personal papers reveal facts and figures about real people leading real lives. Look for such papers within your extended family and in archives and manuscript collections throughout the world.

Even if your ancestors left no written trace, seek out personal papers of their contemporaries, people living in the same geographic area at about the same time. Find an original or transcribed diary of a pioneer woman who made the trek from Independence, Missouri, to the Oregon Territory when your great-great-grandmother did and learn about her experiences. Search for a written account of the activities of your ancestor's regiment or company during the Civil War in a regimental history or in original statements of comrades in pension files of the era. A bonus of finding business account books for a community may be a mention of purchases by your ancestor.

Why read about people who aren't even related to you? Your ancestors may be mentioned in personal papers of other residents of their community. Even if they are not, learning about the climate, social conditions, industries, or other details of your ancestors' immediate area may help you understand more about them. For instance, if your ancestors were tobacco farmers in Virginia but you cannot find a trace of them after they left that area, it may help to study the papers and diaries of their neighbors. The neighbors may mention that several families moved on to southern Kentucky for better tobacco land, providing you a clue about where to look for your lost ancestors. Mention of a cholera epidemic in a doctor's record book may help you determine a possible cause of death for an ancestor. Reading about other people in the area you are researching gives you a better understanding of your own ancestors' lives.

Begin Close to Home

Since a proven genealogy begins with you, start by looking around your home or your parents' home for papers about your own birth, education, military service, marriage, and other life events. You may find original vital records or newspaper clippings, diaries, old letters, or other items. As you locate these objects, be sure to record them on your research log, enter them in your genealogy database program, and note the exact location where they are filed or stored.

Ask your parents or grandparents if they possess or know of any family documents such as letters a relative may have written home during twentieth-century wars like Vietnam, Korea, or World Wars I and II. Take your request to the child or family that a grandparent last resided with; they may have kept some items upon the death of the parent. Discussions about present-day letters or teenage diaries may prompt memories of a packet of Spanish-American War letters or an old Bible.

As you express an interest in family history to relatives, you may be surprised to find other original records in their possession. When I first became interested in genealogy

Finding Personal Papers in Libraries and Archives

Unless you have a lot of time and money, you probably can't visit every repository in the areas where your ancestors lived, much less all the areas where their descendants migrated. But you can search indexes of a good number of repositories online and then write those repositories or hire a researcher to make on-site copies of the documents you need. Harvard's Widener Library offers a series of excellent online research guides by Fred Burchsted, including "Finding Personal Papers in United States Repositories" *(www.people.fas.harvard.edu/~burchst/FPPiUSR.html)* and "Research Guides for Finding Sources in History" *(www.people.fas.harvard.edu/~burchst/)*. Some of the sites Burchsted recommends are available free of charge to anyone through the Internet. Others may be offered through your local university or public library, either at the library or through home access as a library-card holder.

Here are a few general sources for finding personal papers or documents throughout the United States:

- WorldCat OCLC (Online Computer Library Center) Online Union Catalog, introduced in 1971, consists of merged catalogs from libraries around the world. It includes holdings such as books, manuscripts, periodicals, films, and photographs. Access to WorldCat is usually gained through a university or public library; some libraries offer remote access to WorldCat from patrons' locations by verifying a username and password. Check with your local library to see whether it offers WorldCat.

- National Union Catalog of Manuscript Collections (NUCMC—pronounced *nuckmuck*) is a free cataloging program for archives and manuscript materials run by the Library of Congress. Access to the approximately seven hundred thousand catalog items in the Research Libraries Group (RLG) Union Catalog is provided by the Library of Congress *(lcweb.loc.gov/coll/nucmc/nucmc.html)*.

- University of Idaho Library Special Collections and Archives provides a list of links to Web sites of worldwide repositories that contain original sources for researchers *(www.uidaho.edu/special-collections/Other.Repositories.html)*.

years ago, I visited my grandfather and asked questions about his parents and siblings. This prompted him to leave the room for a few minutes and return with an old Bible that had belonged to his mother, Naomi. This was not a traditional family Bible with pages for record keeping, but it did contain a one-page loose-leaf handwritten list of family information—Naomi's, her husband's, and her children's names and birth dates, and her marriage date and place. Also tucked away within the Bible's pages were my great-grandfather's original discharge from the Union Army in 1865, several papers Naomi had kept regarding her widow's military pension, and a title for a 1921 Ford Coupe that had belonged to one of her sons. Until I asked questions about our family, I did not have an inkling that these papers were stored in my grandfather's house.

Search Public or Private Collections

Long-time genealogists have learned to add the cautionary phrase "that I know of" to the end of many sentences. You'll hear, "I have no German ancestors, *that I know of*," or "There are no Bibles or diaries or letters written by my family members, *that I know of*." We all learn from experience that it's good to keep an open mind about possibilities we have not completely exhausted. Even though you find no evidence of family documents in your immediate family's possession, they may still exist someplace, and that "someplace" may be many states away from where your ancestors lived. A transcribed discussion about the old plaza in Santa Fe, New Mexico, and various mountain men, including Tim Goodale, Ceran St. Vrain, and L. B. Maxwell can be located at the University of California Berkeley campus's Bancroft Library, rather than at a more logical location in a New Mexico library or archive. Materials made their way westward as families migrated, and in today's mobile society, you may find a family diary, Bible, or business papers in almost any locale nationwide.

Most of the vast number of personal papers housed in libraries, archives, and museums have not been published and are not available on the Internet. But the wonderful resources of the World Wide Web can help you locate many of these incredibly rich resources. Chapter 13, "Using Libraries and Archives Effectively," provides in-depth details about accessing and using online catalogs, but here are a few examples of using Internet resources in your quest for personal papers.

NUCMC Search

Using the advanced search form of the National Union Catalog of Manuscript Collections (NUCMC) *(lcweb.loc.gov/coll/nucmc/nucmc.html)*, a query is entered for *Groton Massachusetts*. Query results include several records, three of which are relevant for Groton, Massachusetts:

- Collection of miscellaneous correspondence (1862–1904) from George S. Boutwell, a United States Senator and Representative from Groton—collection held by Rutherford B. Hayes Presidential Center, Fremont, Ohio.

- Oral history of Groton School, 1885–1985, including interviews with some of its more famous graduates—collection held by Groton School Library, Groton, Massachusetts.

- Correspondence, court records, and other papers (1775–1856) of Timothy Farrar (1788–1874) and his father, Timothy Farrar (1747–1842), of New Hampshire, including an item regarding counterfeiting in Groton, Massachusetts—collection held by New England Historic Genealogical Society, Boston, Massachusetts.

While someone might very well check with the Groton School Library for an oral history of that school, researchers might not intuitively try the New England Historic Genealogical Society in Boston for personal papers of a New Hampshire family and probably would not search a manuscript collection in Ohio for letters of a politician from Groton, Massachusetts. The value of NUCMC is that it can reveal original records in locations that you may not have considered.

WorldCat Search

WorldCat combines the catalogs of libraries worldwide and includes entries for all kinds of holdings beyond traditional books—photographs, videos, manuscripts, and even theses and dissertations. Using WorldCat's advanced search feature, a query for *Missouri history* narrowed to find only theses or dissertations yields numerous entries. One example is a 1984 doctoral thesis at Wayne State University by Richard Edmond Bennett entitled "Mormons at the Missouri: A History of the Latter-day Saints at Winter Quarters and at Kanesville, 1846–52; A Study in American Overland Trail Migration." The WorldCat entry further lists ten libraries in Iowa, Idaho, Nebraska, Texas, Utah, and Wyoming that own copies. You can learn more about WorldCat in Chapter 13.

Regional Catalogs

Be sure to search repositories in the area you are researching. Many regional archives and libraries provide information about their holdings, offer online catalogs to their collections, and show helpful finding aids on their Web sites. For example, the St.

Louis Mercantile Library Web site *(www.umsl.edu/mercantile/)* presents a detailed calendar of its special collections, describes its nationally relevant Herman T. Pott National Inland Waterways Library and John W. Barriger III National Railway Library, and directs researchers to its holdings, which are catalogued in the University of Missouri St. Louis online catalog *(www.umsl.edu/services/library/)*.

Finding Transcribed or Published Papers

All genealogists wish they could find an old trunk in someone's attic chock-full of family Bibles, certificates, ancestors' diaries, letters, or other memorabilia. Many are lucky enough to locate one or two of these items. But what if you descend from illiterate farmers who left very few possessions? You might be surprised to learn that even poor families often owned a Bible in which they recorded births, marriages, and deaths. Before vital statistics registration in the twentieth century, these Bible records were often the only record of life events. And even if Papa and Mama could not read or write, their son still may have written letters home from the war for someone else to read for them. You may be fortunate enough to locate such treasures if you search diligently.

If you are unable to locate personal papers within the family, expand your search to the Internet. Numerous sources exist for historical records or personal papers, including many online transcriptions of diaries, letters, or family information from old Bibles. Start with a general search. For instance, the Google search results shown in Figure 5.2 represent 177 Web sites that contain the terms *Bible* and *"Cumberland County, Virginia,"* many citing a family Bible as the source of information about an individual with a Cumberland County connection.

Bible Records

The National Society Daughters of the American Revolution (NSDAR) has long worked diligently to gather and transcribe old family Bible records, which are housed at the DAR Library in Washington, D.C. Search the DAR Library catalog online *(dar.library.net/)* to determine whether a volume of transcriptions exists for the area you are researching. If you can't go to Washington to look at the book, try searching for a duplicate in large libraries in your community or at the state repository that houses the DAR collection for your state or region.

At its Web site, the Library of Virginia provides scanned images of more than six thousand family Bible records from Virginia. Some are typewritten transcriptions by

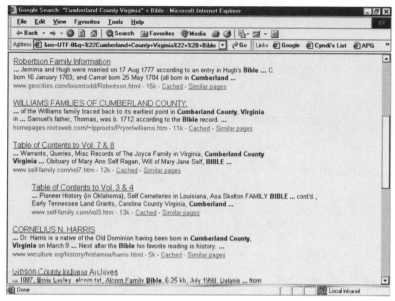

Figure 5.2 Locality search for Bible records

members of the Depression-era Works Progress Administration Historical Inventory Project in Virginia. Others are images of actual original family Bibles. If you have Virginia ancestry, be sure to search for Bibles in the online Library of Virginia Archives and Manuscripts catalog *(eagle.vsla.edu/bible/virtua-basic.html).*

Search GenWeb County Sites

Many of the USGenWeb Project's state or county pages offer links to transcriptions or abstracts of family records on Web sites hosted by a variety of organizations or individuals. These records include family Bibles, military records, biographies, family histories, family group sheets, memorabilia, and wills. You should check county pages or message boards for localities where your ancestors lived, where the family originated, where the family ended up, and even where collateral lines migrated. Any of these sites just might offer personal papers that provide the missing link you've been seeking to solve your family mystery.

To find a USGenWeb state or county site, go to the state list shown in Figure 5.3 *(www.usgenweb.com/statelinks-table.html)* and click the name of a state. The state GenWeb page displays (see the Iowa GenWeb page shown in Figure 5.4), and on that

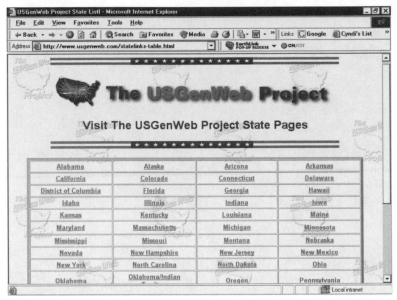

Figure 5.3 USGenWeb state pages

Figure 5.4 Iowa GenWeb page

page you'll find a link to a list of county pages and a link to archives and special projects for the state. Either of these links eventually takes you to the abstracted or transcribed family records for a specific county.

From the Iowa GenWeb page, you can click the County List link to bring up a list or a map of counties in Iowa. Then click on a link to a county to visit that county's GenWeb page, where you'll find the family records. You can also click the link to Iowa's GenWeb Archives and Special Projects, where you'll read about federal and state census transcription projects, a project devoted to orphan train riders and another to Iowa family memorabilia that has been lost or found. The Iowa GenWeb Archives and Special Projects site also contains a link to the Iowa GenWeb Archives, and there you'll find links to the state's county archives projects. Clicking on the Linn County link results in a list of biographies and other records for that county (see Figure 5.5). Any of the biographies or other text files can be opened, read, copied to your word processor, or printed.

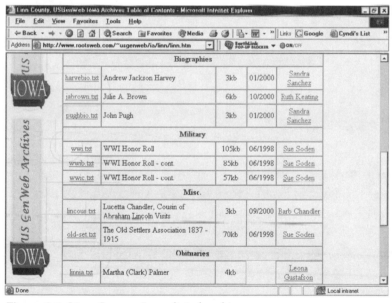

Figure 5.5 Linn County, Iowa digital archives

Ancestry.com/RootsWeb.com Message Boards

RootsWeb.com message boards hosted by Ancestry.com are similar to bulletin boards you see in your neighborhood grocery store. Instead of selling cars or giving away puppies, people post messages to these boards that contain personal records, such as Bibles, military discharges, wills, and others. To locate a county or state message board at RootsWeb or Ancestry.com, access *boards.ancestry.com/* and enter the name of a state or county (see Figure 5.6). Click a link on the resulting list to access the topic or county message board you want to search.

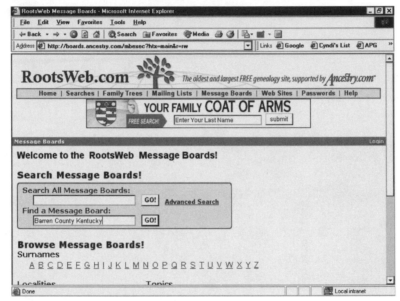

Figure 5.6 Find a RootsWeb message board

When you go into a state or county message board, every message posted on that board displays, and your screen looks like the one in Figure 5.7. To see only Bible records, click on the drop-down menu to the right of View Message Type and select Bible.

You can more effectively search a RootsWeb message board by using the Advanced Search feature. When your message board appears, click the Advanced Search link at the top of the screen to access a screen like the one in Figure 5.8. Select the radio button next to your board name, enter a name in the Find Messages Containing field, and choose the record type you want to find. The search in Figure 5.8 scans the text of all Biography category messages in the Barren County, Kentucky, board. Remember that the resulting message title and brief description may not contain the name you entered. Be sure to click the message link and read the entire message or transcript.

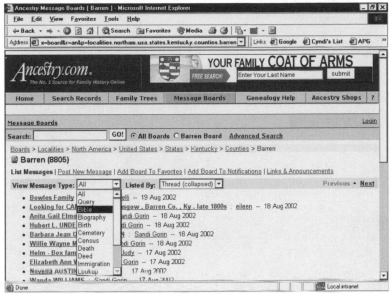

Figure 5.7 Display Bible records in a RootsWeb message board

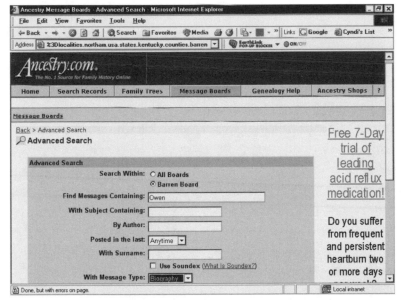

Figure 5.8 Advanced Search for an ancestor in a RootsWeb message board

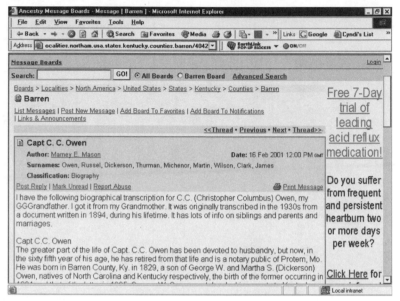

Figure 5.9 Biography transcript from a RootsWeb message board

The search for the name Owen in Barren County (Kentucky) Biography messages resulted in one transcription of a biography for Capt. C. C. Owen, transcribed from an 1894 document written during Owen's lifetime. Figure 5.9 shows the transcript of this RootsWeb Message Boards Biography result.

Transcribed Historical Records

The Depression-era Works Progress Administration (WPA) devoted some of its resources to inventorying, indexing, and transcribing historical records throughout the United States, including family Bibles, county courthouse records, and newspapers. WPA-employed writers also gathered information and wrote guidebooks to states or regions. In many states, the Federal Writers' Project of the WPA interviewed and collected information from former slaves. These narratives were gathered together as the seventeen-volume *Slave Narratives: A Folk History of Slavery in the United States from Interviews with Former Slaves.* These slave narratives provide important facts and details of life in the pre–Civil War South, mentioning both African-American and white family members and neighbors.

The Library of Congress has made more than twenty-three hundred of these slave narratives and more than two hundred black and white photographs of former slaves available online with its project *Born in Slavery: Slave Narratives from the Federal Writers' Project, 1936–1938*. Browse or search these important personal papers at the Library of Congress American Memory Web site *(memory.loc.gov/ammem/snhtml/snhome.html)*.

WPA Federal Writers' Project

Many results of the federal government's Works Progress Administration Federal Writers' Project can be found across the United States, from the Library of Congress to state libraries or county courthouses. A Google search of the phrase *Works Progress Administration Federal Writers Project* results in about twenty-nine thousand hits. To find slave narrative transcripts, inventories, indexes, state guides, or other materials for an area you're researching, try a Google search that adds the state name, using a phrase similar to *Works Progress Administration Federal Writers Project New Mexico*.

This particular search for New Mexico WPA records reveals a descriptive summary of twelve linear feet of WPA collection records housed at the New Mexico State Records Center and Archives. These original records include information about, to name just a few items, folk songs, social life and customs, topography, place names, old cattle trails and ranches, county histories, an inventory of federal archives in New Mexico, a 1941 Historical Records Survey list of publications, and a 1938 *Guide to Depositories of Manuscript Collections*. Similar information about your area of research would be invaluable.

The Periodical Source Index

Thorough genealogists always check the PERiodical Source Index (PERSI) for references to any articles about their ancestors or to topics or locations of interest. PERSI is an index of genealogical and historical periodical articles created and updated regularly by the Allen County Public Library in Fort Wayne, Indiana. It is an invaluable source of published records. Articles indexed in PERSI range from the 1700s to the present, and the index catalogs about fifty-five hundred different periodicals written in English and French (Canadian entries).

PERSI is available in print form at many genealogical libraries. Some libraries also provide access to the CD-ROM or online versions via a library computer. The CD-ROM version of PERSI, available for purchase by individuals for home use, is published by Ancestry.com. Ancestry.com also offers a paid subscription that includes access to its online version of PERSI at *www.ancestry.com/search/rectype/periodicals/persi/main.htm.*

How does PERSI work? You can search it by any combination of surname, given name, or article title keyword; by state, county, article title keyword, or record type for U.S. articles; by province, article title keyword, or record type for Canadian articles; by nation or area, article title keyword, or record type for foreign localities; or by article title keyword or record type for methodology articles. The resulting listing provides the information needed to locate the article: its title, the publication it appears in, and the volume and number. Clicking on the periodical title link displays detailed information about the publication: its publisher and address, number of issues per year, PERSI code, which issues are available at Allen County Public Library, and whether other large repositories include the publication in their collections.

A sample search of PERSI's Surname section for all articles relating to the surname Wilcox with *diary* as the article title keyword (see Figure 5.10) turns up three matches: a Civil War diary of Charles E. Wilcox (Capt.) published in the *Illinois Historical Journal*, a Civil War diary for W. H. Wilcox of Illinois published in the *Grand Prairie Historical Society Bulletin*, and a Civil War diary for William H.

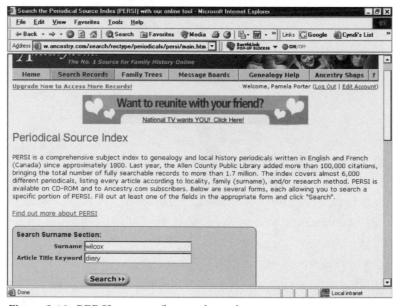

Figure 5.10 PERSI surname/keyword search

Wilcox, 77th Illinois, in Arkansas, published in the *Jefferson County Historical Quarterly*. These search results are shown in Figure 5.11. Clicking on the periodical title for *Grand Prairie Historical Society Bulletin* reveals that the journal is produced twice a year and that the Family History Library, State Historical Society of Wisconsin, New York Public Library, and Allen County Public Library hold at least partial collections of the publication beginning with volume 1 in 1958, as shown in Figure 5.12. Simply click on a library's name link to display the mailing address for the library.

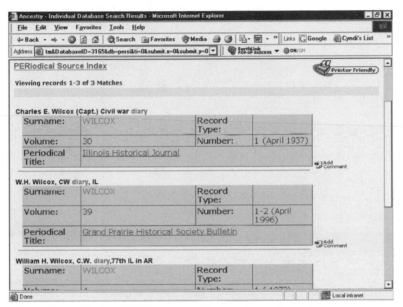

Figure 5.11 Typical PERSI surname/keyword search results

Once you have searched PERSI and found the title and identifying information about an article, you can locate the entire article itself. Local library genealogical collections may have the periodical you need. If you can't locate a publication locally, you can order a copy from the Allen County Public Library Foundation by downloading a PERSI order form from *www.acpl.lib.in.us/database/graphics/order_form.html* and mailing it and a modest fee for photocopying and handling. You can also contact the publisher directly to see whether you can order a copy of the article or that particular issue.

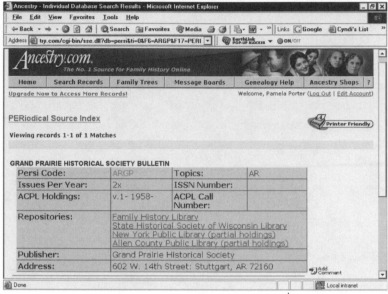

Figure 5.12 PERSI publication information

Surely, by now you are convinced that learning more about your ancestors than their vital record dates and their "begats" is a fulfilling pursuit. The many details of their lives that can be gleaned from interviews, Bibles, diaries, letters, and other personal papers are well worth the effort.

It is amazing how much you can find out about your ancestors and the history they lived through using the Internet. From how to conduct a better interview with family members, to locating Bibles and letters, to articles that mention your ancestors, the Internet provides the source material or its possible location.

CHAPTER 6

Acquiring Vital Records

Since genealogical research begins in the present and works backward to the past, some of the first records you need are vital records. This chapter helps you locate birth, marriage, divorce, and death records and points you to sites that help you order photocopies of the documents. You will also learn about funeral homes and virtual cemeteries that can provide death evidence.

> **Vital records** are birth, marriage, divorce, and death documents that record these important life events. Some genealogists humorously refer to them as "hatched, matched, and dispatched" records.
>
> **Vital statistics** are numbers that relate to deaths, births, and marriages as they affect the population. Many states' vital statistics programs track such things as the child mortality rate, the number of marriages and divorces, and the numbers of deaths caused by certain diseases, among other things.

Locating Vital Records Sources for an Area

Laws that govern record-keeping procedures for vital statistics vary among states in the United States. For the most part, the keeping of vital records at the state level is a twentieth-century occurrence, although some records do exist for prior periods, usually recorded in county government offices such as the probate court. It's important to learn the dates when vital records registration formally began in the area you are researching and whether records are held at the county or the state level.

A good starting place for learning about available vital records for the state you're researching is the Vital Records Information Web site *(www.vitalrec.com),* which provides details about vital records in the United States, such as dates when registration began and the cost and procedure for ordering birth, death, marriage, or divorce records from each state. This Web site lists the state agency responsible for vital records registration and its contact information, including an e-mail address and link to the state's Web site. A brief history of vital records registration in the state is also provided. For example, for New Hampshire (shown in Figure 6.1), birth, death, and marriage records since 1883 are available from the Bureau of Vital Records, but some vital records since 1640 can be obtained from the town clerk's office in the town where the event occurred. Divorce records since 1808 can be ordered from the State of New Hampshire or from the Clerk of the Superior Court in the county where the divorce occurred.

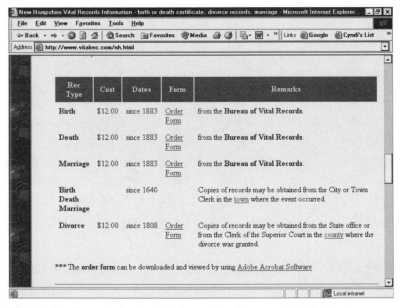

Figure 6.1 State vital records information from *www.vitalrec.com*

What County Is It In?

It is often necessary to know what county a town or city lies within when looking for vital records. Use the U.S. Geological Survey's Geographic Names Information System (GNIS) at *geonames.usgs.gov/* for the United States and its territories. Just enter a feature name (town, city, mountain, or other geographic feature) and a state to determine the county in which the feature lies.

This Vital Records Information Web site also provides links to online forms for ordering a certificate from the appropriate agency, contact information for county clerks or county vital records offices within a state, contact information for city vital records offices (if applicable), and links to related online vital records indexes or sources such as those on Ancestry.com or USGenWeb.

The FamilySearch Web site provides Research Outlines for U.S. localities and for many foreign countries. Not only do these online guides contain embedded links to vital records office Web sites, but they also provide information about which records for the area are available on microfilm or in published indexes through the Family History Library. To find a Research Outline for the area you're researching, go to *www.familysearch.org*, click the Search tab at the top of the screen, click Research Helps, click the beginning letter for the area (for example, G for Germany), and then click the link for the research guide (for instance, Germany—Research Outline). You will find information and links for vital records, or birth, death, and marriage records.

For information about vital records in countries outside the United States, try using a phrase similar to *"vital records" + Norway* in a search engine. Some Web sites, such as JewishGen, the Home of Jewish Genealogy, provide information about or links to vital records offices in foreign countries (see *www.jewishgen.org/infofiles/#Vitals*).

Using Online Vital Records Indexes or Abstracts

Quite a few indexes or abstracts of birth, marriage, divorce, and death records are spread across the Internet. There is no one place to search for all records from every state or country. This section shows you how to find records from the area you are researching and then analyze what you find.

Online Birth and Death Records

A few states maintain vital records indexes online for anyone to search. However, since the September 11, 2001 terrorist attack on the United States, many states have reconsidered their laws about privacy and the availability of vital records to the public. Some state laws mandate that only next of kin or a direct descendant be allowed to obtain copies of birth or death information. Other laws are so restrictive that you must almost know the very information you hope to find in order to receive a copy of the certificate. Many state laws regarding vital records are currently in flux; not only is public access to indexes at risk of being removed, but in some instances, access to the records themselves is being restricted. To find out about current availability of an area's records or indexes, consult the specific agency's Web site or contact the agency.

Birth Records

It's easy to find some states' birth records or indexes online. To look for birth records for South Dakota, I perform a Google search with a phrase similar to *online birth records South Dakota*. The resulting searchable database for the state of South Dakota (*www.state.sd.us/applications/ph14over100birthrec/index.asp*) explains that it contains just fewer than one hundred thousand birth records of individuals born more than a hundred years ago. Searching for a Joseph E. Taylor results in one birth record, shown in Figure 6.2, for Joseph Edgar Taylor, male, born 19 January 1867 in Clay County to Elizabeth Eaton and Lamb Barnett Taylor. It is important to read any FAQ or Help files to understand how the information is presented. Although the genealogical standard is to present dates in a day-month-year format, such as 1 June 2002, many databases do not follow this standard.

The file date for this record is 27 September 1943. Why would the birth record of someone born in 1867 be filed as late as 1943? Supplemental information on this Web site states that South Dakota's vital records registration did not start until July 1905, but that persons born before that date were given the opportunity to file their records after 1905. Genealogists sometimes find these delayed birth certificates for individuals born before official birth registration began in a state. Often people filed such records because they needed proof of age to qualify for Social Security benefits beginning in the 1930s.

The information obtained from any Web site is not the original record (unless it is an actual scanned image of the birth certificate posted by a reliable source). The clerk entering the data from the original record may have made data-entry errors or misread the handwriting on the document. You should try to obtain a copy of the original birth certificate to verify the abstracted information in the index and to see whether other information is available beyond that included in the online index. Depending on state requirements, an original birth certificate may contain information such as the number of other births for the child's mother, the hospital or location where the birth occurred, the mother's and father's ages and birthplaces, and the attendant or physician present at birth. Usually, the Web site of the state in question provides information about how to order a birth certificate.

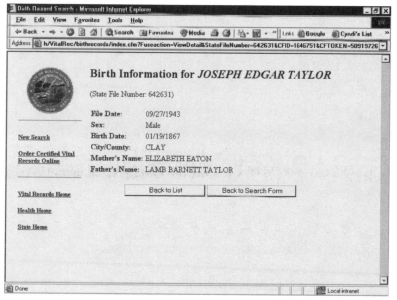

Figure 6.2 South Dakota birth information

Death Records

A death certificate can provide important facts about a person's life, such as name, birth date and place, parents' names, race, military service, educational level, marital status, spouse's name, death date and place, and cause of death. Actual details included on a death certificate vary from state to state. Most online death indexes or abstracts do not include all the particulars from a death certificate, but merely a summary or a few facts. However, usually the information from an index helps you request and obtain a copy of the actual death certificate.

My friend Mike's great-great-grandfather, Elias Francis, immigrated to New Mexico from what is now Lebanon just before 1900 and was still living at the time of the 1920 U.S. census. Not knowing when or where he died, we decided to look for an online record of his death in New Mexico. A Google search for *online death records New Mexico* turned up a USGenWeb Archives project, the New Mexico Death Index Project (1899–1940) *(www.rootsweb.com/~usgenweb/nm/nmdi.htm).* Perusing this index, I located a listing for Elias Francis, who died 14 March 1930 in Bernalillo County at age seventy-three years, six months (see Figure 6.3). Since the Elias Francis I am seeking was listed as age sixty-two in the January 1920 New Mexico census and since members of his family moved from Valencia to the adjacent Bernalillo County during the 1920s, this entry in the online death index probably refers to the same individual.

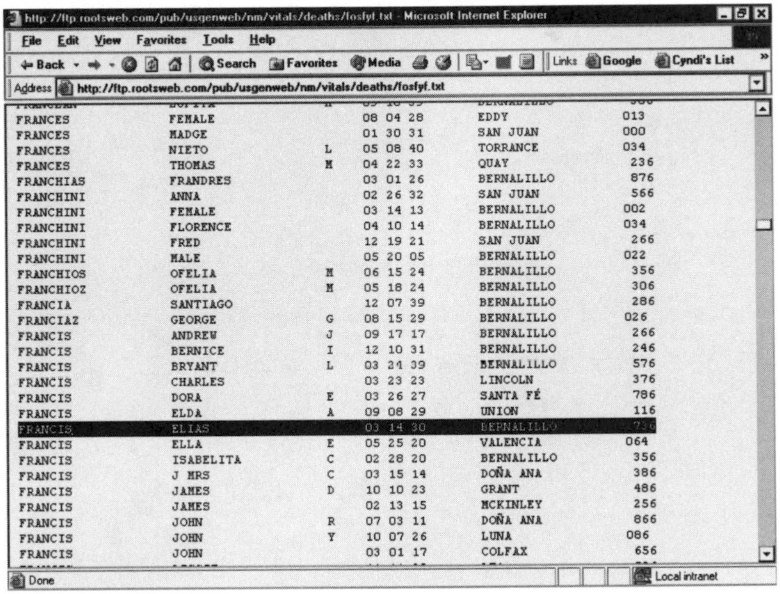

FRANCES	FEMALE		08 04 28	EDDY	013
FRANCES	MADGE		01 30 31	SAN JUAN	000
FRANCES	NIETO	L	05 08 40	TORRANCE	034
FRANCES	THOMAS	M	04 22 33	QUAY	236
FRANCHIAS	FRANDRES		03 01 26	BERNALILLO	876
FRANCHINI	ANNA		02 26 32	SAN JUAN	566
FRANCHINI	FEMALE		03 14 13	BERNALILLO	002
FRANCHINI	FLORENCE		04 10 14	BERNALILLO	034
FRANCHINI	FRED		12 19 21	SAN JUAN	266
FRANCHINI	MALE		05 20 05	BERNALILLO	022
FRANCHIOS	OFELIA	M	06 15 24	BERNALILLO	356
FRANCHIOZ	OFELIA	M	05 18 24	BERNALILLO	306
FRANCIA	SANTIAGO		12 07 39	BERNALILLO	286
FRANCIAZ	GEORGE	G	08 15 29	BERNALILLO	026
FRANCIS	ANDREW	J	09 17 17	BERNALILLO	266
FRANCIS	BERNICE	I	12 10 31	BERNALILLO	246
FRANCIS	BRYANT	L	03 21 39	BERNALILLO	576
FRANCIS	CHARLES		03 23 23	LINCOLN	376
FRANCIS	DORA	E	03 26 27	SANTA FÉ	786
FRANCIS	ELDA	A	09 08 29	UNION	116
FRANCIS	ELIAS		03 14 30	BERNALILLO	736
FRANCIS	ELLA	E	05 25 20	VALENCIA	064
FRANCIS	ISABELITA	C	02 28 20	BERNALILLO	356
FRANCIS	J MRS	C	03 15 14	DOÑA ANA	386
FRANCIS	JAMES	D	10 10 23	GRANT	486
FRANCIS	JAMES		02 13 15	MCKINLEY	256
FRANCIS	JOHN	R	07 03 11	DOÑA ANA	866
FRANCIS	JOHN	Y	10 07 26	LUNA	086
FRANCIS	JOHN		03 01 17	COLFAX	656

Figure 6.3 New Mexico death index

However, this online file includes the important advice that "These files should only be used as guides for ordering copies of the originals from the New Mexico State Health Department. Transcription and typographical errors are possible." Now that we have located a county and date of death, Mike should order a copy of his great-great-grandfather's death certificate from the New Mexico Vital Records Department, and he will probably learn even more facts about Elias Francis's life—his parents, his wife, and even the status of his health before his death.

Online Searchable Death Indexes

If you're not sure an online index exists for the death records of a state you are researching, try this Web site: Online Searchable Death Indexes for the USA—a Guide for Genealogists and Other Researchers *(home.att.net/~wee-monster/deathrecords.html)*. It provides links to general databases such as the Social Security Death Index and RootsWeb's Cemetery Database, as well as links to state and county online death and obituary indexes.

Online Marriage and Divorce Records

Marriage records are sometimes easier to access than birth or death records, probably because they are less likely to be used for fraudulent purposes. While birth and death records for most states are recorded at the state level, marriages and divorces often may be found at the county level. Again, individual state laws determine which agency or court is responsible for marriage or divorce records. For example, Missouri marriage records are issued and recorded by the Recorder of Deeds of the county and its divorce records are filed with and maintained by the Clerk of the Circuit Court. In Massachusetts, the Registry of Vital Records and Statistics maintains marriage records for the entire state from 1911 to the present and copies of divorce records are available from the probate court where the divorce was granted.

Marriage Records

In most cases, a marriage license was issued to the bride and groom, and when they were married, the minister or officiant returned a form with the date and location to be recorded at the county courthouse or town hall. In some states, the groom and another party willing to ensure that no impediments to the marriage existed signed a marriage bond. Most online marriage indexes simply extract the date of the marriage, the names of the bride and groom, and information about the exact location of the recorded marriage document. This is enough to point you to the original marriage record, whether on microfilm through your local LDS Family History Center, or in its original form at the county courthouse or state archives.

A marriage record provides the names of the bride and groom and the date of marriage, but what else can it tell you? It might also include the bride's and groom's dates of birth, parents' names, and witnesses to the marriage. If one of the intended was underage, a handwritten note of permission from a parent or guardian may accompany the marriage record at the county courthouse or town hall.

Online marriage indexes can lead you to the original record. For example, I wanted to locate an 1800s marriage record for Allen Smith and Susan Carter in Barren County, Kentucky, so I used Google to search for *Kentucky marriages online.* The search resulted in a long list, including Kentucky's Vital Records Index *(ukcc.uky.edu/~vitalrec/),* which includes marriages only from 1973 to 1993. Looking further at the Google hits, I found a link to a site named GenWed.com, which contains a marriage database of early records from Barren County, Kentucky.

As you see in Figure 6.4, this database contained a record for Allen Smith and Susan Jane Carter, 4 December 1834, in Barren County. I learned Susan's middle name—

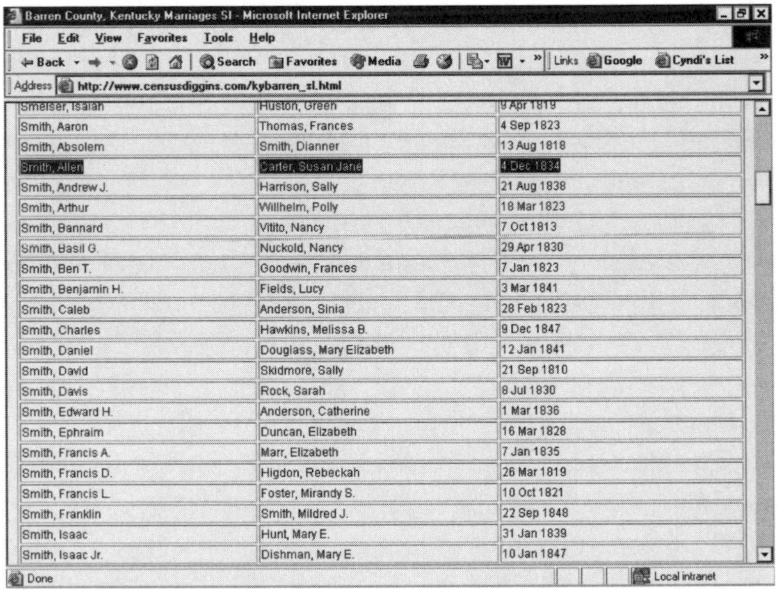

Smelser, Isaiah	Huston, Green	9 Apr 1819
Smith, Aaron	Thomas, Frances	4 Sep 1823
Smith, Absolem	Smith, Dianner	13 Aug 1818
Smith, Allen	Carter, Susan Jane	4 Dec 1834
Smith, Andrew J.	Harrison, Sally	21 Aug 1838
Smith, Arthur	Willhelm, Polly	18 Mar 1823
Smith, Bannard	Vitito, Nancy	7 Oct 1813
Smith, Basil G.	Nuckold, Nancy	29 Apr 1830
Smith, Ben T.	Goodwin, Frances	7 Jan 1823
Smith, Benjamin H.	Fields, Lucy	3 Mar 1841
Smith, Caleb	Anderson, Sinia	28 Feb 1823
Smith, Charles	Hawkins, Melissa B.	9 Dec 1847
Smith, Daniel	Douglass, Mary Elizabeth	12 Jan 1841
Smith, David	Skidmore, Sally	21 Sep 1810
Smith, Davis	Rock, Sarah	8 Jul 1830
Smith, Edward H.	Anderson, Catherine	1 Mar 1836
Smith, Ephraim	Duncan, Elizabeth	16 Mar 1828
Smith, Francis A.	Marr, Elizabeth	7 Jan 1835
Smith, Francis D.	Higdon, Rebeckah	26 Mar 1819
Smith, Francis L.	Foster, Mirandy S.	10 Oct 1821
Smith, Franklin	Smith, Mildred J.	22 Sep 1848
Smith, Isaac	Hunt, Mary E.	31 Jan 1839
Smith, Isaac Jr.	Dishman, Mary E.	10 Jan 1847

Figure 6.4 Barren County, Kentucky marriage index

Jane—and found a date of 4 December 1834. But was this the date of marriage, the date when the bride and groom obtained a license, or the date of the return? And wasn't it likely that other important information was included on the original license?

Because I know that this marriage occurred in Barren County, Kentucky, in December 1834, I was able to search the Family History Library online catalog *(www.familysearch.org/Eng/Library/FHLC/frameset_fhlc.asp)* and determine that Barren County marriage records of this period have been microfilmed and are available through my local Family History Center. I ordered the microfilm from Salt Lake City, and when it arrived, I viewed the microfilmed image of the original marriage record recorded in Barren County. I was glad I did! The original marriage record revealed that Allen Smith was married to Susan Jane Carter on 4 December 1834 by Andrew Nuckols. George W. Carter acted as surety (bondsman), and the bride's father, James Carter Sr., gave consent for the marriage, a sure indication that Susan was underage. Witnesses to the marriage were William H. Carter and George W. Carter. The marriage was recorded on 15 December 1834.

Looking at the original of this marriage record provided not only the bride's middle name, but her father's name, and possibly her two brothers' or other close relatives' names. The online index entry gave me what I needed to find the original record, but did not provide nearly the goldmine of information contained in the marriage record itself. This is one example of how the Internet can help speed along genealogical research, but should not be the end-all of our efforts.

Divorce Records

Divorce decrees may be issued in a variety of courts. For earlier time periods, you may have to look in the Acts of the State Legislature for information about a divorce, since that is where they were granted in some states up until the early to late 1800s. Today, most divorces are granted in a court at the county level. Again, you must make an effort to find out the applicable laws and court for the area you are researching.

If I am interested in obtaining information about a divorce granted in Colorado, a visit to the Web site of the Colorado Department of Public Health and Environment *(www.cdphe.state.co.us/hs/marriage.html)* informs me about records availability. There, I learn that divorce, separation, and annulment records from 1900 to the present are available from the Department of Public Health and Environment, except for those from 1940 to 1967. A dissolution granted during those years must be obtained from the clerk of the district court for the county where it was decreed. The Web site contains links to a chart and maps that identify the appropriate district court for any Colorado county.

I also learn from this Web site that an online index to Colorado divorces from 1968 to 2002 is available at *www.quickinfo.net/madi/comadi.html*. A search of this index yields the names of the petitioner and respondent in a divorce suit, the county abbreviation, the decree date and type, and a docket number. With this information from the online index, anyone can easily request a copy of the decree from the Colorado Department of Public Health and Environment.

Ordering Copies of Vital Records

Often, birth, death, marriage, or divorce records have not been microfilmed and are not available as digitized documents online. In that case, you may have to order a copy directly from the Vital Records office in the state you are researching. What you receive varies from state to state. You may obtain a copy of the original record, certified by the agency as being an exact duplicate. Instead of a photocopy, you may receive a typed form completed in the office that handles vital records and certified as an accurate record of the event. Some states even send a photocopy of the original record, but clearly mark it "for informational purposes only." If you have a choice, it's always best to look at the original record or an exact reproduction of it because errors can be made when transcribing or abstracting records. Additionally, a so-called transcription may not include all the information in the original document.

Most localities provide a Web site with information about ordering vital records, pricing, addresses, or online options. Try a search engine with a phrase like *Saskatchewan vital records* to find a Web site for the area you are researching.

Other Online Sources of Vital Records

RootsWeb

RootsWeb offers user-contributed databases of more than nine million birth, death, marriage, and divorce records *(userdb.rootsweb.com/regional.html)*. The database list, representing information from numerous countries and states, can be sorted by category of record or by country/state/region. If you sort the list by category, you can click the category title (Marriage Records, Birth Records, etc.) to bring up a search tool for that type of record, like the example shown in Figure 6.5.

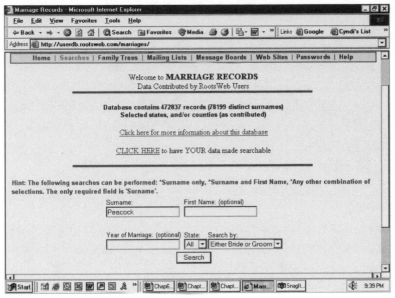

Figure 6.5 Search of a user-contributed marriage database at RootsWeb

For weekly updates about the latest information or databases added to RootsWeb, be sure to subscribe to the free online *RootsWeb Review*. To subscribe, visit the RootsWeb home page *(www.rootsweb.com)* and click the Subscribe link under Getting Started. When an e-mail form appears, type the word *subscribe* in the Subject field, and leave the message area blank. Send the subscribe message, and you should begin receiving *RootsWeb Review* in your e-mail box within a few days.

USGenWeb and WorldGenWeb
The USGenWeb Marriages Project site *(www.rootsweb.com/~usgenweb/marriages/)* links to marriage indexes or abstracts contributed by project volunteers. You may also find vital records abstracted and contributed by volunteers at WorldGenWeb's Online Digital Archives *(www.worldgenweb.org/archives/)*.

International Vital Records
If you need information about vital records in a country outside the United States, try searching Google or another search engine for a term similar to *vital records + Germany*. The Vital Records Information site *(www.vitalrec.com/links2.html)* also provides links to foreign vital records sources.

Subscription or Paid Services

Commercial subscription services like Ancestry.com *(www.ancestry.com)* or Genealogy.com *(www.genealogy.com)* offer online indexes or abstracts of vital records from many states. Ancestry.com subscriptions, available on a quarterly or annual basis, offer access to many published vital records sources. Genealogy.com's subscription service provides online access to the same information it publishes and sells on CD-ROMs, and it is possible to subscribe for only a month to try the service. Many libraries also provide access to these commercial services through computers at the library, free of charge to patrons.

Origins.net

The Web site *www.origins.net* provides access to databases of vital records information for Scotland, England, and Ireland. Some indexes can be searched free of charge, but you have to pay online with a credit card to see the actual record images or to order hard copies from Origins. Paying for many foreign services is usually surprisingly easy with a credit card.

Traipsing through Virtual Cemeteries

Cemetery gravestones or markers are simply another form of death record, and there are all kinds of cemetery records online to help with your genealogical research. A gravestone is only as reliable as the source of its information, so resist the urge to believe everything you see on a cemetery marker, even if it *is* carved in stone. Always try to verify with another source the names, dates, or relationship information that you obtain from a gravestone.

That said, online virtual cemeteries could still help you locate missing ancestors who just disappeared. Quite a few organizations and individuals have made it a priority to record the information on gravestones in cemeteries around the world and post the information on the Internet. This section describes just a few of them. To find a specific cemetery online, try a Google search similar to *cemeteries Metcalfe County Kentucky*.

Analyzing Burials in a Cemetery

Remember the nineteenth-century immigrant Francis family in New Mexico? A search of Interment.net Cemetery Transcription Library *(www.interment.net)* for

New Mexico cemeteries reveals twenty-one people with the Francis surname buried at Mount Calvary Cemetery in Albuquerque. You see in Figure 6.6 that the results provide the address and a brief history of Mount Calvary and even its latitude and longitude, making it easy to locate the burial ground on a map. Having learned from the online New Mexico death index that Elias Francis died in Bernalillo County, it stands to reason that he and some of his family members are buried there, too.

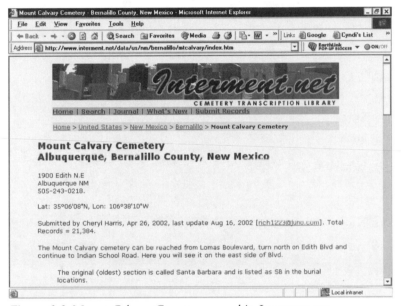

Figure 6.6 Mount Calvary Cemetery record in Interment.net

Unfortunately, many cemetery databases or publications are arranged alphabetically by surname rather than by the order in which people are buried. Since most people are buried beside spouses, parents, children, or other family members, rearranging the burials in alphabetical order results in the loss of valuable clues to relationships. You can get around this by carefully analyzing burial data.

In the case of the Francis burials, I enter the names, dates of birth and death, and cemetery section and row information into a simple spreadsheet or table of columns and rows. This way, the burial information can be sorted in different ways and analyzed for clues. First, in Figure 6.7, I sort it by cemetery section and row to see which Francises are buried close to one another.

Surname	First Name	Birth Date	Death Date	Section	Row
Francis	Jason Philip	d. 1976	baby	Sec. AD	Row 1
Francis	Felicita	b. 20 Jan 1911	d. 6 Mar 1998	Sec. B	Row 1
Francis	Floyd N	b. 13 May 1915	d. 3 Jun 1997	Sec. B	Row 1
Francis	Elizabeth 'Corky'	b. 22 Jul 1905	d. 12 Nov 1987	Sec. EC	Row 3
Francis	Michael M	b. 25 Sep 1899	d. 17 Nov 1987	Sec. EC	Row 3
Francis	Mary 'Mickey'	b. 21 Jun 1921	d. 16 Mar 1985	Sec. I	Row 10
Francis	Elias	b. 1857	d. 1930	Sec. NE-Cal	Row 8
Francis	Ethel G	b. 26 Jul 1916	d. 21 Nov 1991	Sec. NE-Cal	Row 8
Francis	Filomena	b. 1888	d. 1931	Sec. NE-Cal	Row 8
Francis	Narciso	b. 1881	d. 1973	Sec. NE-Cal	Row 8
Francis	Paulie H	b. 1863	d. 1946	Sec. NE-Cal	Row 8
Francis	Fred N Sr	b. 29 Apr 1911	d. 7 Sep 1997	Sec. North Circle	Row 12
Francis	Margaret C	b. 1918	d. 1972	Sec. North Circle	Row 12
Francis	Fred D	b. 25 Sep 1949	d. 9 Jan 1978	Sec. North Circle	Row 13
Francis	Isabel	b. 27 Jul 1939	d. 22 Aug 1976	Sec. North Circle	Row 13
Francis	Albert D	b. 19 Nov 1932	d. 18 Aug 1970	Sec. South	Row 16
Francis	Anthony L	b. 1 Jun 1952	d. 14 Oct 1995	Sec. South	Row 18
Francis	Andrea B	b. 1911	d. 1990	Sec. South	Row 19
Francis	Salim N	b. 1905	d. 1995	Sec. South	Row 19
Francis	Esther A	b. 1879	d. 1961	Sec. SW	Row 8
Francis	Naman M	b. 1884	d. 1951	Sec. SW	Row 8

Figure 6.7 Francis burials sorted by cemetery section and row

A quick glance shows that Elias and four other Francises are buried in Section NE-Cal, row 8. While this is not proof that these individuals are related to one another, it is a strong indication.

How can possible relationships among the five Francis burials in the same section and row be determined? Eliminating all but the Francises in Section NE-Cal, Row 8, in Figure 6.8, I sort the data again by birth date.

Sorting these people by birth date shows only six years' age difference between Elias and Paulie H., raising the possibility that they were husband and wife. The same is true for Narciso and Filomena Francis, with only seven years' age difference. It seems possible that Elias and Paulie H. are the parents of Narciso, given the ages. And Ethel G. Francis appears to be of a different generation, so perhaps she is a daughter or daughter-in-law of Narciso and Filomena.

Of course, it is important to gather further proof of these relationships—proof that can be obtained from death certificates, marriage records, other vital records, or obituaries. But simply rearranging the information obtained from an alphabetical cemetery database can shed new light on possible family relationships.

Surname	First Name	Birth Date	Death Date	Section	Row
Francis	Elias	b. 1857	d. 1930	Sec. NE-Cal	Row 8
Francis	Paulie H	b. 1863	d. 1946	Sec. NE-Cal	Row 8
Francis	Narciso	b. 1881	d. 1973	Sec. NE-Cal	Row 8
Francis	Filomena	b. 1888	d. 1931	Sec. NE-Cal	Row 8
Francis	Ethel G	b. 26 Jul 1916	d. 21 Nov 1991	Sec. NE-Cal	Row 8

Figure 6.8 Francis burials in Section NE-Cal sorted by birth date

Finding Online Cemetery Databases

To find a cemetery transcription project that includes burials for your area of research, look first at area genealogical society or county GenWeb sites. Then use a search engine by entering a phrase similar to *cemeteries + Oswego New York*. Here are just a few of the available online cemetery resources that help genealogists:

- **The Association for Gravestone Studies:** This organization of more than twelve hundred members supports and teaches cemetery preservation through workshops and information posted at its Web site *(www.gravestonestudies.org)*. Visit this site to learn about marker designs and symbolism, and even how to identify individual stone carvers in an area. You'll also find publications about how to photograph cemetery markers or take rubbings from them without damaging the stones.

- **Cyndi's List of Genealogy Sites on the Internet—Cemeteries and Funeral Homes:** Cyndi's List *(www.cyndislist.com/cemetery.htm)* provides quite a number of links to all kinds of information about cemeteries and funeral homes, including directories and transcriptions.

- **Find a Grave:** Visit the Find a Grave Web site *(www.findagrave.com)* to search its 3.7 million grave records.

- **Headstone Hunter:** Need a photograph of a headstone in a distant state? The service at *www.headstonehunter.com* matches volunteers willing to photograph headstones in their area to others who need a photograph.

- **Interment.net:** The Interment.net Cemetery Transcription Library *(www.interment.net)* provides more than 3 million cemetery records from around the world.

- **International Jewish Cemetery Project:** The International Association of Jewish Genealogical Societies (JewishGen) has created a project with the goal of cataloging every Jewish burial site throughout the world. The International Jewish Cemetery Project Web site *(www.jewishgen.org/cemetery/)* explains the project and provides links to regions throughout the world. The JewishGen Online Worldwide Burial Registry (JOWBR) eventually will be a searchable database of individual burials.

- **National Veterans Cemeteries:** Burial information for national cemeteries across the United States can be found at Interment.net's site *(www.interment.net)*.

- **Obituary Central's Cemetery Search:** Obituary Central is an important project that abstracts obituaries from published sources and makes them available on the Web at *www.obitcentral.com*. It also provides CemSearch, a tool that searches for a surname through thousands of online cemetery sources. Access CemSearch at *www.obitcentral.com/cemsearch/*.

🍃 **RootsWeb's Cemetery Records Database:** Another user-contributed database at RootsWeb, these cemetery records are searchable by surname, first name, or location. Search the more than six hundred thousand records at *userdb.rootsweb.com/cemeteries/.*

Funeral Home Records

Funeral home records can be valuable genealogical sources, providing the deceased's name, date and place of birth, date and place of death, burial location, parents' names, veteran status, and Social Security number. Such records may also list next of kin and provide information about who paid the account. I sought out the funeral home record of a bachelor brother of my great-grandfather and found a list of his nieces and nephews, each of whom had paid a portion of his funeral bill.

Some funeral home records may be online in the form of transcribed records submitted by volunteers. Figure 6.9 shows a sample transcription of Antill Funeral Home records in Cameron, West Virginia, found at *www.rootsweb.com/~wvmarsha/antill.htm.* To find online records for the area you are researching, try a search phrase like *funeral home records + West Virginia.*

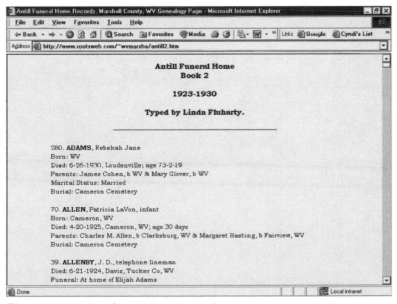

Figure 6.9 Online funeral home record

If you do not find the funeral home records you need on the Internet, you have to contact mortuaries in your ancestor's area to request information or hard copies. Mark Barker, a licensed funeral director in Tennessee, describes funeral home records and methods for gaining access to them in an article at *www.tngenweb.org/misc/funeralhomes.htm.*

To locate a funeral home in the area you are researching, use an online funeral directory service, such as *www.funeralnet.com* or *funeralhomesdirectory.com.*

By now, you've undoubtedly realized the value of acquiring records of your ancestors' births, marriages, deaths, and other life events, and you're ready to explore the Internet to see just how many online references you can find to someone in your own family. Remember, in order to keep it simple and to avoid getting lost among the vast array of resources, create your research plan and stick to it.

CHAPTER 7

Finding Ancestors in the Census or Other Lists

ONCE YOU EXHAUST THE SEARCH FOR EASY-TO-FIND VITAL RECORDS identifying an ancestor's birth, marriage, and death, you can fill in more life details by looking at lists such as U.S. or state censuses or jurisdictional tax lists. Compiled for specific purposes—usually taxation or representation—these lists help account for ancestors at regular intervals. You may track an ancestor from year to year in a county property tax list, or every ten years in the U.S. federal census.

The U.S. Census

The U.S. Constitution requires that a nationwide count of the population be taken every ten years to determine representation in the House of Representatives; the census has occurred since 1790. Before 1850, these census schedules recorded only the name of the head of household. Other members of the household were accounted for only by age groups and sex. As you can see in the online census image in Figure 7.1, this 1790 census of Groton, Massachusetts, lists the head of family and provides only the numbers of free white males sixteen years and older (including the head of the family), free white males under sixteen, free white females (including heads of families), all other free persons, and slaves. Beginning in 1850, the U.S. population schedule of the census recorded the name of every free person in a household, but it wasn't until 1880 that the relationship of each person to the head of household was identified.

Extant U.S. population census schedules from 1790 to 1930 and the census of 1885 **103**

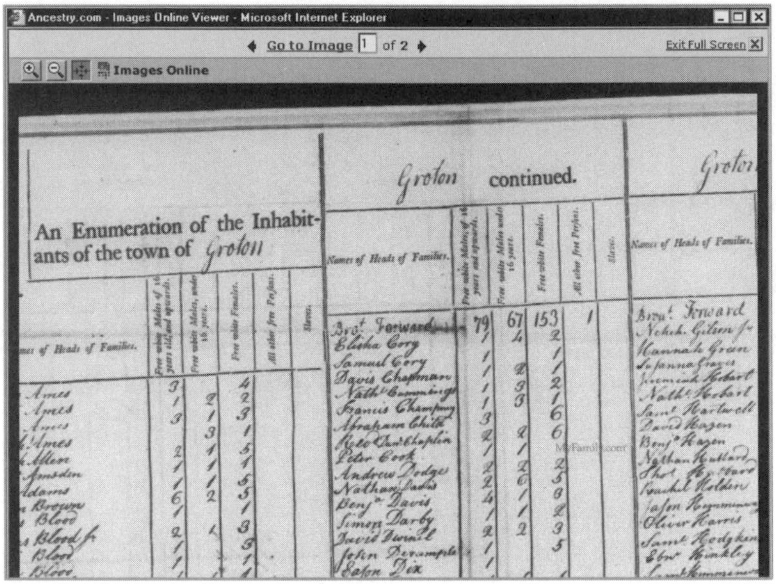

Figure 7.1 1790 census example

All about the Census

If you have any questions about the early censuses, the National Archives and Records Administration's online publication "1790–1890 Federal Population Censuses—Part 1" at *www.archives.gov/publications/microfilm_catalogs/census_schedules/1790_1890_federal_ population_census_part01.html* should answer them. This article addresses issues such as privacy restrictions on access to the census, where to find the census on microfilm, what is included in the various census schedules, privately printed indexes to the censuses, Soundex or Miracode indexes, and enumeration district descriptions. It also provides helpful research hints and a list of useful publications about the census. The National Archives' microfilm rental program is described, and instructions are provided for purchasing microfilm. There's even a list of abbreviations and terms used in Soundex cards, like *Sgd* for step-granddaughter or *Wt* for waiter.

Another online NARA article, "How to Use NARA's Census Microfilm Catalogs," at *www.archives.gov/research_room/genealogy/census/using_census_microfilm_catalogs.html* describes and tells how to use microfilmed indexes for the 1880–1920 censuses.

(a special census that enumerated only Colorado, Florida, Nebraska, Dakota Territory, and New Mexico Territory) are available on microfilm at the National Archives and Records Administration (NARA) in Washington, D.C., at NARA regional facilities throughout the nation, at the Family History Library, and at major regional libraries or archives. Unfortunately, all but about 1 percent of the 1890 census returns were destroyed by a fire and resulting damage in Washington, D.C. Part of the 1890 Special Union Veterans and Widows supplemental schedule does survive (read about it later in this chapter). The law does not allow a census to be released to the public until seventy-two years after it is taken, so the 1940 census will not be available until the year 2012.

In addition to the population count, special nonpopulation schedules were mandated during certain census years. The 1850–1880 censuses and the 1885 census include a mortality schedule with information about persons who died in the twelve months preceding the census. Special slave schedules in 1850 and 1860 account for the numbers of slaves for each slave owner, but do not list their names. An agricultural schedule from 1850 to 1880 counts crops, animals, farm production, and other information about farms. An industry and manufacturing schedule for 1810, 1820, and 1850–1880 provides statistics about local businesses and manufactured products. An 1880 special schedule enumerates and describes "defective, dependent, and delinquent" classes, namely, the insane, idiots, deaf-mutes, blind, homeless children, inhabitants in prison, and paupers and indigents. (While these terms seem harsh by today's standards, they were the terms in use at the time.) The 1850–1870 social statistics schedules report about churches, schools, and other community institutions.

The originals of these special census schedules are located at the National Archives; the Daughters of the American Revolution Library in Washington, D.C.; and throughout the United States at various libraries and archives. Some have been microfilmed and are available through NARA or the Family History Library.

Census Online

Census Online (*www.census-online.com/links/*) provides almost twenty thousand links to online censuses for the United States, Canada, England, Ireland, Scotland, and Wales. Some lead to commercial sites where a subscription is required to access actual digitized images (such as Ancestry.com and Genealogy.com, described below). Some links lead to Web sites where individuals have posted indexes or abstracts of census records for an area. Some also lead to records transcribed for the USGenWeb Census Project, described later in this chapter.

Using the Soundex

The Soundex is a coded index based on the way a surname sounds, which groups similar names together regardless of spelling. This allows researchers to find like names that are spelled differently, such as Smith, Smyth, or Smythe. Soundex indexes are available for most U.S. census records for the years 1880 and 1900–1930, but not for all states. For more information about the Soundex available for each census year, refer to the National Archives and Records Administration's Web site at *www.archives.gov/publications/microfilm_catalogs/census_schedules/1790_1890_federal_population_census_part01.html*.

A Soundex code consists of a letter and three numbers, such as F-652. The letter is always the first letter of the surname, and the three digits are determined by the Soundex guide below. Zeroes are added to the end of a Soundex code, if necessary, to produce a four-character code. The basic rules for determining the Soundex code for a surname are shown in the list below. For more details, see NARA's "Soundex Indexing System" article online at *www.archives.gov/research_room/genealogy/census/soundex.html*.

- **Write the first letter** of the surname.

- **Assign a number** to each letter after the first until the code is four characters long. Number values are assigned to letters as follows:

      1 B, F, P, V
      2 C, G, J, K, Q, S, X, Z
      3 D, T
      4 L
      5 M, N
      6 R

- **Disregard the letters** A, E, I, O, U, H, W, and Y. Some examples:

    Francis = F652 (F, 6 for the R, 5 for the N, 2 for the C)

    Reynolds = R543 (R, 5 for the N, 4 for the L, 3 for the D)

    Law = L000 (L, ignore the A and W, and add three zeroes to create a four-character code)

    Lowe = L000 (L, ignore the O and W and E, and add three zeroes to create a four-character code)

- **Double letters:** If a name contains double letters, treat them as one letter (for example, the double Ts in Litton should be treated as only one T, so the name is coded L350).

- **Side-by-side letters:** If side-by-side letters have the same Soundex code, use the number only once (for example, in the name Jackson, coded as J250, the C, K, and S letters are all represented by the number 2, but only one 2 should be used in the Soundex).

- **Names with prefixes:** If a surname has a prefix, such as Van Cortland, De los Santos, or Le Compte, code the name both with and without the prefix because the surname may be listed under either code. Note, however, that Mc and Mac are not considered prefixes, so their codes begin with M. Example: Van Cortland could be coded as V526 under listings for VanCortland (V, ignore the A, 5 for N, 2 for C, ignore the O, 6 for R) or C634 under listings for Cortland (C, ignore the O, 6 for R, 3 for T, 4 for L).

- **Consonant separators:** If a vowel (A, E, I, O, U) separates two consonants that have the same Soundex code, the consonant to the right of the vowel is coded. Example: Tymczak is coded as T-522 [T, ignore the Y, 5 for the M, 2 for the C, ignore the Z (see side-by-side rule above), 2 for the K]. Since the vowel A separates the Z and K, the K is coded (even though both C and K have the same Soundex code—2).

  If H or W separate two consonants that have the same Soundex code, the consonant to the right of the H or W is *not* coded. Example: Burroughs is coded B620, not B622 [B, ignore the U, 6 for the R, ignore the second R (see double letters rule), ignore the O and U, 2 for G, ignore the H, ignore the S (it's the same code as the G—2—and it's the consonant to the right of the H)].

As you see in the Law and Lowe examples above, similar names are coded the same and grouped together in a Soundex index, allowing you to find names you might not otherwise locate.

Some genealogy database programs, such as Legacy Family Tree or Reunion, have built-in Soundex calculators. You can also access the following free online Soundex calculators:

- JewishGen's JOS Soundex Calculator *(www.jewishgen.org/jos/jossound.htm)*

- AncestorSearch Surname to Soundex Converter *(www.searchforancestors.com/soundex.html)*

- RootsWeb's Soundex Converter *(resources.rootsweb.com/cgi-bin/soundexconverter)*

Unless you look at an actual digitized image of a census, remember to take what you read with a grain of salt. Data-entry errors can occur, and some Web sites may include only abstracts of selected surnames or ethnic groups, rather than a transcription of the entire census for the area. With these caveats in mind, the Census Online Web site is a great help for locating indexes, abstracts, transcriptions, and actual census images.

So You Want to Talk Like a Genealogist?

Here are a few definitions that will help you understand what librarians, archivists, and fellow researchers are trying to tell you.

- **Abstract:** A statement that summarizes the essential facts in a record. "She provided an abstract of John Jones's will."
- **Extant:** Still in existence; not lost or destroyed. "The 1920 census is extant for all states."
- **Extract:** A portion of information exactly recorded from a document or record. "I have prepared an extract of the Adamson household information from page 209 of the census."
- **Transcription:** An exact handwritten or typed duplication of an entire record, including headings, insertions, notes, capitalization, and cross-outs. "A transcription of the Jones deed will have to suffice; I was not allowed to make a photocopy of it."

When you enter the Census Online Web site, click the name of the state or country you want to access. Your screen will be similar to the one for Alabama, shown in Figure 7.2, and a list on the left side indicates the number of censuses available for each county.

When you access the state of interest, click the county name to display the links for that area. In Figure 7.3, links for Barbour County, Alabama, include extracts of 1860 mortality and slave schedules, an extract of black households in the 1870 federal census of the county, an extract of the 1910 federal census, and an index to the 1850 federal census. Each of these links can help pinpoint a Barbour County ancestor and may even identify the exact page of the census, making it easy for a researcher to find and view the original record.

AccessGenealogy.com

Like Census Online, this Web site *(www.accessgenealogy.com/census/)* provides links to online censuses in the United States, including some town enumerations used for incorporation purposes.

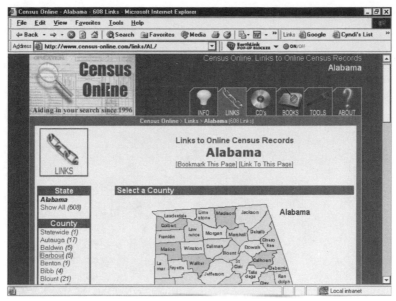

Figure 7.2 Census Online links to Alabama census records

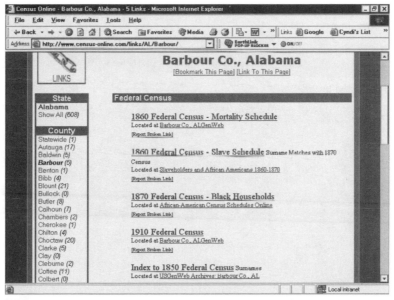

Figure 7.3 Census Online links to Barbour County, Alabama, census records

Cyndi's List of Genealogy Sites on the Internet

Links at Cyndi's U.S. Census category list *(www.cyndislist.com/census.htm)* are organized by decennial census year and connect to articles about researching the census; the online NARA catalog of microfilmed censuses; HeritageQuest.com's CD-ROM and microfilm census products descriptions; printable census forms; and online census indexes, abstracts, and transcriptions.

Census Extraction Forms

You should record information from the census records that you view, and special forms can help. Each decennial census contained different information, and customized extraction forms exist for each federal census or special schedule and for many state censuses. Download free forms from these sites:

- Access Genealogy *(www.accessgenealogy.com/census/freecensusforms.htm)*

- Ancestry.com *(www.ancestry.com/save/charts/census.htm)*

- Census Tools *(censustools.com/)*

- FamilySearch.org *(www.familysearch.org)*. Click Search, then Research Helps. Click Sorted by Document Type and scroll down to Census Forms.

- Family Tree Magazine *(www.familytreemagazine.com/forms/download.html)*

- Genealogy.com *(www.genealogy.com/00000061.html)*

Accessing Census Images Online

A census is one of the first sources beginning genealogists learn to use. The National Archives site *(www.archives.gov)* provides an online catalog for each census year, but these simply describe the microfilmed versions of the census. The National Archives does not provide any electronic access to the federal censuses in its collections. In the past, this meant a visit to a regional branch of the National Archives, your local Family History Center, or a library to view the census records on microfilm. But thanks to

International Censuses

The censuses of a few countries are available online. To find the one you're looking for, try a Google search of a phrase similar to *1865 census + Norway.* Cyndi's List of links to census-related sites worldwide at *www.cyndislist.com/census2.htm* can also help. Here are some links to resources or actual censuses for countries outside the United States:

- Australia—links to online census records of Australia (*www.users.on.net/proformat/census.html*)

- Canada—links to online census records of Canada (*www.census-online.com/links/Canada/*)

- Canada—1901 (*www.archives.ca/02/02012202_e.html*)

- England—links to online census records of England (*www.census-online.com/links/England/*)

- Norway—1660, 1801, 1865, 1875, 1900 (*digitalarkivet.uib.no*). To view in English, click on English. Census is available by clicking Categories, then Censuses.

- Norway—1865, 1875, 1900 (*draug.rhd.isv.uit.no/folketellinger_engelsk_britisk.html*)

- Sweden—1890 (five counties) (*www.foark.umu.se/census/Index.htm*)

- United Kingdom—1901 (searches are free, but there is a charge to view details or to download images) (*www.census.pro.gov.uk/*)

technology, some census indexes and actual census images are now available twenty-four hours a day on the Internet. You can view, save, or print these digitized census images, and after saving one, you can even open it in a photo retouching or drawing program to enhance its readability.

Ancestry.com Online Census Images

Individuals can purchase a quarterly or annual subscription to Ancestry.com's U.S. Census Images and Indexes online service, allowing access to digitized federal censuses from home computers twenty-four hours a day. Currently, Ancestry.com provides indexes and images of censuses from 1790 to 1850, 1920, and 1930; images and a partial index of the 1860 census; and images of the 1870–1910 censuses. To view a sample census image at Ancestry.com, visit *www.ancestry.com/search/rectype/census/usfedcen/main.htm.*

Genealogy.com U.S. Census Collection Online

For a monthly or annual fee, individuals may subscribe to Genealogy.com's U.S. census collection, which currently includes images for 1790–1910 and 1930. Several censuses are indexed, and the other years can be browsed by locality (usually county, district, or township). These images can be viewed, saved, or printed for future reference. For more information, see *www.genealogy.com/uscensussub.html.*

HeritageQuest Online

HeritageQuest Online from ProQuest is another provider of subscription Internet access to U.S. federal censuses. Census images now available include 1790–1930, with indexes being added regularly. For more information, see *www.heritagequestonline.com.*

Library Access for Online Censuses

If you use census records frequently, you may be willing to pay a subscription fee for continual access to U.S. census records from every locality. But if you have only occasional need of census images, try visiting your local library—they just might have a subscription for patrons' use that won't cost you anything.

Accessing Online Census Indexes or Abstracts

Before you start reading a census line by line to find a name in the county or city you are researching, you might like to know that indexes or abstracts can help you go right to the exact page and line where your ancestor's information is recorded. How can you find an online index or abstract of the census for a state or county you are researching? A search of Google for the phrase *"census index"* results in about 127,000 hits for everything from state and federal censuses of the United States to the Swedish census of 1890 to an English census of 1801. To narrow your search a bit further, try adding a location name to your search phrase—*"census index"* + *Dorset England,* for example.

USGenWeb Census Project

Genealogists are generous with their volunteer hours, and one result is the USGenWeb Census Project. Hundreds of volunteers transcribe or proofread census transcriptions that are uploaded to the USGenWeb Census Project Archives for free access by any researcher. To see an online census inventory of transcribed records at this site, access *www.us-census.org/inventory/inventory.htm;* a list of states appears in the left window. Click the state you are researching to bring up a list of counties.

Some USGenWeb Census Project volunteers transcribe a census word for word; others simply extract the names and identify page numbers where they can be found. A few scan and upload the actual census image to the USGenWeb Census pages. Figure 7.4 shows the links to Illinois census records available at this Web site. Notice that the 1850 Adams County file is only a partial transcription and that actual scanned images are available for that particular census.

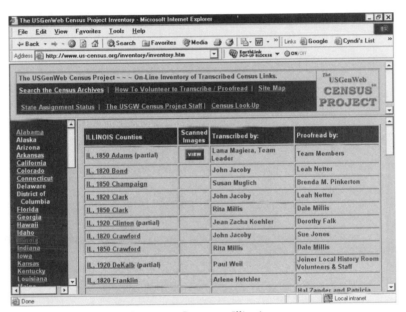

Figure 7.4 USGenWeb Census Project—Illinois

Using the USGenWeb indexes, transcriptions, and scanned images is easy once you understand how the process works. Here's how to find the record for Elizabeth Abeny in the 1850 Adams County, Illinois index and transcriptions, and how to view the original image.

First, click the underlined link for the county name and census year. USGenNet's Safe-Site FTP (file transfer protocol) server with file names for Adams County displays in a new window, similar to the one shown in Figure 7.5. Most USGenWeb census indexes and transcriptions work this way, bringing up a list of index and page number files. Next, just double-click to open the file labeled indx-a-d.txt since the

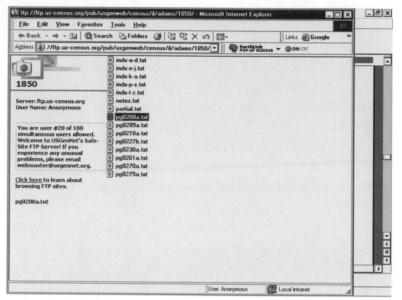

Figure 7.5 FTP Server files—index and transcriptions

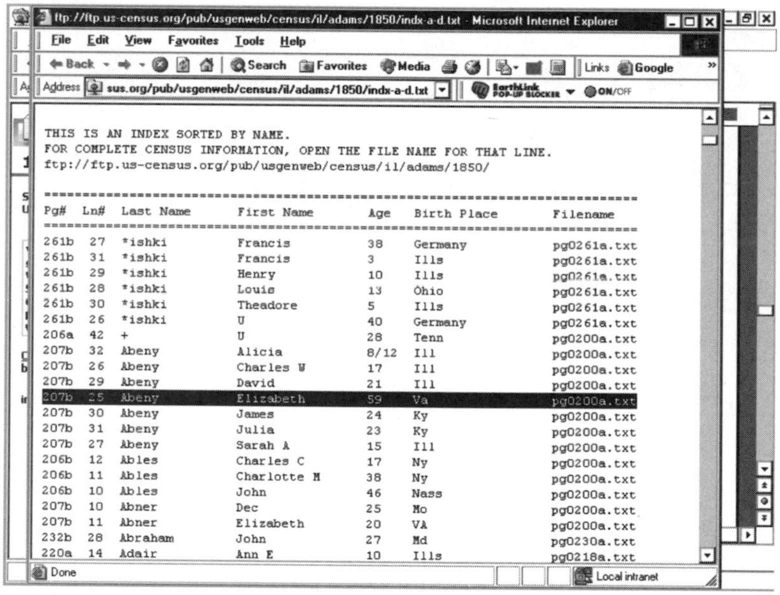

Figure 7.6 USGenWeb census index file

surname Abner should be included in an index of names from A to D. The index file opens, and you see the alphabetical listing that includes Elizabeth Abeny (Figure 7.6). According to this index, Elizabeth Abeny's census enumeration appears on page 207b, line 25, of the 1850 Adams County, Illinois, census.

Make note of the page and line number, and close the index file. Back at the window with FTP file names, look for the file that contains the transcription of page 207b of the census. There is a file named pg0200a.txt, with the one next to it named pg0209a.txt. The pg0200a.txt file begins with page 200a and ends before page 209a, so double-click to open the pg0200a.txt file. Figure 7.7 shows the actual census transcription. Note that there is more information off to the right that does not fit on the screen, so use the scroll bar at the bottom of the screen to move to the far right to see all the information. Locate the transcribed census information for Elizabeth Abeny on line 25 of page 207b; you learn that she resided in household number 140, family number 141, and that she was fifty-nine years old, a female born in Virginia.

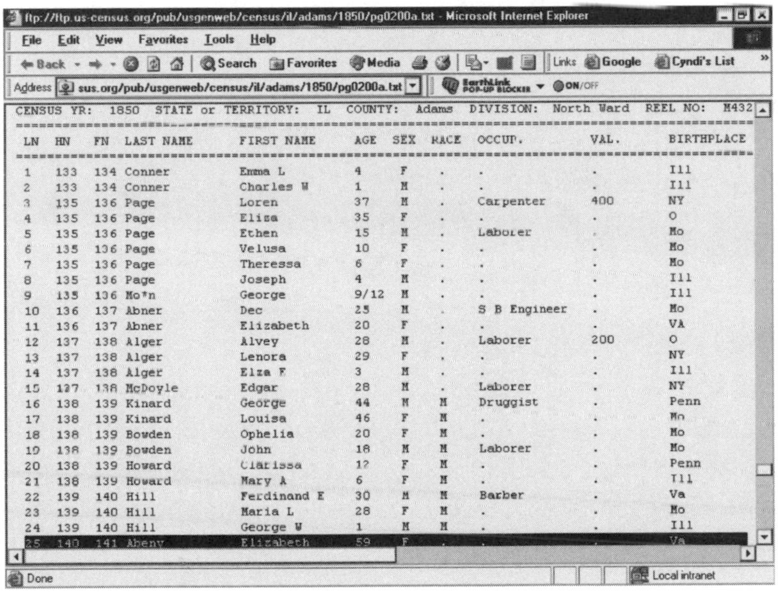

Figure 7.7 USGenWeb transcribed census file

Following good research procedure, you should look at the actual census rather than trusting only the transcribed version. This particular census at USGenWeb's Census Project is available to view. Back at the Illinois page, just click the View button beside the 1850 Adams County census, and another window with file names displays. Clicking on file name 0207b.qif brings up the scanned image of page 207b (see Figure 7.8).

If the actual census image is not available online, look for the microfilmed version at your local library or order it for viewing at your local Family History Center.

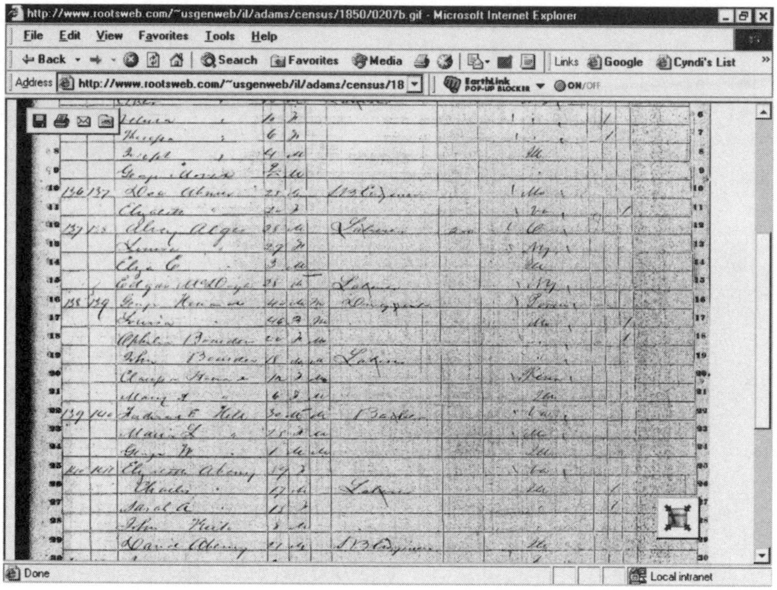

Figure 7.8 USGenWeb census image

RootsWeb User-Contributed Databases

Volunteers also contribute random census indexes, extracts, or transcriptions to RootsWeb's databases *(userdb.rootsweb.com/regional.html)*. You may find an entire census here, such as the Swedish 1890 census, or you may find an extracted list of a single surname for an area census, such as the Atkinson surname in the 1881 Cumberland County, Nova Scotia census.

FamilySearch.org's Census Abstracts

FamilySearch.org recently added free searchable census extracts for 1880 United States, 1881 British Isles, and 1881 Canada to its Web site *(www.familysearch.org/ Eng/Search/frameset_search.asp?PAGE=census/search_census.asp)*. Originally offered by the Church of Jesus Christ of Latter-day Saints for sale on CDs (and still available as such), these records include much of the information from the original censuses. Unlike the microfilmed 1880 Soundex that indexes only households with children age ten and under, the FamilySearch database offers an every-name index, providing an opportunity to locate ancestors whose names had not been indexed before.

The powerful search engine also allows searching by only a first or last name, and narrowing by birthplace, birth year, and census state, county, and town. This helps you find people previously unlocatable in the 1880 Soundex. For example, if you seek an ancestor named Martha born in 1851 in Kentucky whom you suspect resided in Carter County, Missouri, during the 1880 census, you enter those items in the query screen. The search may result in finding a woman named Martha living with a husband near a family you know to be your Martha's family of origin. Further research may prove that this is indeed the Martha you were seeking.

The FamilySearch 1880 searchable abstract database also allows a search by last name only, enabling you to search for all Porters born in Canada enumerated in a specific Michigan county. As a unique research tool, these census databases are well worth the cost of the CDs. As a free research tool on the Internet, they should be used regularly.

Ancestry.com's U.S. Census Indexes

If you or your library subscribes to Ancestry.com's U.S. Census Images and Indexes service, you have access to its online collection of federal census indexes, state census indexes, and indexes to nonpopulation schedules, such as mortality, veterans, and slaves, for most of the United States and part of Canada. For the most part, indexes range from the colonial era to 1870. For a list of the censuses indexed in this collection, see *www.ancestry.com/search/rectype/census/ais/censuslist.htm*.

Even without a subscription, you can search the Ancestry.com census indexes at *www.ancestry.com/search/rectype/census/ais/main.htm*. You should see a list of results similar to those shown for the surname Westmoreland in Figure 7.9. But unless you have a paid subscription at home or access through a local library, you are not able to click the census links in this list to bring up actual index data like that shown in Figure 7.10. This information arms you with the facts you need to find and view the original microfilmed or digitized census record—the state, county, and locality (usually township) of the census and the page number.

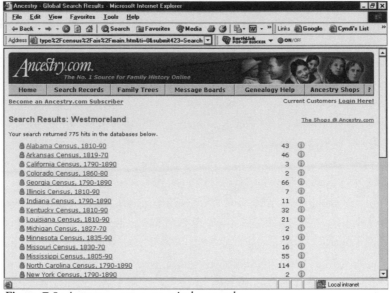

Figure 7.9 Ancestry.com census index search

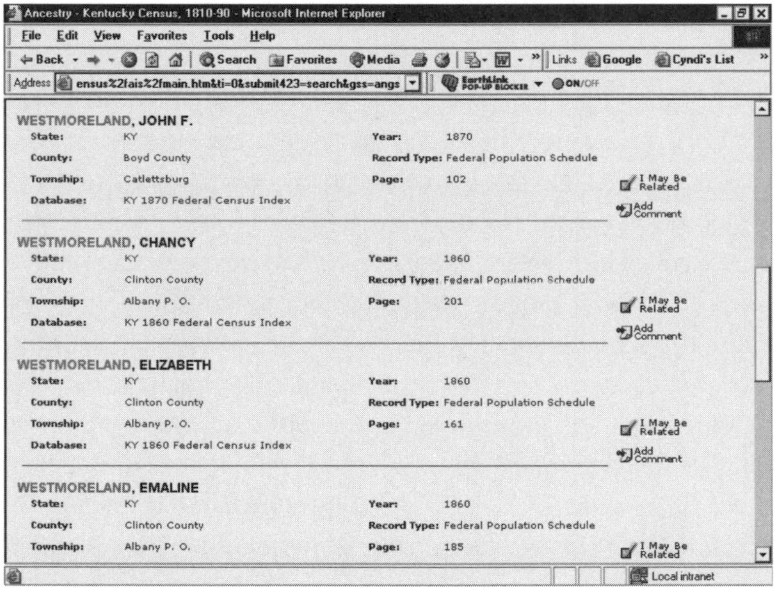

Figure 7.10 Ancestry.com census index results

Census Substitutes

The U.S. census has occurred every ten years since 1790, but many schedules have been lost or destroyed through the years. For instance, of the 1790 census records, no Delaware, Georgia, Kentucky, New Jersey, Tennessee, or Virginia schedules survive, and only partial records survive for other states. Due to a fire in the facility that housed the 1890 census, almost no records at all survive for that census, a critical time of immigration, growth, and industrialization for the United States. But some census substitutes are available.

Ancestry.com's 1890 Census Substitute

Ancestry.com, assisted by the National Archives and Records Administration and the Allen County (Indiana) Public Library, provides an online substitute for the 1890 census at *www.ancestry.com/search/rectype/census/1890sub/main.htm*. This collection comprises extant fragments of the 1890 census (spotty records from ten states and the District of Columbia), state censuses for 1885 or 1895, special veterans schedules for 1890, Native American tribal censuses for years around 1890, city and county directories, alumni directories, and voter registration records. This is another of Ancestry.com's paid subscription services, so you must either subscribe or access the service at your local library.

A search of the 1890 Census Substitute for anyone by the surname Twidwell in any

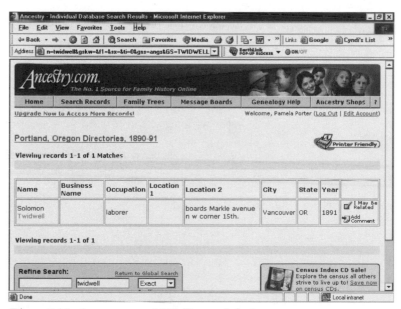

Figure 7.11 Ancestry.com 1890 Census Substitute

state returns just one result, shown in Figure 7.11, an abstract of an entry in the 1890–91 Portland, Oregon directory. This city directory entry abstract records a Solomon Twidwell, laborer by occupation, who boards on Markle Avenue at the northwest corner of 15th in Vancouver, Oregon. Knowing this information, a researcher can follow up by searching the 1880 and 1900 Oregon censuses and other county or state contemporary records.

The 1890 Census Substitute collection at Ancestry.com is not all-inclusive, but it does contain important clues for people who lived in cities or areas that were covered by the sources that make up the collection. To view a list of upcoming databases that will be added soon, visit *www.ancestry.com/search/rectype/census/1890sub/upcoming.htm*.

1890 Special Veterans Schedule

The 1890 Veterans Schedule identifies Union Civil War veterans (and a few Confederates mistakenly included) or their widows living in 1890. It features the soldier's, sailor's, marine's, or widow's name; the veteran's rank, company, regiment (or vessel), date of enlistment, date of discharge, length of service, disability incurred during the Civil War; and that veteran's or widow's post office address at the time of the census in 1890. This special schedule survives for about half of Kentucky and all states alphabetically from Louisiana through Wyoming, plus Washington, D.C. It is available on microfilm at National Archives facilities, the Family History Library, and libraries throughout the United States. To determine whether a veterans schedule is available for a particular county, look at the National Archives' online catalog of the 1890 special schedule at *www.archives.gov/publications/microfilm_catalogs/census_schedules/1790_1890_federal_population_census_part08.html*.

You may be able to find an abstracted or transcribed online version of the 1890 veterans schedule for the county you are researching. Be sure to check USGenWeb's Census Project *(www.rootsweb.com/~census/states.htm)* for a transcription, scanned image, or link to an 1890 special veterans census. You might also try using a search engine with a phrase similar to *1890 veterans census + Michigan.*

An online transcription may be similar to the one in Figure 7.12, the 1890 Wayne County, Missouri veterans census contributed for use in the USGenWeb Archives by Linda L. Green. This is actually an abstract, since it is incomplete, including only the veteran's or widow's name and unit but omitting the rest of the information given in the schedule. However, it does provide enough information to investigate the veteran's military service, which you'll learn more about in Chapter 10, "Finding Clues to Military Service." By now, you know that a good genealogist uses indexes, abstracts, or transcriptions as a means of locating the original record, which may contain more information.

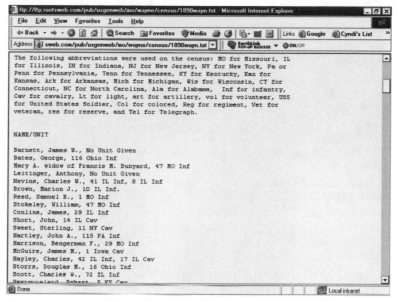

The following abbreviations were used on the census: MO for Missouri, IL for Illinois, IN for Indiana, NJ for New Jersey, NY for New York, Pa or Penn for Pennsylvania, Tenn for Tennessee, KY for Kentucky, Kan for Kansas, Ark for Arkansas, Mich for Michigan, Wis for Wisconsin, CT for Connecticut, NC for North Carolina, Ala for Alabama, Inf for infantry, Cav for cavalry, Lt for light, art for artillery, vol for volunteer, USS for United States Soldier, Col for colored, Reg for regiment, Vet for veteran, res for reserve, and Tel for Telegraph.

NAME/UNIT

Barnett, James W., No Unit Given
Bates, George, 116 Ohio Inf
Mary A. widow of Francis M. Bunyard, 47 MO Inf
Leitinger, Anthony, No Unit Given
Nevins, Charles W., 41 IL Inf, 8 IL Inf
Brown, Marion J., 10 IL Inf.
Reed, Samuel B., 1 MO Inf
Stokeley, William, 47 MO Inf
Conline, James, 29 IL Inf
Short, John, 14 IL Cav
Sweet, Sterling, 11 NY Cav
Hartley, John A., 115 PA Inf
Harrison, Bengerman F., 29 MO Inf
McGuire, James M., 1 Iowa Cav
Hayley, Charles, 42 IL Inf, 17 IL Cav
Storrs, Douglas M., 16 Ohio Inf
Scott, Charles W., 72 IL Inf

Figure 7.12 1890 Wayne County, Missouri veterans census abstract

Tax Lists

Many early censuses are no longer extant, but tax lists can be good substitutes. In fact, annual tax lists can help fill in information between decennial censuses. As an example, no 1790 or 1800 censuses survive for Virginia, but a great number of tax lists for counties in the state do exist. Publishers have compiled these tax lists to create substitutes for Virginia and other states lacking censuses. Many of the original lists are available on microfilm at archives or libraries in the area where they were created.

How can a tax list help you? These early tax lists of tithable property, like the one in Figure 7.13, usually list information such as the name of the person charged with the tax; the names of free male tithables above the age of sixteen in the household; the numbers of blacks of certain ages; and the number of horses, carriage wheels, or other taxable items at the time. This at least allows you to pinpoint a head of household at a given time and provides some supplemental information about other taxable persons or property in the household.

You may be able to find abstracts, transcriptions, or digitized images of tax lists online. A Google search for *"Virginia tax lists"* yields about three hundred results, including the Binns Genealogy, LLC, Web site of 1790/1800 Virginia Tax Lists

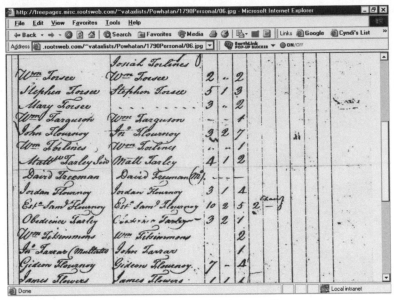

Figure 7.13 1790 Powhatan County, Virginia tax list

(homepages.rootsweb.com/~ysbinns/vataxlists/). A search of the 1790 index of Powhatan County at this site for William Fitzsimmons locates a William Fitsimmons on page 6 of the 1790 Powhatan County Personal Tax List. The actual tax list is available as a digitized image, as seen in Figure 7.13. Wm. Fitsimmons is listed both as the person charged with the tax and as a free male tithable above the age of sixteen. He must also pay taxes on two horses. William Fitzsimmons does not appear in the index of the 1800 Powhatan County Personal Tax List, meaning that he is too old to pay taxes any longer or that he has died or moved away.

Tax lists can be helpful as census substitutes, and they are essential tools for determining when an individual or family moves into or out of a county. Try searching with Google for a phrase similar to *Kentucky tax list + Barren County* to find early tax lists for the area you are researching, particularly if the census for that time is not extant.

A Census Research Project

Remember the Francis family research project from Chapter 1? In that phase of the research project, I located an online obituary for Naphie Francis-Baca. Now I want to learn her birth date, birthplace, and her parents' names. Following the same steps as in the research strategy steps and decisions diagram from Chapter 1 (Figure 1.1), I decide to use a fact found in her obituary—that she taught in the 1920s in Seboyeta, New Mexico—to search for her family in U.S. census records of New Mexico, beginning with the 1920 census and working back.

My first task is to determine which county to search for Seboyeta. I can use the Geographic Names Information System (GNIS) of the U.S. Geological Survey (USGS) to find the county where Seboyeta is located. Accessing GNIS at *geonames.usgs.gov/pls/gnis/web_query.gnis_web_query_form*, I enter *Seboyeta* as the feature name and *New Mexico* as the state or territory, then click Send Query.

Search results, shown in Figure 7.14, include eight places with Seboyeta in their names—a populated place (town), a valley, a stream, a school, a post office, a mine, a dam, and a reservoir. Most are in Cibola County or the adjacent Valencia County. A click on Seboyeta (populated place) in Cibola County reveals that it was settled in 1749; it lies 4.4 miles north of Paguate at an elevation of 6,387 feet; and its variant names include Cebolleta, Gebolleta, and Grebolleta. The GNIS also provides a latitude and longitude in case I want to enter this place in a mapping program or Global Positioning System (GPS) device. I can click on other links to see a digitized USGS topographic map of the Seboyeta area or to view a black-and-white aerial photographic map of the area. (To learn more about GPS devices or the USGS Web site, see Chapter 14, "Putting Your Ancestors in Context.") I have now learned what I needed about Seboyeta —that it lies in Cibola County for my next research step

Mrs. Francis-Baca's obituary listed a surviving brother as Narciso Francis Jr., so I'm going to take a leap of faith and assume that her father was Narciso Francis. According to her obituary, Naphie Francis was teaching in Seboyeta before her marriage in the 1920s, so she may appear in her father's household in the 1920 census. Because Ancestry.com's index lists only heads of household, I search the 1920 census index for Narciso Francis in Cibola County, New Mexico. This query returns no results at all, so I search again for Narciso Francis in New Mexico, without specifying a county.

This time a single record is located for the query—a Narciso Francis, age thirty-eight, birthplace Syrian Arab Republic, is enumerated in Cebolleta Township, Valencia County, New Mexico, on page 4A, Enumeration District 188, Image 1033. The 1920 census index result for Narciso Francis is shown in Figure 7.15.

This Ancestry.com index provides the National Archives microfilm roll number, county, page number, enumeration district, and image number where Narciso Francis's census enumeration can be located. Clicking on the View Image Online link

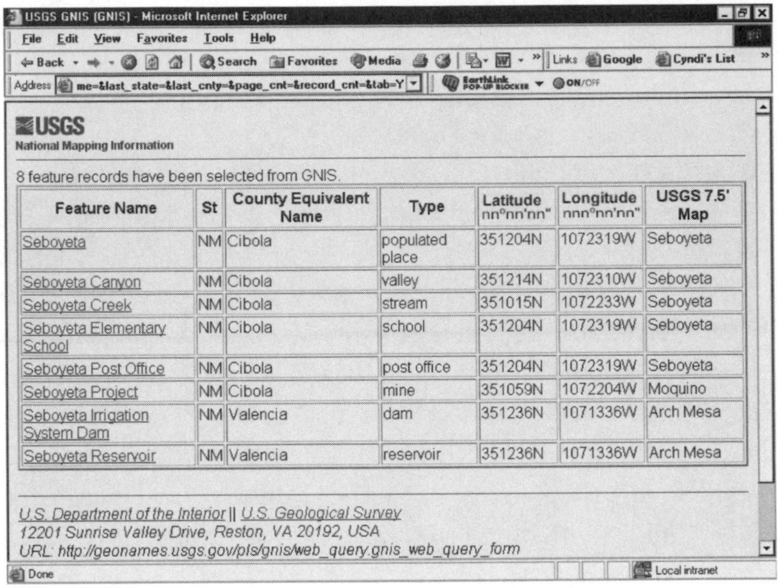

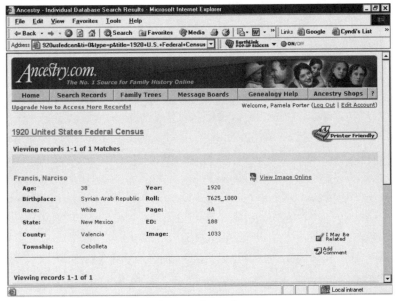

Figure 7.14 USGS GNIS search results

Figure 7.15 1920 census index search results

displays the actual digitized image of this census page, shown in Figure 7.16. I zoom in to enlarge the names and find Narciso Francis, his wife, and children on lines 34–42. Bingo! The first daughter is Nafy Francis, female, white, age fourteen, single, born in New Mexico, both parents born in Syria. I've struck gold with this census record, and there is a wealth of information to mine from it.

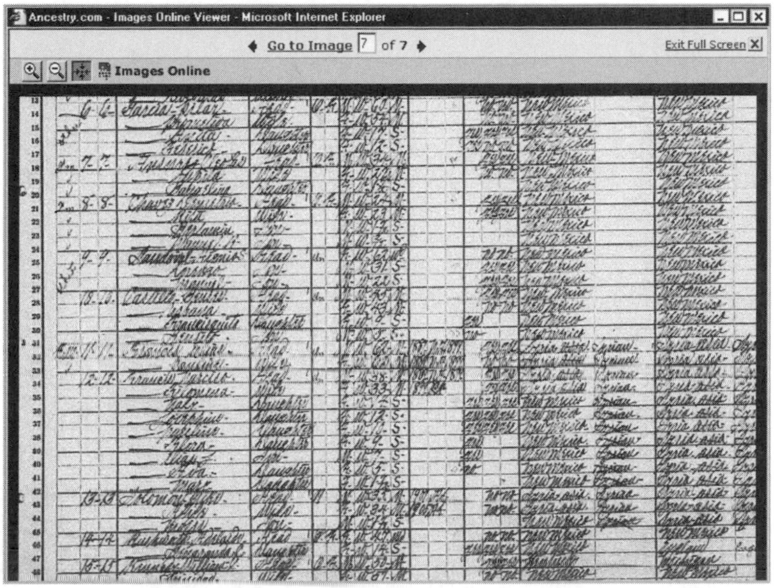

Figure 7.16 Online census image

The 1920 census provides the parents and siblings of Naphie Francis-Baca, their ages and birthplaces, and the birthplaces of their parents. The census indicates that the mother tongue of the entire family was Syrian, that Naphie's father, Narciso, was born in Syria, immigrated to the United States in 1889, and was naturalized in 1899, and that her mother, Filomena, also born in Syria, immigrated in 1899 and was still an alien at the time of the 1920 census. Mr. Francis was a merchant with a grocery store.

Another family immediately preceding the Narciso Francis family catches my eye—that of Elias and Pauline Francis, both also born in Syria and immigrating to the United States in 1887 and 1889, respectively. They were both age sixty-two, and Elias was a farmer. Although no relationship is stated between the Elias Francis and the Narciso Francis families, it is highly likely that they are related since they lived next to one another, were born in the same country, immigrated at the same time, and all spoke Syrian as their native language. Elias and Pauline Francis, at age sixty-two, are old enough to be the parents of Narciso, age thirty-eight. If I check the 1910 and the 1900 New Mexico censuses, I may be able to find Narciso living in the Elias Francis household and verify that he is a son. This has led me to identify possible grandparents for Naphie Francis-Baca.

For now, let's answer two important questions before moving on.

Question 1: Didn't people know how to spell in the past? And the answer is—not like we do today. There were fewer literate people in earlier centuries before school attendance became mandatory, and people often wrote things down just as they sounded. I can be relatively certain that the Naphie Francis-Baca of the online obituary is the same Nafy Francis in Narciso Francis's household in 1920, even if her name is spelled differently. Don't they both sound like "Naf-ee"? The census taker may have misspelled names even if the family correctly spelled them for him.

And what about Seboyeta/Cebolleta? It's another case of spelling it like it sounds. A quick search on the Internet for *Seboyeta New Mexico history* finds an online excerpt from *The WPA Guide to 1930s New Mexico* stating that the community name may have derived from the Spanish word *cebolleta* (tender onion). The spelling of *Seboyeta* represents the English phonetic pronunciation of the Spanish word. The important thing to take away from these spelling variations is this: *Spelling doesn't count in genealogy!* Don't obsess over a spelling that couldn't possibly be your ancestor because you don't currently spell your name that way. Consider the possibilities.

Question 2: If Seboyeta was in Valencia County in the 1920 census, why does the GNIS database show it in Cibola County today? No, the town didn't move, but the county lines did. Seboyeta was indeed located in Valencia County, New Mexico, in 1920. Today, it lies in Cibola County, which was created in 1981 from most of western Valencia County. No wonder I found no record of Narciso Francis in Cibola County in 1920—that county did not even exist until 1981! It's a good thing I searched for him in Valencia County, too, or I would never have found him and his family.

In genealogy, it's vital to learn about the area you are researching. Before you start searching in a new area that you're unfamiliar with, visit the USGenWeb site to learn about that area. Another useful resource is the Research Helps link at the LDS FamilySearch site *(www.familysearch.org)*. Click on the Search tab, then the Research Helps link for an alphabetical list sorted by place. Then click the first letter of the place you want and scroll down the list. For example, to find the New Mexico resources, click on N to display a list of places that start with the letter *n,* and scroll down to the New Mexico listings. There you find historical background about the area, statewide sources and indexes, and my favorite, a New Mexico Research Outline that describes major sources of information about families in New Mexico. FamilySearch has Research Outlines for a great many places worldwide, making the outlines good places to begin when you're researching a new area.

Census and tax lists provide researchers with a snapshot of a family at a given point in time, fleshing out details about marital status, personal belongings, age, number of children and even military service. These basic building blocks of genealogy start you well on your way to piecing together an entire family. If you like what you find in the census records, then head on to your next stop—the county courthouse. In the next chapter you'll learn how to find even more personal details about those ancestors.

CHAPTER 8

Visiting the Courthouse

IF YOU HAVE COMPLETED YOUR CENSUS RESEARCH AND LOCATED A family in a particular area at a given time, you should next explore the local records available for that family. Records obtainable at the local level may vary from county to county; certainly, they vary by state or country. However, the same basic types of records are created in every locale.

Just think of the times in your life that you have gone to your town hall or county courthouse. You may have requested a marriage license, perhaps received a divorce decree, or filed paperwork for adoption or guardianship of a minor child. As executor of a relative's will, you may have filed settlement papers for the estate. If you have bought or sold land or real property, you or your representative has recorded these transactions and the deed at the county courthouse. Perhaps you've been involved in a minor civil lawsuit. The records of this exist at the county courthouse. As a good citizen, you've surely registered to vote and paid your taxes. These records are on file at the county courthouse.

Get the picture? Many records resulting from your actions have been filed at your county courthouse. Your ancestors left behind valuable genealogical information at their county courthouses, too. If you aren't digging through those records, you're missing some revealing details about your people.

Finding the Right Courthouse

How do you find the courthouse where your ancestors filed their deeds, paid their taxes, or conducted other business? It's not always simply a matter of which county they lived in—sometimes geography made it easier for them to travel to the courthouse in the next county. Moreover, rural land or towns that lay in a particular county in the 1800s may not remain in that same county today—county boundaries change over time.

You have already learned about vital records in Chapter 6, so you know where to look for birth, marriage, and death records. The USGenWeb site is a good starting point for finding out about other records available at the county level. Visit *www.usgenweb.com/statelinks-table.html,* and click the link for the state you're researching. Most GenWeb state sites provide general information about a county's date of formation, county seat, and parent counties, and offer links to more information about each county. The Connecticut GenWeb site in Figure 8.1 is an example.

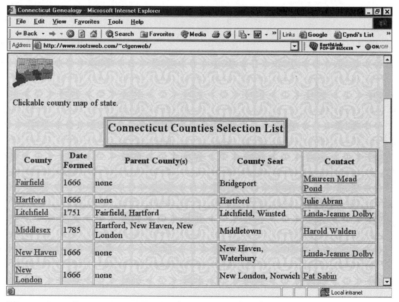

Figure 8.1 Connecticut GenWeb county information

Some GenWeb sites go beyond telling you where you can find county records. Many have indexes or abstracts of the records. The Hampshire County, West Virginia GenWeb site *(www.rootsweb.com/~wvhampsh/)* contains an index to the County Court

Minute Book for 1788–1789. The Hickman County, Kentucky, GenWeb site (*www.rootsweb.com/~kyhickma/*) has abstracts of deeds and court records. These are just two examples from the hundreds of Web sites that are part of the US GenWeb project.

The LDS Research Outlines mentioned at the end of Chapter 7 are also valuable sources for learning about a state's resources and the types of records available for that state. These outlines can be purchased for a nominal fee at Family History Centers around the world, or you can view them at the FamilySearch Web site (*www.familysearch.org/Eng/Search/RG/frameset_rhelps.asp*).

Political Divisions and Records

Most countries are divided into smaller political areas where responsibility for local records lies. In the United States, there are federal-level records, such as census, immigration and naturalization, federal court cases, and military. Next are the state-level records, such as state censuses, state militia, incorporation, and vital records registration. At the next level in most states, you find county-level records, which may consist of anything from reports of stray livestock, to lists of the area insane or indigent, to land deeds and tax records. Some services are also offered at the city or town level, including business licenses or school records.

In New England and some other parts of the United States, a town is a legally defined area with definite boundaries and almost all land is part of a town or a city—as soon as you exit one town, a sign welcomes you to the next. In these areas, you often find most local records at the town level, rather than the county. In that case, instead of just visiting the county courthouse, you should stop by either the virtual town hall on the Internet or the brick and mortar one in the town itself.

Some cities in the United States do not lie within a county, but are stand-alone political divisions. Baltimore, St. Louis, and several cities in Virginia are good examples. The City of St. Louis separated from St. Louis County in 1876. If your ancestors lived within St. Louis city limits before that date, you can find their records at the St. Louis County Courthouse. After 1876, you have to look in City of St. Louis records.

Did the County Move?

When researching a family, it may appear that they moved from one county to another several times over the years. In fact, they may have remained on the same piece of land, but the county boundaries changed, placing them in different counties. As populations grew and shifted, new counties were formed, taking land from the parent county (or counties). Here is a typical evolution of counties:

- Washington County, Northwest Territory (now Ohio), was formed in 1788 as an original county.
- Ross County was formed from Washington County in 1798.
- Fairfield County was formed from Washington and Ross counties in 1800.
- Athens County was formed from Washington County in 1805.
- Hocking County was formed from Athens, Ross, and Fairfield counties in 1818.

Depending on where your ancestor was living in Hocking County in 1818, earlier records pertaining to that family (such as land, tax, and probate records) could be in any of four Ohio counties—Athens, Fairfield, Ross, or Washington.

How do you know which county courthouse records to search? Determine the county boundaries for the period you are researching and as they are today. Most USGenWeb state sites list counties, their dates of formation, and other counties from which they were formed. A search engine query of a term such as *"county boundary*

AniMap Plus County Boundary Historical Atlas Software

If you want to locate a town that no longer exists on modern maps or pinpoint a location that may have been in two or more counties over the years, the AniMap Plus software program can help. This CD-ROM program from GoldBug Software *(www.goldbug.com)* displays more than 2,300 maps showing changing county boundaries in the forty-eight adjacent states since colonial times. The SiteFinder element of the program helps you identify more than 799,000 places in the United States, including cities and towns, railroad stations, cemeteries, plantations, farms and ranches, and mining camps. You can even plot a place on the county maps to see which county it lay in as boundaries changed. Overlays show railroads, waterways, and township/range grids for public land states. View the maps on your screen, export them to a bitmap (.bmp) file for use in a word-processing or paint program, or print paper copies.

changes" + *Oregon* may turn up online maps or descriptions of changing county lines. William Dollarhide and William Thorndale's book, *Map Guide to the U.S. Federal Censuses, 1790–1920* (Baltimore: Genealogical Publishing Co., Inc., 1987) provides maps showing county boundary changes every ten years when the census was taken. Your local library may have a copy of this book, or you can order it online from Genealogical Publishing Company at *www.genealogical.com.* AniMap Plus software displays and prints county maps, showing the changing boundaries and allowing you to plot a specific place and visualize which counties it lay in over time. You may have to check the courthouses in several counties for records of an ancestor who lived in an area where the boundaries changed over time.

Which Courthouse Should You Check?

As you see in Figure 8.2—Wayne County, Missouri—which county courthouse you should visit depends on where your ancestors were living at a given time. If they settled in 1843 in northwestern Wayne County and remained there, you should probably check records in Wayne, Ripley, Shannon, Carter, Reynolds, and possibly Iron and Madison counties. If you know they settled specifically on Brushy Creek in an area that is today just across the Wayne County line in Carter County, check at least those counties—and probably Shannon and Reynolds counties for the 1843 period.

Figure 8.2 Changing boundaries in Wayne County, Missouri

Some citizen responsibilities, such as paying school taxes or recording deeds to a piece of property, had to be carried out in the appropriate county or town. But be aware that ancestors may have conducted other business at a more convenient location. If their county seat was over a river that flooded in spring or was at the opposite end of the county from their residence, they may have opted for the shorter or easier trip to the next county's courthouse when obtaining a marriage license or having a document notarized. Looking at topographical maps of an area can help you determine which courthouses may be relevant to your research.

Finding the Records

Once you've narrowed your search to the appropriate county, how do you know the types of records available there? You may be able to avoid an actual trip to the county courthouse by finding the records you need as digitized images online or on microfilm. Many county records have been filmed and are available through various state archives or libraries, historical societies, or LDS Family History Centers worldwide.

State Archives or State Library

Start with the state archives or library for the area you're researching. For links to state historical societies and state archives throughout the United States, visit *web.syr.edu/~jryan/infopro/hs.html;* for links to state-level records repositories, visit Cyndi's List *(www.cyndislist.com/lib-state.htm#States).* You may find a listing of microfilmed county records available for a state and, by browsing those records, determine what types of records exist at the county level.

An example of helpful information at a state Web site is the Missouri State Archives' searchable Local Records Inventory Database, a compiled inventory of local government records, at *www.sos.state.mo.us/CountyInventory/index.asp.* Browsing county records gives you a sense of the types of transactions recorded in local town halls or courthouses, including land and property tax assessment, court minutes, inquests, road petitions, and school censuses. The Missouri State Archives Web site also provides a roll-by-roll listing of microfilmed records by county at *www.sos.state.mo.us/archives/resources/county/croll.asp.*

Many other states have similar finding aids. Anyone with Virginia ancestry can benefit from the extensive online finding aids and digitized records of the Library of Virginia *(www.lva.lib.va.us/).* Its What We Have page shown in Figure 8.3 points researchers to an online catalog, collection guides to Virginia county and city records, a burned record counties database, an index to city and county wills and administrations, and information about West Virginia and Kentucky records (states that were once part of Virginia). A good starting place is the Library of Virginia collection guides at *www.lva.lib.va.us/whatwehave/local/index.htm.*

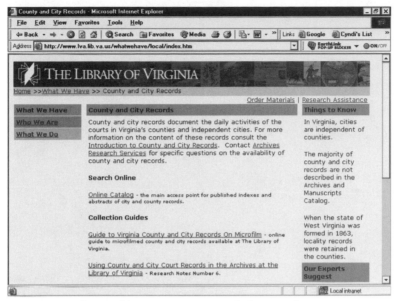

Figure 8.3 Library of Virginia—county and city records

Family History Library

The Family History Library (FHL) offers microfilm rental at its Family History Centers around the world. You can use the FHL catalog at these Centers or access it online at *www.familysearch.org*. Just click the Search the Family History Library Catalog link under Family History Library System.

When you start researching in a new county, it is helpful to view or print lists of all available records for that county and to familiarize yourself with them. To find a courthouse record in the FHL Catalog, use the Place Search option. The guidelines in Figure 8.4 help you locate the type of courthouse records you seek. If you want records for a city rather than a county, enter the county *and* the city. You may need to search more than one locality to find all records of a given type. For example, birth records may exist at the state level, the county level, and the city level. Search the FHL Catalog for the types of records listed in Figure 8.4. Where State, County, or City appears in italics, enter the name of the locality you are searching.

Online Sources

Like vital records and other records covered in this book, most county courthouse records are not yet available online as transcribed or digitized records. You'll probably

Record Type	FHL Catalog Search Phrase
Births and deaths	*State*—Vital records (births, deaths, coroner) *State, County*—Vital records *State, County*—Obituaries *State, County*—Cemeteries *State, County, City*—Vital records
Civil and criminal court records	*State, County*—Court records *State, County*—Public records (justice of the peace, etc.) *State*—Court records (for Spanish and French records and early records)
County business records (roads, treasurer's payments, etc.)	*State, County*—Public records *State, County*—Court records *State, County*—Land and property
Deeds and land records	*State, County*—Land and property *State, County*—Maps *State*—Land and property (early land grants)
Divorces (In many states, divorces in early times were granted by the state legislature. Today they are usually granted in a circuit court or court of common pleas.)	*State, County*—Vital records (divorce) *State*—Vital records (divorce)
Marriage	*State*—Vital records *State, County*—Vital records *State, County, City*—Vital records
Military records	*State*—Military records *State*—Military history *State, County*—Military records
Naturalization	*State, County, City*—Naturalization and citizenship *State, County*—Naturalization and citizenship *State*—Naturalization and citizenship
Professional licenses	*State, County*—Occupations *State*—Occupations
School records	*State, County*—Schools *State*—Schools
Tax records	*State, County*—Taxation *State*—Taxation
Wills and probate records	*State, County*—Probate records (wills, bonds, letters, etc.)

Figure 8.4 Searching the Family History Library Catalog for locality records

A Few Online Courthouse Records

Comb state archives and county Web sites for online indexes or records, and use a search engine to look for specific county records. Many indexes cover multiple counties or an entire state, but the records are usually located at the county level. You may be lucky enough to find indexes and transcribed or digitized records for the county you are researching similar to some of these:

- Index to Texas Probate Records (covers several Texas counties) *(three-legged-willie.org/texas.htm)*

- Delaware Public Archives Probate Index Database Search (1680–1925): *(www.state.de.us/sos/dpa/collections/probate.htm)*

- Massachusetts Probate Records Online Indexes *(www.mass-doc.com/probate_pub_index.htm)*

These types of records are not limited to the United States. For example, you can find a Danish Probate Index for four counties of Denmark at *ddd.sa.dk/dprob/*.

have to go to the county courthouse or town hall to view the records or order microfilmed copies at your local Family History Center.

One of the best uses you can make of the Internet for county research is to browse Web sites about the county or its records. Try a Google search of a type of record and a county name, such as *"probate records" + Taos.* This particular search netted a description of Taos County, New Mexico records from 1847 to 1959 that are held by the New Mexico State Records Center and Archives in Santa Fe *(elibrary.unm.edu/oanm/NmAr/nmar%231974-030/nmar%231974-030_m3.html)*, including those of the county clerk, assessor, county commissioners, treasurer, justice of the peace, probate court, coroner, school superintendent, and school board. At the site, more details about the Taos records are described, such as

deeds, chattel mortgages, notarial records, licenses, bonds, mining claims, and partido contracts; voter lists; election results; bylaws; and a register of stray animals. The register also contains materials on Indian depredations in the Taos area (1856–1889).

County commissioners' records include proceedings and a poll tally of the special election of delegates to the Constitutional Convention of 1889. Probate records include proceedings, wills and estates, guardianships, and two adoptions (1905, 1906).

Such information helps researchers know what kinds of records they may expect to locate in this particular county, perhaps sparking an idea for a search not previously considered.

Now you know how to ferret out those interesting and varied records at the county courthouse or town hall. Don't overlook any source of information about an ancestor. Even a record of stray cattle can provide an important clue—it's evidence that the person finding the animal was in the county at that time.

CHAPTER 9

Coming to America: Immigration, Naturalization, and Ethnic Sources

THE UNITED STATES IS A NATION OF IMMIGRANTS. UNLESS *ALL* YOUR ancestors were Native Americans, you have at least one ancestor who came here from another country. Whether you are German-American, Lithuanian-American, Norwegian-American—or any other type of hyphenated American—the time will come when your research must leave the shores of the New World and you must look back to your origins across the sea.

Immigration and Naturalization Basics

Until 1819, no national policy existed regarding records of people entering the Colonies or the United States. The few records that survive are scattered among myriad libraries, archives, and other repositories. Fortunately, many of the existing records have been published.

Passenger Lists
Luckily for genealogists, the federal government required in 1819 that masters of ships entering the United States give a list of all passengers to customs officials in the port of arrival. These Customs Passenger Lists included the passenger's name, age, sex, occupation, and nationality. Most lists also recorded any births or deaths that

139

What You Need to Know Before You Jump the Pond

Finding ancestors in the Old World is the driving force for some genealogists. It is natural to want to take the line as far back as possible. It is certainly exciting to find a passenger list or a marriage record in a different country for someone who has the same name as your ancestor. But how do you know that the John Young in the baptism record in Scotland is your John Young who moved to Washington County, Ohio? You need to have something besides your ancestor's name to give you clues to correctly identify him in a different location. The basic pieces of information you need before you attempt to find your ancestor overseas are

- **Name**, including given names, surname, nicknames, and any variations on his name.
- **Date**, preferably the birth date, but if you cannot find that, look for a date of another event that happened in the country of origin.
- **Origin**, in more specific terms than *Ireland* or *Germany*.
- **Associates**, those people whom your ancestor lived near, worked with, married, etc. People rarely migrate by themselves. Your ancestor's neighbors and associates may have come to America with him.

It is also helpful to know your ancestor's occupation and religion. Learn the family stories—they often have at least a kernel of truth in them. The bottom line: find everything you can about your ancestor here before you try to move to the other side of the pond.

occurred at sea. The lists vary from year to year and from one shipping line to another since the captains used no official form.

In 1883, immigration matters were transferred from the State Department to the Department of Treasury. Although "Customs Passenger Lists" became "Immigration Passenger Lists," the two lists were virtually identical until 1893. Beginning that year, masters of ships were required to provide much more detail about their passengers—name; age; sex; marital status; occupation; nationality; last residence; final destination; whether or not they had been in the United States previously (and if so, where and when); and the name, address, and relationship of any relative they were joining in the United States. In 1903, the passenger's race was added to the form, and starting in 1906, the passenger's town of birth was recorded.

Suggested Resources for More Information on Immigration and Naturalization

We could fill an entire book on immigration and naturalization. In fact, many people have. Two of the better ones are

- *They Came in Ships*, 3rd edition, by John Philip Colletta (Provo, Utah: Ancestry, 2002)

- *American Naturalization Records, 1790–1990: What They Are and How to Use Them*, by John J. Newman (Bountiful, Utah: Heritage Quest, 1998)

Also, visit the National Archives Immigrations Records page *(www.archives.gov/ research_room/genealogy/immigrant_arrivals/passenger_records.html)* for an overview of the records held by the National Archives in Washington, D.C., and a brief history of different periods in American immigration law.

Naturalization

Naturalization is the process of becoming a legal citizen of a land other than the one where you were born. Although many people who came to America became legal citizens, many others did not. Becoming naturalized was a three-step process:

1. The immigrant filed a Declaration of Intent to Become a Citizen. Information on these declarations, sometimes called first papers, includes the applicant's name, country of birth or allegiance, and sometimes, the date and port of arrival. More recent papers may include age, occupation, personal description, date and country of birth, residence, and last foreign residence.

2. After meeting residency requirements, usually from three to five years, the applicant filed a petition for citizenship.

3. The court admitted the applicant to citizenship and issued a certificate of naturalization.

Before 1906, all of these papers could be filed in any court of record—federal, state, or local.

Finding Immigration Records on the Internet

Passenger lists greatly outnumber naturalization records on the Internet, perhaps because passenger lists are readily available on microfilm and naturalization records are buried in volumes of court records. County GenWeb sites and state archives Web sites have the largest number of naturalization records available online. A major site is the Kings County (Brooklyn, New York) Clerk's Office Index to Naturalization Records 1907–1924 *(www.jgsny.org/kingsintro1.htm),* which includes the names of over 250,000 people who were naturalized or who filed their intent with the State Supreme Court. For links to many online naturalization records, see Cyndi's List's Immigration and Naturalization page *(www.cyndislist.com/immigrat.htm).*

Ellis Island Records

Millions of Americans can trace their ancestry through Ellis Island. It was a joyful day in genealogy when the Ellis Island Foundation launched the American Family Immigration History Center Web site *(www.ellisisland.org).* Commonly called the Ellis Island Database, this site, shown in Figure 9.1, contains abstracts and digitized images of the passenger lists of ships arriving at Ellis Island and the port of New York from 1892 to 1924—more than twenty-two million entries.

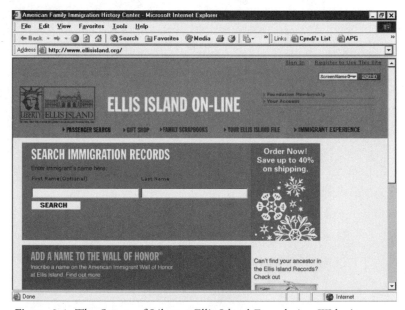

Figure 9.1 The Statue of Liberty–Ellis Island Foundation Web site

It is easy enough to start a search. From the home page, enter the name of the person you are looking for. You must enter the last name; the first name is optional. (To view the results, you must register, which is free.) A search for William Smith gave 3,704 records. Obviously, this is too many to look through. Clicking on Close Matches Only or Alternate Spellings Only produces shorter lists of results, but removes all exact matches.

For best results, limit the search by other means. Set a range of years of arrival, ethnicity, age at arrival, port of departure, or ship name. You can set any of these restrictions, but you have to set each one separately—you cannot select two or more at the same time. I want to limit my William Smith search to those who arrived between 1910 and 1915, age twenty to twenty-five years, having departed from ports in the United Kingdom. First, I click on the Year of Arrival button and enter the range of years. At this point, I have to run the search; I can't set the other limits first. After running this intermediate search, I set the age at arrival, search again, then limit the ports of departure to the United Kingdom. When I am done with all four searches, I have narrowed the list to fifty, with the first five displayed (see Figure 9.2).

I am interested in the William Smith of Glasgow, Scotland—entry number five. I click his name to see his abstracted passenger record. This gives me his name, ethnicity, place of residence, date of arrival, age on arrival, gender, marital status, ship name, and

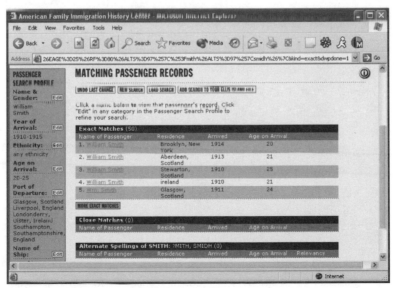

Figure 9.2 Results of the William Smith search after it is narrowed

port of departure. This is a great amount of information, but it isn't everything on the ship manifest. I click on View Original Ship Manifest to see a scanned image of the actual list. Here I read that he was a constable, he could read and write, his nationality was British, his race was Scottish, and his last permanent residence was Glasgow, Scotland. Those are great facts, but they pale in comparison to the listing of the name and complete address of his nearest relative or friend in the country he came from: Brother, G. Smith, 18 Grove St., Glasgow. William gave his final destination as Newark, New Jersey. This isn't surprising, considering that the second half of his entry lists the name and address of the relative or friend he was joining as "Mother, A. Smith, 225 Mt. Pleasant Ave., Newark, New Jersey."

You can read a text version of the manifest by clicking on View Text Version Manifest, which gives you an abstract of the entire passenger list, in order. It doesn't include all the information on the list—it includes only the name, gender, age, marital status, ethnicity, and place of residence—but it is a convenient way to read the list for associated names, such as other family members, friends, and neighbors who may be migrating together. Clicking on Ship brings up a photo and brief history of the ship in question—in this case, the *Columbia.*

The JewishGen site has a more robust search engine for the Ellis Island database. As you can see in Figure 9.3, "Searching the Ellis Island Database in One

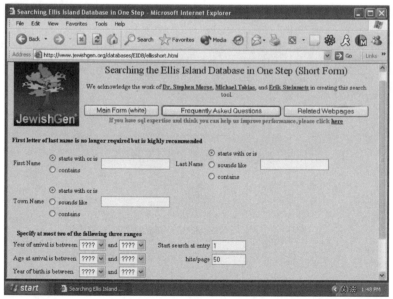

Figure 9.3 "Searching the Ellis Island Database in One Step" search screen

Step" *(www.jewishgen.org/databases/EIDB/ellisshort.html)* does exactly that—it allows the user to search by name, town name, year of arrival, age at arrival, and year of birth all at once. You may search the first name, last name, and town name by "starts with or is" or "contains." You may also search the last name and town name by "sounds like." This flexibility can help you overcome difficulties presented by different spellings. This search engine, developed by Stephen Morse, Michael Tobias, and Erik Steinmetz, gives the results in a concise mannter. Each hit gives a link to the Passenger Record, Text Manifest, Scanned Manifest (the Original Ship Manifest), and Ship Image on the Ellis Island site. This search engine will eventually be incorporated into the Ellis Island Database site.

Immigrant Ships Transcribers Guild

Although the Ellis Island database is the largest, it is by no means the only source of passenger lists on the Internet. Another major source is the Immigrant Ships Transcribers Guild (ISTG) Web site *(istg.rootsweb.com)*. This all-volunteer effort has transcribed the lists for almost five thousand ships, representing thousands of passengers. Begin your search by clicking on one of the passenger list volumes.

After reading the copyright notice and clicking on the agreement, you see the main page for one of the ISTG passenger list volumes (see Figure 9.4). You can search for

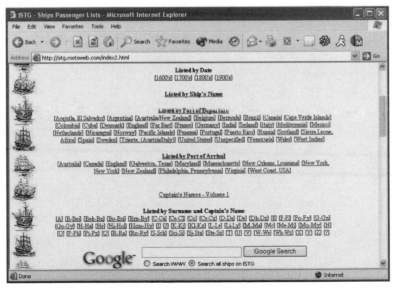

Figure 9.4 Immigrant Ships Transcribers Guild volume page

passenger lists in several ways. Each volume has links to display the lists included in that volume by date, ship's name, port of departure, port of arrival, captain's name, and captain and passenger surname. The most useful displays are by surname and by ship's name. You can also use the search engine at the bottom of the page to search all the volumes at once.

The surname index gives you links to all the ships that contain that surname. In looking for my Tracy ancestors in the surname index for volume 5, I find lists for four ships with Tracys aboard and two other ships that had Tracey passengers. I click on the link to the ship *Constitution* and am taken to the transcript of the *Constitution*'s passenger list from 25 May 1857 from Liverpool to New York, shown in Figure 9.5. I then use my Web browser's Find feature to look for Tracy. Each entry on the passenger list has a line number, as shown in Figure 9.6. If that number has an asterisk next to it, be sure to scroll down to the bottom of the list, where you'll find a comment about that specific entry (smudged ink, difficult handwriting, etc.).

For each of the volumes, you can look by ship's name, which is very useful because so many families have handed down the name of the immigrant's ship. You may look through the list of ships for each volume or use the search feature. If you're looking for a ship named after a person, such as the *Alexander Barclay*, it may be less confusing to look through each volume's list, rather than using the search feature.

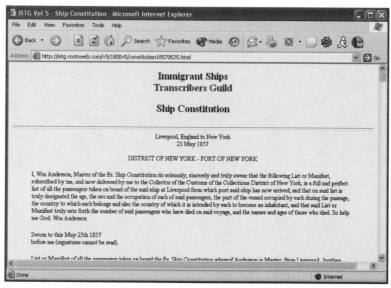

Figure 9.5 ISTG passenger list transcription

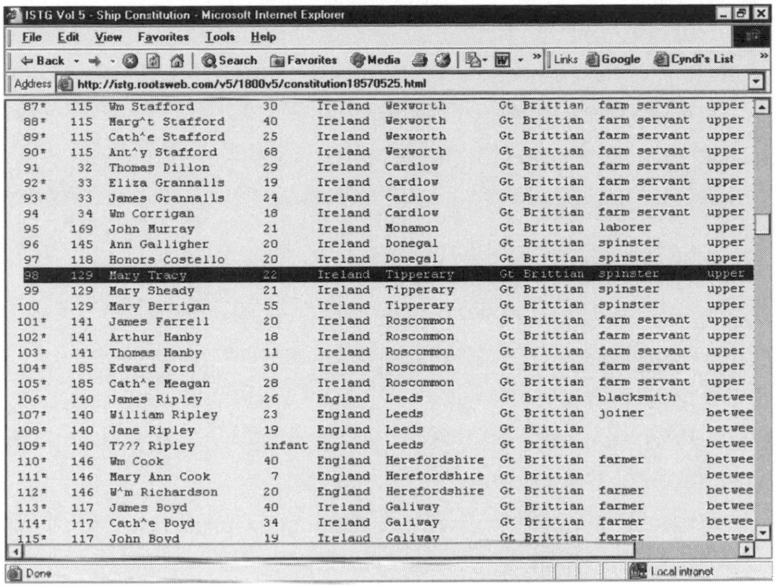

87*	115	Wm Stafford	30	Ireland	Wexworth	Gt Brittian	farm servant	upper
88*	115	Marg^t Stafford	40	Ireland	Wexworth	Gt Brittian	farm servant	upper
89*	115	Cath^e Stafford	25	Ireland	Wexworth	Gt Brittian	farm servant	upper
90*	115	Ant^y Stafford	68	Ireland	Wexworth	Gt Brittian	farm servant	upper
91	32	Thomas Dillon	29	Ireland	Cardlow	Gt Brittian	farm servant	upper
92*	33	Eliza Grannalls	19	Ireland	Cardlow	Gt Brittian	farm servant	upper
93*	33	James Grannalls	24	Ireland	Cardlow	Gt Brittian	farm servant	upper
94	34	Wm Corrigan	18	Ireland	Cardlow	Gt Brittian	farm servant	upper
95	169	John Murray	21	Ireland	Monamon	Gt Brittian	laborer	upper
96	145	Ann Galligher	20	Ireland	Donegal	Gt Brittian	spinster	upper
97	118	Honors Costello	20	Ireland	Donegal	Gt Brittian	spinster	upper
98	129	Mary Tracy	22	Ireland	Tipperary	Gt Brittian	spinster	upper
99	129	Mary Sheady	21	Ireland	Tipperary	Gt Brittian	spinster	upper
100	129	Mary Berrigan	55	Ireland	Tipperary	Gt Brittian	spinster	upper
101*	141	James Farrell	20	Ireland	Roscommon	Gt Brittian	farm servant	upper
102*	141	Arthur Hanby	18	Ireland	Roscommon	Gt Brittian	farm servant	upper
103*	141	Thomas Hanby	11	Ireland	Roscommon	Gt Brittian	farm servant	upper
104*	185	Edward Ford	30	Ireland	Roscommon	Gt Brittian	farm servant	upper
105*	185	Cath^e Meagan	28	Ireland	Roscommon	Gt Brittian	farm servant	upper
106*	140	James Ripley	26	England	Leeds	Gt Brittian	blacksmith	betwee
107*	140	William Ripley	23	England	Leeds	Gt Brittian	joiner	betwee
108*	140	Jane Ripley	19	England	Leeds	Gt Brittian		betwee
109*	140	T??? Ripley	infant	England	Leeds	Gt Brittian		betwee
110*	146	Wm Cook	40	England	Herefordshire	Gt Brittian	farmer	betwee
111*	146	Mary Ann Cook	7	England	Herefordshire	Gt Brittian		betwee
112*	146	Wm Richardson	20	England	Herefordshire	Gt Brittian	farmer	betwee
113*	117	James Boyd	40	Ireland	Galiway	Gt Brittian	farmer	betwee
114*	117	Cath^e Boyd	34	Ireland	Galiway	Gt Brittian	farmer	betwee
115*	117	John Boyd	19	Ireland	Galiway	Gt Brittian	farmer	betwee

Figure 9.6 Detail of ISTG passenger list transcription

Other Passenger Lists on the Internet

The Ellis Island database and the Immigrant Ships Transcribers Guild aren't the only sites on the Internet with passenger list information. Here are some others to visit:

- Bremen Passenger Lists 1920–1939 *(db.genealogy.net/maus/gate/shiplists.cgi?lang=en)*
- Cyndi's List—Immigration and Naturalization *(www.cyndislist.com/immigrat.htm)*
- Joe Beine's What Passenger Lists Are Online? *(home.att.net/~wee-monster/onlinelists.html)*
- Hamburg Emigration Lists (index is free, but you must pay for details) *(www.hamburg.de/LinkToYourRoots/english/start.htm)*
- Norwegian Emigration Lists *(digitalarkivet.uib.no/)*. To view in English, click on English. Emigration lists are found by clicking on Categories, then Emigrants.

A Real Family Example

The U.S. census can be a big help in determining a family's arrival date in the United States. The earliest census in which I could locate my friend Mike's family was the 1900 federal census of Valencia County, New Mexico, shown in Figure 9.7 from Ancestry.com's online census images. This census provides the following information about the Francis family:

- Elias Francis, head of household, white male, born September 1857, age forty-one, married twenty-two years, born in Turkey, both parents born in Turkey.

- Pabla Francis, wife, white female, born May 1858, age forty-two, married twenty-two years, mother of three children, one child living, born in Turkey, both parents born in Turkey.

- Narciso Francis, son, age twenty-one, white male, born January 1879, single, born in Turkey, both parents born in Turkey.

The census further shows that Elias Francis had immigrated to the United States in 1888, had lived in the United States for twelve years (in 1900), and was a naturalized

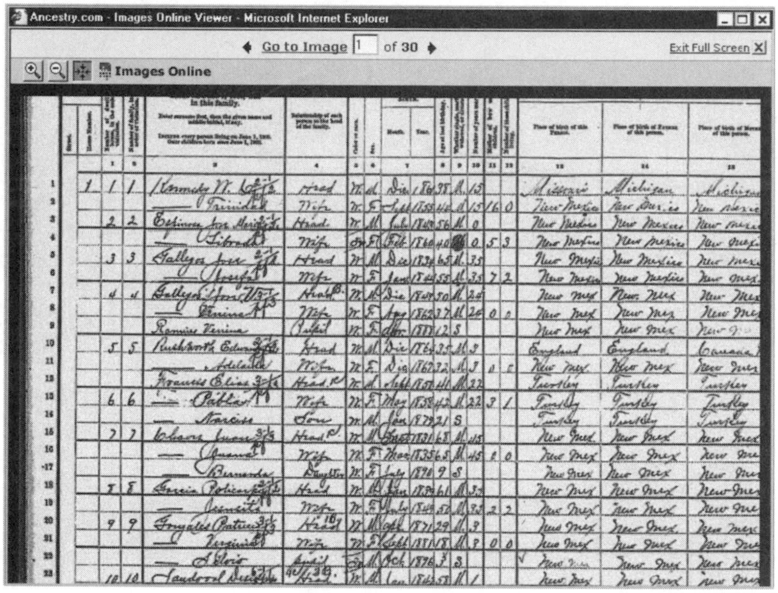

Figure 9.7 1900 federal census of Valencia County, New Mexico

citizen. His occupation is identified as "Merchant—General Merchandise." Pabla Francis and son Narciso are listed as immigrating in 1894 and living in the United States for six years. Narciso's occupation is also identified as "Merchant—General Merchandise."

Later census immigration information for the family varies. The 1910 federal census of Valencia County records Elias and Pablita Francis as immigrating in 1888, and Narciso in 1890. The 1920 census records all three family members as immigrating in 1899 and gives their birthplace as Syria rather than Turkey.

A search of the Ellis Island database *(www.ellisisland.org)* provides two results of an Elias Francis immigrating between 1892 and 1900, shown in Figure 9.8. The second one, immigrating in 1895 at age 37, looks like a possible match for our New Mexico Elias Francis, born in 1857. Clicking on the link for the second Elias Francis results in the display of the passenger record shown in Figure 9.9. This person arrived in New York on 21 October 1895 aboard the ship *La Champagne,* which had departed from the port of Le Havre, Seine-Inferior, France. He was a thirty-seven-year-old married male. Did he travel alone, or was he accompanied by a family?

When clicking on the View Original Ship Manifest button, a digitized image of the *La Champagne* passenger list displays, with an option to purchase a copy of this original page from the Ellis Island Foundation. But there is also an option to view a text version

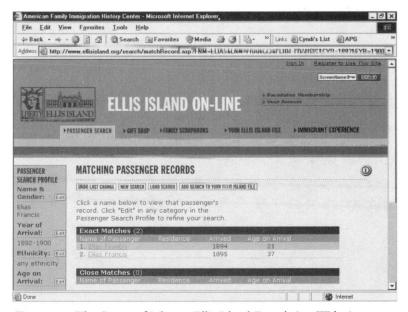

Figure 9.8 The Statue of Liberty–Ellis Island Foundation Web site showing Elias Francis results

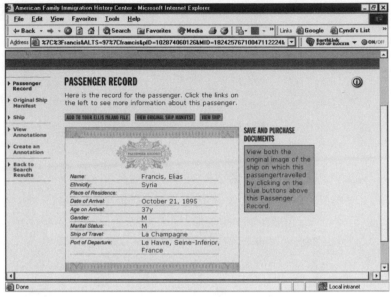

Figure 9.9 The Statue of Liberty–Ellis Island Foundation Web site showing Elias Francis passenger record

of the manifest, shown in Figure 9.10. Immediately under the name Elias Francis on line 450 is the name Nacif Francis, male, age fifteen, of Syria. Wondering if the ship manifest includes other potential members of Elias Francis's family, I decide to search it more closely. I find that coming into Ellis Island on the *La Champagne* from Havre on 21 October 1895 were the following Syrian passengers with the surname Francis:

- Line 450. Elias Francis, age 37, male, married
- Line 451. Hasula Francis, age 36, female, married
- Line 452. Yapour Francis, age 11, male
- Line 453. Nacif Francis, age 15, male

This is probably a family since they are listed on consecutive lines of the ship's manifest, but are they the same as the Elias and Pabla Francis family with their son Narciso Francis in the 1900 Valencia County, New Mexico census? What happened to the boy, Yapour, by 1900? According to Pabla, she was the mother of three children, but only one, Narciso, was still living in 1900. The names are not exactly the same, but it

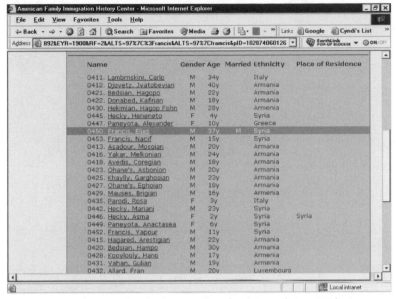

Figure 9.10 The Statue of Liberty–Ellis Island Foundation Web site showing text passenger list

is not unusual for immigrants to change their names in a new country. Pabla Francis appeared in later New Mexico records as Pablita and Paulina in what was at the time a U.S. territory of many Spanish-speaking natives. Could the Spanish name Narciso have been a variant of the Syrian Nacif? I found nothing on the Internet to confirm or deny my hunch that this is indeed the same family.

Because not every record is available on the Internet, I took a trip to the New Mexico State Records Center and Archives and found several original civil dockets from the Second Judicial District Court of Valencia County in which "Elias Francis and Nasef Francis, a co-partnership doing business under the firm name and style of Elias Francis & Son" filed suits against debtors as early as 1903. The 1900 census reveals Elias and Narciso Francis as merchants, and this 1903 court record names Elias and Nacef Francis as businessmen, a good indication that they are one and the same. The name Nacef is strikingly similar to the immigrant, Nacif Francis, entering Ellis Island at age fifteen in 1895. More work needs to be done to verify that Pabla, Pablita, or Paulina Francis is the same as the Hasula Francis entering Ellis Island in 1895 with Elias and Nacif, but things look promising.

What about the conflict in the birthplace of Turkey versus Syria given in the censuses and Ellis Island records? Elias Francis's 1930 obituary in the *Albuquerque Journal* newspaper gives his place of birth as Mount Lebanon, Syria. Mount Lebanon comprises the central part of present-day Lebanon, and Elias's descendants claim a Lebanese-Christian heritage. Modern-day Syria lies between Lebanon and Turkey, all of which in the past were part of the Ottoman Empire. Just as county boundaries have changed within the United States, international boundaries have changed among countries of the world. The immigrant Francis family's birthplaces may have changed as country boundaries changed.

Ethnic Sources at Home and Abroad

Ethnic pride has taken hold in the United States. Beyond the heritage festivals that showcase ethnic culture and history (and lots of good food), a growing amount of literature about ethnic groups in America is available both in print and online. It's not only fun to learn about your ancestors' customs and culture, but it is also important to look at how ethnicity may change your research strategies. Different ethnic groups, whether in the United States or abroad, have varying materials that are useful to genealogists. If you take advantage of these resources, your research will become more efficient and successful.

General Help

Before you dig very deeply into your ancestors' ethnic roots, you must learn the basics about researching that ethnic group. The Church of Jesus Christ of Latter-day Saints has made this information readily available at the FamilySearch Web site *(www.familysearch.org)*. To find these Research Helps, go to *www.familysearch.org/Eng/Search/RG/frameset_rhelps.asp* or, from the main page, click on the Search tab, then click on Research Helps. From there, select the location you are interested in and the document of interest. The Research Outline gives you an excellent place to start. Figure 9.11 shows the selection of Research Helps for Italy.

One of my neighbors wanted help with her Italian research. She had learned a little bit about the family from her grandmother, who had emigrated from Italy. My neighbor had found all that she could about the family in the United States, but with her grandmother having been such a recent immigrant (arriving in the mid-1950s), she was quickly ready to make the jump to the old country. Having no experience in Italian research myself, I showed my neighbor the Italian Research Outline. We

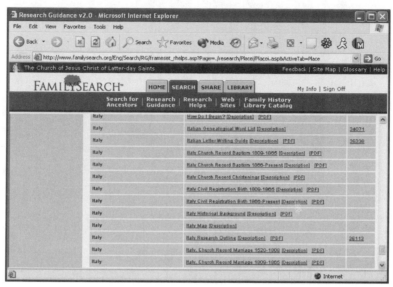

Figure 9.11 FamilySearch Web site showing the Italian Research Helps

learned about Italian research strategies, civil registration, church records, Italian history, and major genealogical collections. In all, there were thirty-three subjects that we could read about on the Italian Research Outline. The outlines for most other nationalities are just as robust.

Other types of Research Helps are also available at the FamilySearch site. My neighbor found the Italian-Latin Genealogical Word Lists to be very helpful in reading the records that she ordered through our local Family History Center. She also downloaded the Italian Letter-Writing Guide to help her compose letters to offices in Italy requesting copies of records.

Other good sources for help in starting your ethnic research are genealogical societies that specialize in a particular ethnic group. The German-Bohemian Heritage Society Web site *(www.rootsweb.com/~gbhs/)* has a page of resources for German-Bohemian research, as well as a brief article that describes the organization.

Many general genealogical societies have ethnic special-interest groups. The Hamilton County Chapter of the Ohio Genealogical Society *(members.aol.com/ogshc/)* has African-American, English, German, and Irish special-interest groups. These groups can often point you toward specific ethnic resources for that area, such as ethnic church records and cemeteries. To find genealogical societies, look at the

World GenWeb

Based on the US GenWeb model, the World GenWeb site *(www.worldgenweb.org)* provides information, data, and queries from around the world. It is categorized into seven regions—North America, South America, Europe, Africa, the Middle East, Asia, and Australia. Not all countries have a World GenWeb site, but you should always look for one whenever your research leads you outside the United States.

Federation of Genealogical Societies Society Hall *(www.familyhistory.com/societyhall/)* and Cyndi's List pages for a particular ethnic group (such as the Norway page at *www.cyndislist.com/norway.htm*).

Specific Ethnic Groups

If you are just starting your African-American research, consider yourself fortunate. There have been more guides to and records dealing with African-American genealogy in the last two years than at any other time. One Web site that you must visit is AfriGeneas *(www.afrigeneas.com)*. The site features numerous articles on African-American genealogy, discussion groups, and abstracts of records. The search feature is easy to use, and the site is incredible. Another rich resource is the Freedmen's Bureau Online *(www.freedmensbureau.com)*. The Bureau of Refugees, Freedmen, and Abandoned Lands, commonly called the Freedmen's Bureau, was the federal agency set up at the close of the Civil War to supervise relief efforts in the former Confederate and border states, the District of Columbia, and the Indian Territory. Freedmen's Bureau Online allows you to search for marriage records, records relating to Freedmen's labor, and records of "murders and outrages." This site, as well as AfriGeneas and Cyndi's List—African-American page *(www.cyndislist.com/african.htm)*, contains numerous links to other sites of interest to African-American researchers.

If your ancestors hailed from eastern Europe, the Federation of East European Family History Societies Web site *(www.feefhs.org)* is a must-see. The site contains more than six thousand data files with more than one million central and eastern European surnames and locations. The FEEFHS Resource Guide page *(www.feefhs.org/masteri.html)* has a section called Ethnic, Religious and National

Finding Good Sites for Your Ethnic Group

No matter how small your ethnic group, a Web site is probably devoted to it. Cyndi's List has numerous ethnic links. Look for the country of interest; if you don't find it, look under a region such as Asia or eastern Europe. Use the pages at World GenWeb—many have links to related sites. Be certain to look for genealogical and historical societies for links to relevant sites. Of course, you can always use Internet search engines.

Cross-Indexes, which provides links to resources for particular locations or religious groups. What this site lacks in graphics, it more than makes up for in information. JewishGen *(www.jewishgen.org)* is the major site for Jewish research, including eastern Europe. You will learn more about it in Chapter 11, "Discovering Ancestors at Work and Worship."

Are your ancestors from the British Isles? Among the numerous sites for that region of the world are GENUKI and the British Isles GenWeb. GENUKI *(www.genuki.org.uk)* has data and links for the United Kingdom and Ireland. The British Isles GenWeb *(www.britishislesgenweb.org)* has data, queries, and a location finder—essential for putting your ancestor in the right place—as well as links to the ten British Isles country projects (Channel Islands, England, Falkland Islands, Gibraltar, Ireland, Isle of Man, Northern Ireland, Scotland, St. Helena, and Wales).

Discovering your ethnic roots is exciting and rewarding. Making the connection with your immigrant ancestors and learning about their customs and heritage adds so much to your understanding of who they were—and who you are. Once you have researched all you can about their lives on these shores, use the power of the Internet to travel to their world.

CHAPTER 10

Finding Clues to Military Service

EVEN IF YOUR ANCESTORS WERE TOO POOR TO OWN LAND OR VALUABLE personal belongings, chances are that one or more of them served in some arm of the U.S. military within the past two-hundred-plus years. Men as young as sixteen or as old as sixty may have participated in local militia units. However, most men who served were between the ages of eighteen and thirty. Don't overlook military records in your genealogical research. They can reveal vital statistics, ancestors' locales, health histories, and politics. Some files, such as pension files and claims applications, may even contain *original* birth, marriage, or death records. Many types of records exist relating to military service. Start with records you can find in the attic—or with clues from family stories—then use the resources in this chapter to find out more.

Types of Military Records

There are multitudes of military records, and you will greatly increase your effectiveness as a family history researcher if you educate yourself about them. That way, you'll know the difference between a compiled service record and a pension file—and you'll be better able to analyze the information you locate in military records.

The National Archives and Records Administration (NARA) is the official repository for records of military personnel who served in the U.S. Army, Air Force, Navy, Marine Corps, and Coast Guard. Records from the Revolutionary War to the beginning of the twentieth century are held by NARA in Washington, D.C. For information about the

Military Service Timeline

An Ancestor Born Circa:	May Have Served In:
1745–1765	Revolutionary War (1775–1783)
1782–1797	War of 1812 (1812–1815)
1750–1877	Indian Wars (1780s–1890s)
1816–1830	Mexican War (1846–1848)
1831–1847	Civil War (1861–1865)
1868–1880	Spanish-American War (1898)
1869–1884	Philippine Insurrection (1899–1902)
1887–1900	World War I (1917–1918)
1911–1927	World War II (1941–1945)
1920–1935	Korean War (1950–1953)
1935–1955	Vietnam War (1965–1973)

types and dates of military records available for research and how to request by e-mail the forms you need for ordering these records, go to NARA's Web site at *www.archives.gov/research_room/obtain_copies/veterans_service_records.html.*

Later military records, primarily those dating from the twentieth century forward, are maintained by NARA's National Personnel Records Center (NPRC) in St. Louis, Missouri. Access to modern military records is limited to the veteran, the next of kin, or a representative of the veteran. Visit *www.archives.gov/facilities/mo/st_louis/ military_personnel_records.html* for information about the military records NPRC holds and to download the forms you need to order them.

Federal, State, or County?

Military records for your ancestor can be found in all three major divisions of government—federal, state, and county. For instance, in 1777, Virginia authorized pensions for disabled Virginia soldiers and widows of men killed during the Revolutionary War. Separate U.S. federal legislation provided pensions for Continental soldiers in the same war. These records are held by the state of Virginia and by the National Archives, respectively. The records are also available on microfilm at the Library of Virginia.

Remember that during the Civil War, two different national governments existed—the United States, and the Confederate States of America. After the war, the

Forms for Ordering Military Records

You must submit these special forms and fees to NARA when ordering military files:

- Pension file more than seventy-five years old: Form 85, plus $37 for entire file
- Pension documents packet: Form 85, plus $14.75
- Bounty land warrant application file: Form 85, plus $17.25
- Military service file more than seventy-five years old: Form 86, plus $17.00

Order the files above from the National Archives building in Washington, D.C. Forms 85 and 86 are not available as downloadable files online, but you can order them at *www.archives.gov/global_pages/inquire_form.html#part_a* by filling in the request and your mailing address. When you submit this online request, NARA receives an e-mail; you should receive a standard e-mail response that your request has been received. Within a few weeks, your forms should arrive in the mail.

To order modern military records from NARA's National Personnel Record Center (NPRC) in St. Louis, download and print a Standard Form 180 from *www.archives.gov/ facilities/mo/st_louis/military_personnel_records/standard_form_180.html*. Fill out and sign the form, and then fax or mail it to the NPRC. Because these requests must be signed and dated, you cannot submit the form online. If your request involves a service fee, you will be notified. Be patient when you've submitted your form; the NPRC has a huge backlog of requests, and your response may take four to six weeks or longer.

federal government issued pensions to soldiers who served in volunteer or regular U.S. regiments (Union), and those records reside at the National Archives in Washington. However, don't expect to find many Confederate pension records at the National Archives. Those pensions were authorized by individual southern or border states, and you'll have to look for them in the archives of the state where the veteran last lived.

At the state level, the Adjutant General is responsible for military affairs. His office created records such as pension files (in some states), militia records (muster rolls, descriptive rolls, or other items), claims, and registers from military prisons and hospitals. Other records relating to military activities within a state include veterans' homes and state veteran censuses.

The county level has military records, as well. You may find some militia records, and you often discover military discharge records, recorded at the local county courthouse by returning veterans, primarily after World War I and later. Some counties took their own veteran censuses. Many counties had boards or commissions to provide relief to local indigent soldiers and their families.

NARA Research Aids

Figure 10.1 shows NARA's online Genealogy Military Records page *(www.archives.gov/ research_room/genealogy/research_topics/military.html)*, a good place to start learning about the wealth of original military records available for your research. Here you find links to helpful online articles, such as explanations of each type of military record, how to compile a soldier's history, and where to find the records. This Web site provides a link to the NARA print publication *Military Service Records: A Select Catalog of National Archives Microfilm Publications*, which is also available online at *www.archives.gov/ publications/microfilm_catalogs/military/military_service_records.html*. Browse this publication for complete descriptions and microfilm numbers of NARA military holdings, from Revolutionary War rolls to Spanish-American War records.

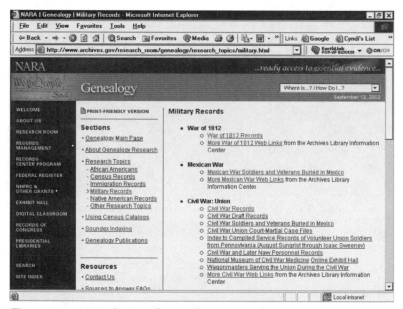

Figure 10.1 NARA's Genealogy Military Records page

NARA's Genealogy Military Records page also features links to NARA resources, including helpful articles from its *Prologue* magazine, such as "Which Henry Cook? A Methodology for Searching Confederate Ancestors," by Desmond Walls Allen (Fall 1995, vol. 27, no. 3). Links to resources outside NARA include such Web sites as *www.dmwv.org/mexwar/documents/docs.htm#reports,* which provides transcriptions of battle reports from the Mexican War of 1846–48.

Finding Private Jones

Because most military records are arranged by unit, one secret to finding them is knowing the organization in which an ancestor served. Knowing your ancestor's unit also helps you better distinguish him from men of the same name. Like so many other facts about your ancestor, the answer may already be in your possession. Obituaries, regimental reunion programs, and pension papers often list the unit. It may even be carved in stone—tombstones can be a source of military information.

Rosters

Rosters, or lists of servicemen, are probably the most common type of military record found on the Internet. At a minimum, any roster tells you the soldier's name and his unit. Some rosters also include rank, age at enlistment, and occasionally, residence. Some online lists are arranged by unit, usually taken from official adjutant general rosters. Others are arranged by county, often compiled from county histories, county discharge records, and cemetery readings.

State libraries, archives, and historical societies have been at the forefront of placing rosters on the Internet. The Wisconsin Historical Society has placed on its Web site searchable digitized images of the *Roster of Wisconsin Volunteers, War of the Rebellion, 1861–1865 (www.wisconsinhistory.org/roster/index.html).* USGenWeb sites often have military rosters. The military page of the Anderson County, South Carolina GenWeb site *(www.rootsweb.com/~scander2/military.html)* contains many rosters, including that of a company that served in the Seminole Wars.

Civil War Soldiers and Sailors System

The Civil War Soldiers and Sailors System (CWSS) at *www.itd.nps.gov/cwss/* contains the largest free database of Civil War soldiers—both Union and Confederate—available on the Internet. It is the result of a cooperative effort among the National Parks Service, the Federation of Genealogical Societies, the Genealogical Society of Utah, and numerous other organizations across the United States. The index of soldiers' names, roughly 5.4 million entries, was compiled from the NARA General Index Cards of the Compiled Service Records, which we'll discuss in detail later. The index of sailors is still being compiled and currently contains only African-American sailors. To look for your soldier, click on the link to Soldiers on the main page. The CWSS soldier search, shown in Figure 10.2, is easy to use. You can search by last name, first name, whether Union or Confederate, state (referring to the unit's origins, not the soldier's), unit, and function (cavalry, infantry, etc.).

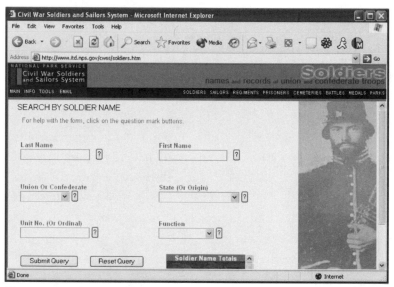

Figure 10.2 CWSS soldier search menu

The CWSS does not allow for wildcard searches; that is, you cannot enter Sm*th and find both Smith and Smyth. However, you can enter the soldier's surname and just the soldier's first initial to find all surname entries with first names that begin with that initial. For example, searching for surname Fitzsimmons with first initial W results in a list of men (Washington Fitzsimmons, William Fitzsimmons, William C. Fitzsimmons, etc.). Some entries contain initials instead of first names, so this way of searching can help you find as many entries as possible. Limiting your search to a particular state is useful, especially when looking for someone with a common surname.

Say I want to find any Francis Hendersons who served from Illinois. I enter the last name Henderson and the initial F, then select Illinois as the state. I get nine results, shown in Figure 10.3.

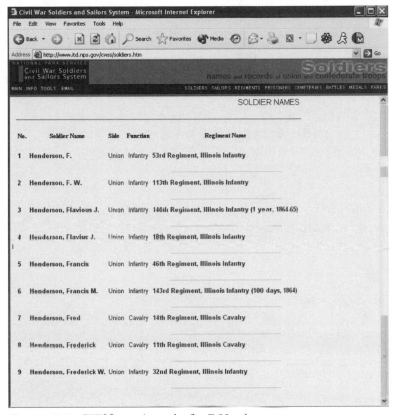

Figure 10.3 CWSS search results for F Henderson

There is a Francis Henderson of the 46th Regiment, Illinois Infantry, and a Francis M. Henderson of the 143rd Regiment, Illinois Infantry. There is also an entry for F. Henderson of the 53rd Regiment, Illinois Infantry, and F. W. Henderson of the 113th Regiment, Illinois Infantry. I do not know the first names of these last two entries, but I now have a lead to look for more information, perhaps with the Illinois State Archives. Clicking on Francis Henderson shows his Detailed Soldier Record (Figure 10.4). Information on this record can include the company the soldier was in, the soldier's rank in, the soldier's rank out, an alternate name, and comments. In this example, Francis Henderson was a member of Company B, was a private upon entry into the unit, was a private when he left the unit, and had the alternate name Francis M. Henderson. This is a clue to me that perhaps he and Francis M. Henderson of the 143rd Illinois were the same man. I must do more investigation to confirm or refute this theory.

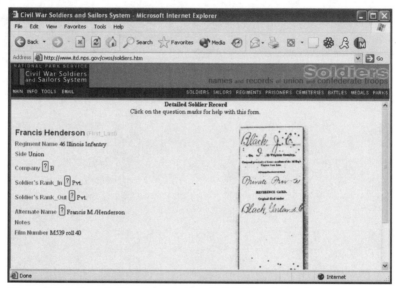

Figure 10.4 Francis Henderson's Detailed Soldier Record

Using my Internet browser's Back button, I return to the results screen (the list of soldier names shown in Figure 10.3). Clicking on Francis Henderson's regiment, the 46th Regiment of the Illinois Infantry, I view a history of the 46th Illinois. Some of the battles in which the unit was engaged, including Shiloh and the sieges on Corinth and Vicksburg, contain links to battle summaries. At the bottom of the unit history, I am given the option to display the entire roster of the 46th Regiment, Illinois Infantry, or to download a file with the information.

If you have already established your ancestor's unit, use the CWSS to find unit histories and battle summaries by selecting either Regiments or Battles from the CWSS main page. The CWSS features a growing database of cemetery information. For example, you can access data on soldiers buried at Poplar Grove National Cemetery, complete with photos of the tombstones. The Prisoners database has information from Fort McHenry and Andersonville.

Compiled Service Records

Compiled service records are available for U.S. volunteer soldiers who served in wars and conflicts from the Revolutionary War through the Philippine Insurrection, 1775–1902, and for Confederates who served during the Civil War. These records do not include members of the regular army, marines, and navy. From the 1890s up to World War I, the War Department extracted information from original muster rolls, post returns, medical files, prison registers, and other records. They organized these abstract cards into compiled service records for individual soldiers. The abstracts may show the person's name, age at enlistment, place of enlistment, place of birth, rank, military organization, term of service, and presence or absence on a particular date. Compiled service records may also include the veteran's date and place of birth, physical description, injuries or illness while in the military, date and place of death, cause of death, burial place, or time spent as a prisoner of war (POW).

Viewing NARA Microfilmed Military Records

If you cannot go to the National Archives in Washington, D.C., you may still be able to look at microfilmed military records. Look at the list of NARA's regional facilities *(www.archives.gov/ facilities/index.html)* for one near you. Libraries often have microfilm of NARA records germane to their local area, so you may find what you're looking for at your local library. Check the Family History Library Catalog online *(www.familysearch.org)* to see whether the microfilm is available there. If so, for a small fee, you can have it sent to your local Family History Center where you can view it. You may also arrange to borrow the NARA microfilm through your local library or have it sent directly to your home. For details on the NARA microfilm rental program, see *www.archives.gov/publications/microfilm_catalogs/how_to_rent_microfilm.html*.

Many indexes to these compiled service records and some of the records themselves have been microfilmed by the National Archives and Records Administration. You can look up the descriptions and microfilm roll numbers in NARA's online *Military Service Records* catalog *(www.archives.gov/publications/microfilm_catalogs/military/ military_service_records_part04.html)* and arrange to view the microfilm locally.

One example of online compiled service records is the 1,235 digitized cards of records for the Rough Riders from the Spanish-American War found with NARA's Archival Research Catalog (ARC) search tool *(arcweb.archives.gov/arc/basic_search.jsp)*. Search for *Rough Riders* to find all matching records in ARC. If you are looking for the compiled service record of a specific Rough Rider, such as Henry Thorp, enter that name in ARC. Figure 10.5 shows the search results.

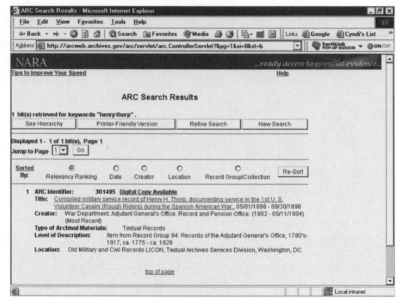

Figure 10.5 ARC search results for Henry Thorp service record

Figure 10.6 shows the digitized images of Henry Thorp's compiled service records. Clicking on the "thumbnail," or small graphic, of one of the compiled service records cards enlarges it to make it legible. Many digitized records on the Internet are accessed in a similar way.

The compiled service record card for Henry H. Thorp's Spanish-American War service shown in Figure 10.7 provides a record of his muster into Company T, 1st Cavalry, U.S. Volunteers in Washington, D.C., 5 May 1898. Henry was "33½" years old and 5 feet 6¼ inches tall; his complexion was fair, his eyes were blue, and his hair was brown. Thorp was born in New York, New York, and he was a physician. He joined for duty 5 May 1898 in Washington, D.C., for a period of two years. He was single, and his parent or guardian was Albert G. Thorp, 345 West 31st, New York City. Wouldn't you like to know the same kinds of details about your ancestor?

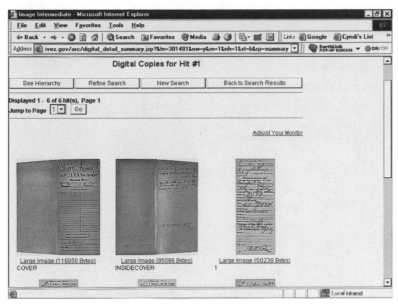

Figure 10.6 Online compiled service record

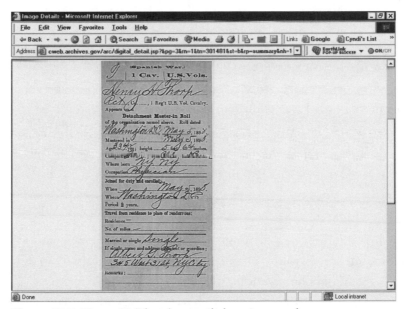

Figure 10.7 Henry H. Thorp's compiled service record

Compiled service records can provide them (although you do not find the names of parents or guardians in most compiled service records).

In addition to the Civil War Soldiers System, other indexes to compiled service records exist on the Internet. Among them are Ancestry.com's Revolutionary War Service Records, War of 1812 Service Records, and Civil War Service Records, all of which require a paid subscription to Ancestry.com *(www.ancestry.com)* or the use of your local library's subscription to AncestryPlus.

Pensions and Other Veterans Assistance

Payment to soldiers didn't always stop with the end of service. The federal government and many states offered pensions to veterans, paid either in cash or in land. Pension files are among the most valuable military records that you can find.

Pension Files

The National Archives has pension applications and records of payment for veterans, their widows, and their heirs, for military service between 1775 and 1916. The U.S. government provided three basic types of pensions based on military service:

- **Disability or invalid pensions**: Awarded to veterans for physical disabilities incurred in the line of duty.

- **Survivor pensions**: Awarded to veterans who served in wartime for specified periods and lived long enough to receive them.

- **Widows' or dependents' pensions**: Awarded to women, children, or parents whose deceased husband, father, or son had served for specified periods or had been killed in war; children usually had to be under the age of sixteen to qualify for a pension.

Individual states may also have granted pensions to veterans who served in the state militia or home guard. Pension files can contain a plethora of historical and genealogical information, including the location and movements of the veteran's unit, battle details, and activities of individuals with whom the veteran came in contact. Files may contain information from muster rolls, diaries, orderly books, or hospital records. The individual's application typically contains his name, rank, unit, dates of service, residence at time of enlistment and at time of application, birthplace, age or date of birth, and even property holdings. A widow's pension application should contain all the same information, plus the widow's maiden name, date and place of marriage, date and place of her husband's death, other husbands of the widow or other wives of the veteran, and names and dates of birth of minor children.

Finding Pension File Indexes Online

Pensions for military service have been awarded by various states and the federal government. You may be able to find abstracted or transcribed pension files for some localities or surnames on the Internet. Try a Google search of a phrase similar to *Confederate pension index + Texas*. Here are some of the pension indexes to be found on the Internet. Some require paid subscriptions.

- Ancestry.com's Revolutionary War Pension Index (subscription) (*www.ancestry.com/search/rectype/inddbs/4691.htm*)

- Genealogy.com's Revolutionary War Pension List (subscription) (*www.genealogy.com/ifa/co_cd145.html*)

- Tennessee State Library and Archives Index to Tennessee Confederate Pension Applications (*www.state.tn.us/sos/statelib/pubsvs/pension.htm*)

- Texas State Library and Archives Commission Index to Confederate Civil War Pension Applications (*www.tsl.state.tx.us/arc/pensions/introcpi.html*)

- Ancestry.com's Civil War Pension Index (subscription) (*www.ancestry.com/search/rectype/military/cwpi/main.htm*)

In pension files, you may find such supporting documents as discharge papers, depositions of witnesses, narratives about the veteran's whereabouts during his service, marriage certificates or family Bible pages, and physicians' reports regarding the veteran's health history, vital signs, and physical description.

Generally, federal pension files for service during the War of 1812, Indian Wars, Mexican War, Civil War, or later are not available on microfilm. You can use NARA finding aids at *www.archives.gov/publications/microfilm_catalogs/military/military_service_records_part22.html* to locate microfilmed indexes to pension application files for the War of 1812, "Old Wars" (1783–1861), the Mexican War (1887–1926), and Indian Wars (1892–1926). Additional NARA-microfilmed pension indexes covering primarily Civil War service include the General Index (1861–1934), arranged alphabetically by surname, and the Organization Index to Pension Files of Veterans Who Served Between 1861 and 1900, arranged alphabetically by state, then by arm of service, by regiment number, and alphabetically by surname.

Ancestry.com makes available to its subscribers a searchable online index of Civil War pension index cards, linked to digitized images of the cards. A sample card is shown in Figure 10.8 for Demetrius Durr and his widow, Annie, who filed for the pension from the state of Missouri. This card provides the information needed to order a copy of the actual Civil War pension file from the National Archives: Soldier's name (Demetrius Durr), widow's name (Annie Durr), the veteran's service information (Company G, 3rd Missouri Militia Cavalry, and Company G, 10th Missouri State Militia Cavalry), date the soldier filed for an invalid pension (19 July 1873), the invalid pension application number (185459) and certificate number (154230), the date the widow filed for a pension (4 January 1903), the widow's application number (1112932) and certificate number (986082), and the state she filed from (Missouri). With this information, a researcher can accurately fill out a

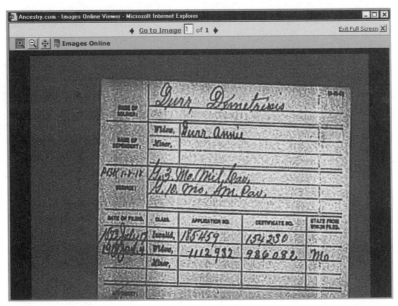

Figure 10.8 Civil War pension file card

Form 85 to request a photocopy of Demetrius Durr's Civil War pension file from the National Archives.

Confederate Pension Files

Confederate veterans usually did not receive pensions from the U.S. government, so few Confederate pension files are available at NARA. (Public Law 85–425, passed on 23 May 1958, did amend the Veterans' Benefits Act of 1957 to include persons who served in the military or naval forces of the Confederate States of America and their widows.) However, many Confederate and border states did provide pensions for former Confederate military service. Check with the appropriate state archives or library for information about Confederate pensions in the state you are researching.

The Texas State Library and Archives Commission's Index to Confederate Pension Applications *(www.tsl.state.tx.us/arc/pensions/introcpi.html)* is one example of an online index. The search results in Figure 10.9 show a Wilson B. Taylor of Bastrop County, Texas. A researcher would have to e-mail the Texas State Library and Archives and provide Taylor's name and pension application number to request a copy of the pension file.

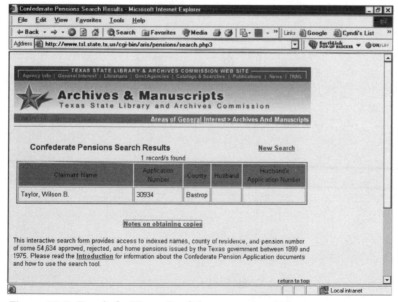

Figure 10.9 Result for Texas Confederate pension index

Bounty Land Warrant Application Files

In order to encourage men to serve in the military, between 1776 and 1855 the U.S. government and some states gave land in specified areas to soldiers and their heirs. For this land, a soldier completed an application that included such information as his name, age, residence when he filed the application, military organization, and term of service. If a widow or heirs applied, their names, ages, and places of residence at the time of the application were given.

In an online article at Genealogy.com *(www.genealogy.com/genealogy/24_land.html)*, excerpted from his book *Revolutionary War Bounty Land Grants,* Lloyd Bockstruck explains the "whys and wherefores" of Revolutionary War bounty land grants and describes the geographical areas awarded by various states and the federal government.

Some eighty thousand pension and bounty land warrant application files are reproduced in NARA's microfilmed series M804, Revolutionary War Pension and Bounty Land Warrant Application Files, 1800–1900. Most of these records relate to pensions, but some are bounty land records. The files are arranged alphabetically by surname. No comprehensive online index exists, so you have to view the microfilm. To determine the

Finding Bounty Land Warrants Online

Spread across the Internet are Web sites with files that index or abstract bounty land grant records for specific surnames or states. To search for your name or area, try a phrase similar to *bounty land index + Smith* or *bounty land index + Kentucky.* Here are a few sample online tools for bounty land warrants:

- Index to War of 1812 Bounty Land Grants in the Illinois Military Tract *(www.lineages.com/vault/BountyLands.asp)*

- Name Index to Military Bounty and Donation Land Grants of Texas, 1835–1888 *(www.mindspring.com/~dmaxey/rep_b&d.htm)*

- The Kentucky Secretary of State Revolutionary War Warrants Database *(www.sos.state.ky.us/intranet/revwscr.asp)*

- The Library of Virginia Revolutionary War Bounty Warrants Searchable Index *(eagle.vsla.edu/rwbw/virtua-basic.html)*

microfilm roll number for the name you want, take a look at the NARA catalog at *www.archives.gov/publications/microfilm_catalogs/military/military_service_records_part19.html.* Bounty land warrant files for service in other wars are also available as original records or microfilm from the National Archives. Look at NARA's Military Records Web page *(www.archives.gov/research_room/genealogy/research_topics/military.html)* for more information.

Soldiers and Veterans Homes

The federal government and many states have homes for aged or infirm veterans. You can usually find the records of defunct facilities at the respective state archives. In fact, a state archives Web site is a good place to start looking for this type of record. While you may find just a listing in the catalog telling you what records are available at the archives, several archives do provide online indexes to their veterans homes. For example, the Arkansas History Commission maintains an online index of the Arkansas Confederate Home at *arkansashistory.arkansas.com/resource_types/military_records/* and the Indiana State Archives has an online index to the Indiana Soldier's and Sailor's Children's Home at *www.in.gov/icpr/archives/databases/issch/index.html.* Of course, look for a Web site of any veterans home still in operation. A search on Google for *Ohio veterans home* provides the URL for the Ohio Veterans Home, whose Web site *(www.state.oh.us/ovh/)* contains a history of the home and an index of people buried in its cemetery.

Military Background Information

You've read in this book about the importance of background research—finding the material that doesn't necessarily mention your ancestor by name but gives you information about events your ancestor may have experienced. Your ancestor's military experiences are no exception, and this section helps you learn more about them.

Unit Histories

A unit history is just that—a history of a particular military unit, usually listing the battles or campaigns in which it was involved. Some unit histories include lists of those taken prisoner, wounded in action, or killed. Many histories tell where the unit was raised, an important clue when you're trying to sort out several men with the same name. A growing number include brief biographies about the soldiers. Although unit histories exist for every war, the Civil War has, by far, the most.

You can find unit histories in many places. You've already read about the Civil War Soldiers System. It's a great site, but don't stop there. The individual state pages on Cyndi's List have military sections, many of which contain links to sites devoted to a specific unit. You can also use your favorite search engine to run a search on a particular unit name.

Diaries, Letters, and Other Manuscripts

Many sites, including state libraries and archives, GenWeb pages, and pages created for a single unit, contain transcripts of soldiers' letters and diaries. These personal papers may not mention your ancestor, but they are an outstanding way to find out what life was like. The letter of Sgt. Erasmus J. Allton, 30th Ohio Volunteer Infantry, to his girl, Miss Catharine Shick, tells of the "disagreeable" weather and the destruction wrought by both Union and Confederate armies *(www.ohiocivilwar.com/stori/30th.html).* Many more letters and diaries are waiting to be read, and you can use the Internet to find them. You'll learn more about online catalogs in Chapter 13, "Using Libraries and Archives Effectively."

Almost every American has at least one ancestor who served in a military conflict. The records created by and for our military ancestors are rich and varied. The Internet has made identifying our veterans easier and has given us better access to a world of military records.

CHAPTER 11

Discovering Ancestors at Work and Worship

OUR ANCESTORS LEFT THEIR HOMELANDS AND CAME TO AMERICA FOR many reasons. Countries ravaged by war, famine, and economic disaster made it difficult for people to support themselves and their families. The social hierarchy made it impossible for some to own their own land or their own businesses. Religious persecution drove the Pilgrims to Plymouth Rock—but the influx of religious and political refugees did not stop then. The promise of religious freedom and tolerance pulled many people to the New World.

Considering the importance of economic and religious factors in the lives of our ancestors, it is little wonder that genealogists can benefit from researching their occupations and religions. The Internet gives you the opportunity to research these areas in general terms and in detail.

Working toward the American Dream

Whether farmer or physician, blacksmith or banker, your ancestors did some sort of work to earn a living. They may not have been wealthy or famous, but the contributions they made to their families and their communities built America. Knowing their religions or occupations helps you find records that identify who they were and where they came from.

175

What's My Line?

Many sources are available to help you find your ancestor's occupation—but the first place to look is in your own home. Whether it is a family album or that old box of stuff in the attic, you probably have a treasure trove of occupational clues close at hand. Take a look at what your ancestor was wearing in those photographs from so long ago. Was it a uniform of some sort? Look at what's in the background of the photograph. Could the shop your great-grandfather was standing in front of be the bakery where he worked? Examine closely the pay stubs, identification cards, correspondence on company letterhead, and countless other items that may have been collected over a lifetime of work and that your family has passed down through the generations. They are all invaluable clues.

Many public sources can also point you toward an ancestor's occupation. You learned about the census in Chapter 7. Beginning in 1850, the census taker was instructed to record occupations. However, this information is often left out of census abstracts, so it is important to look at the census itself, either as a scanned image online or on microfilm at a library.

City directories, like those you learned about in Chapter 4, are excellent sources of occupational information. In addition to being published almost yearly (instead of once every ten years like the census), city directories are often more specific than the census. They tend to list the name of the business, rather than just the type of work the ancestor did. Death certificates and obituaries also often list the deceased's occupation.

Certainly, today's workforce isn't the same as it was when our ancestors were earn-

Was Your Ancestor an Inventor?

You may not have Thomas Edison or Alexander Graham Bell in your family tree, but that doesn't mean you don't have an inventor in your past. Your ancestor may have tinkered part-time in the woodshed instead of all day in a laboratory, but his (or her) inventions should not be overlooked. The U.S. Patent and Trademark Office *(www.uspto.gov)* has an online database of patents from 1790 to the present. The listings for the earliest patents (1790–1975) include a link to full-page images of each page of the patent. The drawback to this site is that to search for the early patents, you must know the patent number. You may be able to find the number in family papers or written on the invention itself.

ing a living. Your third great-grandfather never heard of astronauts or Webmasters. Conversely, many trades that your ancestors may have followed aren't exactly common today. When was the last time you met someone who was a cooper or a cordwainer? Several sites on the Internet can point you toward the meaning of obscure or archaic occupations. Dictionary.com *(www.dictionary.com)* and Merriam-Webster Online *(www.m-w.com)* are both extensive online dictionaries, but for older, out-of-use words, you may need other resources. Two Web sites that may explain what it was your ancestor did are John J. Lacombe's page, A List of Occupations *(cpcug.org/user/jlacombe/terms.html),* and Sam Behling's page, Colonial Occupations *(homepages.rootsweb.com/~sam/occupation.html).* (By the way, a cooper makes barrels and a cordwainer makes shoes or works with leather.)

Not of Their Free Will

Slavery existed on the shores of the New World almost from the beginning of European immigration. Until the end of the Civil War, most African Americans did not have a choice about being employed, but were considered property. A growing number of slave-related records are becoming available. In Chapter 9, you learned about AfriGeneas *(www.afrigeneas.com).* Among the databases in that organization's online library are Georgia Slave Bills of Sale and A Partial Transcription of Inward Slave Manifests for the Port of New Orleans, 1818–1860.

Slaves and Insurance

In August 2000, the California legislature found, in the archives of several insurance companies, insurance policies from the slave era providing insurance coverage to slave owners for damage or death of a slave. In January 2001, California passed a statute requesting that insurance companies doing business in California provide information on the names of slaveholders and slaves. The result, online at *www.insurance.ca.gov/SEIR/main.htm,* is a searchable database for the names of slaves and slaveholders reported by these insurance companies. Scrolling down on that page and selecting Slave Names brings up an alphabetical list of the names of slaves reported by the insurance companies, as shown in Figure 11.1.

The Industry as a Whole

In genealogy, it is often said that you must research the neighbors to find answers about your ancestors. After all, people who live near each other and associate with each other

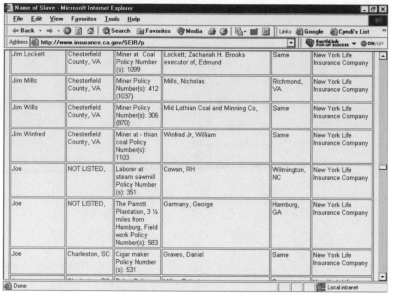

Figure 11.1 Names of slaves insured for damage or death

are likely to have common experiences. Perhaps they migrated together from another location. Perhaps the men served in the same regiment in the military. In Chapter 5, you read about how valuable it is to look for the diaries and other personal papers of the people associated with your ancestors. Your great-great-grandmother may not have kept a diary, but if her friend did, she may mention your great-great-grandmother. At the least, that diary gives you a glimpse into what her life was probably like.

The same can be said for other aspects of our ancestors' lives. Researching on a broad scale leads to new avenues to investigate and provides insight into what life was like for your ancestor. The industry in which your ancestors worked is one such area to explore.

Unions

Labor unions have a long history and tradition in the United States. You won't find rosters of union members on these Web sites, but you are likely to find histories of the union and of the industry its members work in. The AFL-CIO Web site (*www.afl-cio.org*) offers an overview of the labor movement in the United States. If your ancestor was active in any of the many early labor struggles, you might find his name in a local newspaper story or in an arrest record for participating in a strike. The History of the Stonecutters Union (Journeyman Stonecutters

Guilds and Apprenticeships

Guilds developed in medieval Europe to regulate many trades. If you know your ancestor's trade and area of origin, you may be able to locate him in records from these guilds or trade associations. For example, English Origins is a subscription service that provides access to several types of records including the London Apprenticeship abstracts (1531–1850). These Livery Companies of London records contain over 73,000 abstracts containing more than 220,000 indexed names of apprentices in a wide variety of trades *(www.englishorigins.com/help/lonapps-details.aspx)*.

The apprentice system consists of an inexperienced worker learning from a master of the trade. Many of our ancestors went through apprenticeships. A short history of the evolution of apprenticeship in America from the mid-1600s to the present is available from the Department of Labor and Industries at *www.lni.wa.gov/scs/apprenticeship/pubs/past1.htm*.

Association of North America) site *(www.stonecarver.com/union.html)* provides a fascinating history of this profession. The Institute of Industrial Relations Library Web site *(ist-socrates.berkeley.edu/~iir/library/webguides/unionsgd.html)* includes a wonderful list of links to various unions.

A good search on the Internet for information about your ancestor's occupation usually includes a place, a topic, and a time period or other distinguishing factor, such as ethnicity. A colleague of mine has Slovak ancestors who worked in the steel mills in the Youngstown, Ohio area. Her grandparents led her to believe that quite a population of Slovaks were employed by those mills. The search *Youngstown "steel industry" Slovak* on Google resulted in thirty hits, including Adam Russ's paper, "Being Slovak: What It Means to Me" *(www.nd.edu/~aruss/Sociology%20Paper2.htm)*. When you read Russ's paper, you learn not only about his great-grandparents, but also about the Slovak neighborhoods and churches, the steel industry that employed them, and the migration of other Slovaks into the area. This paper is full of clues! Using them, you can continue to research your Slovak ancestors in that area with a search for such things as the names of the steel mills, records of Slovak churches, and immigration records (now narrowed to a specific time)—all of which were listed in this one essay.

Such online essays are often fruitful, although not all will be as specific in their details. For instance, a search on Google for *agriculture Indiana "19th century"* resulted in over nine thousand hits; on the first page of hits was a link to Indiana Farming: Yesterday and Today at *www.connerprairie.org/historyonline/indag.html.* That site lists only one farmer by name (John Goodwin of Brookville) but provides details that enhance our understanding of farmers and farming in Indiana in the 1800s. Horses had replaced oxen by 1850, and hogs, not cattle, were considered "the most valuable animal."

Besides running keyword searches, you should always examine several types of general sites in your search—state libraries, archives, and historical societies. For example, the Idaho State Historical Society *(www.idahohistory.net)* has online articles in its Reference Series, including several about mining and miners in Idaho. Because online exhibits and articles are sometimes tied to special exhibits or events at the library or archive, visiting these sites regularly ensures that you don't miss an opportunity to find the clue that takes you to the next step in your search.

Although you might not find union membership lists online, you can find archives that hold such records. For example, a search for *st louis brewer workers union* results in 1,950 links. Clearly, the search should be narrowed, but luckily the very first link leads to the Henry Tobias Brewers and Maltsters Union No. 6 collection, 1873–1990 (see Figure 11.2). This series of papers at the Western Historical Manuscript Collection in

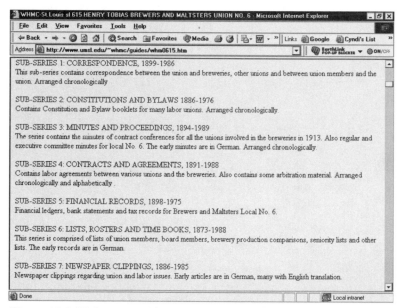

Figure 11.2 Union materials in a manuscript collection

St. Louis includes lists of union members and board members, seniority lists, union membership cards from 1885 to 1933, and other business papers. The Western Historical Manuscript Collection also holds records of other area unions, such as the Carpenters Local No. 5, 1886–1948. This series includes early membership lists (in German) and several membership and dues ledgers from 1886 to 1899. You can search archives or manuscript collections in the area you are researching to find similar records.

If one of your ancestors worked on riverboats, a search for *"riverboat captains"* + *missouri* provides a link to the Riverboats, Steamboats, Sternwheelers, Sidewheelers site *(members.tripod.com/~Write4801/riverboats.html#BOATS).* This site provides lists of riverboats, riverboat captains, riverboat owners, and steamship companies. As shown in Figure 11.3, Samuel Clemens (also known as Mark Twain) is listed, along with the seven ships he piloted. If you search diligently on the Web, you may find your ancestors on similar sites.

Businesses Have Histories, Too

It isn't just people who are interested in their history. Whether to establish a claim as leaders in their industries based on their longevity or to prove to investors that they're

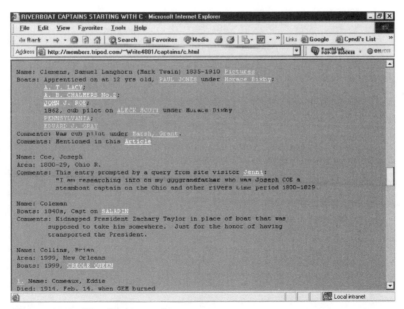

Figure 11.3 Riverboat captains

Fraternal Organizations

Fraternal organizations have been an important part of American life ever since the colonial days. George Washington, Thomas Jefferson, and Benjamin Franklin were all Masons. While you are unlikely to find membership lists online, you may be able to locate the name and address of the organization in the area where your ancestor lived. With luck, that group may have historical membership records it is willing to share. Another good starting place for genealogists is Cyndi's List Fraternal Organizations link *(www.cyndislist.com/soc-frat.htm)*.

not fly-by-night operations, more and more businesses are compiling their histories and making them available to the public. And it's not just megacorporations that include histories on their Web sites. Small, family-run businesses have them, too. The histories that smaller companies post are often more personal than those of their larger counterparts.

Although you are not likely to find specific information about your ancestor, unless he or she was a top executive, company Web sites frequently include a chronology of milestones in the company's past, biographies of officers, and historic photos. Your research will benefit from the clues that business histories can provide. Could your ancestor, whom you cannot find in the 1920 census for Chicago, have been living in Minneapolis, working at the company's new field office? Business histories also often provide a new way to look at your ancestor. Instead of seeing that person as a name and a series of dates, you can see him or her as a real person, earning a living and providing for a family.

Don't despair if the company your ancestor worked for is now defunct. Perhaps it was sold or merged with another company. For example, Boeing Company's Web site contains a history of North American and McDonnell Douglas. If you don't know which company may have purchased your ancestor's company, look at the names of similar businesses in the area. Many online telephone directories allow a search by business type. Often, the name of a company reflects a merger—the Jones Funeral Home purchased the Miller Funeral Home and now calls itself the Jones-Miller Funeral Home.

Workin' on the Railroads

Into the early twentieth century, railroads were the largest employers in the United States. If your ancestors lived in America between the Civil War and the early 1920s, chances are good that at least one worked for a railroad. One clue to railroad employment is your ancestor's Social Security number if he received it before 1963; Social Security numbers beginning with 700 through 728 were reserved for railroad employees.

The key to finding more information about your railroad ancestor is knowing which railroad he worked for. Like other occupations, city directories may give the name of the employer—in this case, the railroad. Death certificates and obituaries may also provide this information. Often what you find is an abbreviation for the railroad, rather than the name itself. Several good sites tell you what that abbreviation stands for— H & R Train's Railroad Road Names & Abbreviations *(www.hrtrains.com/rdname.html);* the Railroad Retirement Board's Abbreviations, Trade Names and Nicknames of Railroads *(www.rrb.gov/funfacts2.html);* and the Piedmont and Western Railroad Club's Railroad Reporting Marks *(www.pwrr.org/rrm/rrm.html).*

Another way to identify railroads is through genealogical mailing lists and message boards. Most people think of these as places to ask about specific ancestors, which is certainly one good use, but you can ask for so much more by using the geographically based mailing lists and message boards. For example, you can post a question such as,

The U.S. Railroad Retirement Board

The U.S. Railroad Retirement Board was established in the mid-1930s and administers the federal pension for eligible railroad employees. You may request copies of the files for workers who were employed by the railroad after 1937. If the employee is still living, the Retirement Board will release the file only with that person's written consent. Your request should include the full name (including the middle name, if known), dates of birth and death, and Social Security number. Because the files are arranged by Social Security number, including that information in your request greatly aids your chances of success. The cost is currently $21. Send your requests to

U.S. Railroad Retirement Board
Office of Public Affairs
844 North Rush Street
Chicago, IL 60611-2092

Read more about the Railroad Retirement Board at *www.rrb.gov.*

"Could you tell me what railroads existed in Tazewell County, Illinois, in 1880?" on the Tazewell County, Illinois mailing list at RootsWeb and on the Tazewell County, Illinois message boards at Ancestry.com and Genealogy.com. You will learn more about mailing lists and message boards in Chapter 16, "Sharing with Others."

My friend Karen's ancestors lived in Murray City, Ohio, and she wondered which railroad served the town and may have employed a collateral relative. A search on Google using the keywords *"murray city" Ohio railroad* yielded several results, including the Murray City Train Depot site *(www.rootsweb.com/~ohathens/murraytrain.htm)*, which told us that the Hocking Valley Railroad served the town. A second search on Google for *"hocking valley railroad"* produced new results, including the site of the Hocking Valley Scenic Railway *(www.hvsr.com)*, which has a detailed history of that railroad.

Although none of the sites we looked at mentioned my friend's relative, they still provided wonderful background about the location and economic conditions—and one important clue to use for further research. Now she can follow up with searches in archives for records of the Hocking Valley Railroad and related companies to try to find her relative. Some of these searches can be done directly through online catalogs of libraries and archives in the region or through a general search in the National Union Catalog of Manuscript Collections (NUCMC), which you will learn more about in Chapter 13, "Using Libraries and Archives Effectively."

Once you have determined which railroad your ancestor worked for or at least narrowed down the possibilities, search for that railroad's Web site. Some railroads, like the Baltimore and Ohio, have museums. In fact, the B&O Museum site *(www.borail.org)* is rich with information. You can get information about obtaining employment records and researching at the Hays T. Watkins Memorial Library and find links to numerous sites related to the B&O Railroad. The Railroad Links Directory at RailroadData *(www.railroaddata.com/rrlinks/)* has more than five thousand railroad-related links. Cyndi's List has a special railroad page *(www.cyndislist.com/railroad.htm)*.

Freedom of Religion

Religious persecution was an important motivating factor in immigration to the United States. And in centuries past, many communities' lives centered on the church or synagogue. It is not surprising, then, that religious records are a rich source of information for many of our ancestors.

What Was the Faith of Your Ancestors?

Religious freedom does not come without some confusion for researchers. The records of one denomination are not necessarily the same types as those kept by another. Therefore, it is vital to determine your ancestor's religious affiliation.

With the United States having such a rich tapestry of religious traditions, how can you know which religion your ancestor practiced? As with other aspects of research, you may already possess some of these sources. Family Bibles, baptismal records, church marriage certificates, and obituaries all may list a denomination. Burial in a church cemetery—while not foolproof—certainly provides a strong indication of church affiliation.

Who Has the Records?

Religious organizations are not required by law to keep their records, nor are they required to make them available to the public. However, most are willing to work with researchers and are making their records available. A growing number appear online.

The USGenWeb Church Records Project *(www.rootsweb.com/~usgenweb/churches/)*, which began in August 2000, is a collection of abstracts of many types of church records from across the United States. The records are arranged by state, then by county. To access these records, scroll down to the bottom half of the page and select the state of interest. Each state's page has links to the various Web sites that are part of this project.

For example, to see if any Allegany County, Maryland records have been abstracted for the USGenWeb Church Records project, I access the site and then click on Maryland. On the Maryland page, I find the Methodist Episcopal Church Register 1838–1840 for Allegany County. I click on the link and find the membership lists for seven different churches, along with explanatory information about where the data came from.

You can find individuals in the Church Records Project through the USGenWeb Archives Search page *(www.rootsweb.com/~usgenweb/ussearch.htm)* or by using the method just described. While the Search page covers numerous databases at once, it is sometimes more efficient to look at the church record pages individually, especially if you are researching a common name. Also, when you read the entire set of records for a particular church, you get a better sense of the associated people. Finding a person with the same name as your ancestor doesn't mean that person is your ancestor. But if you read the entire church membership list, for example, and you see the names of many of his neighbors and associates, you have a clue to help you verify that you have found the correct person.

Many other types of sites offer abstracted church records—individuals, genealogical and historical societies, sometimes the church itself. Finding these records is a matter of constructing a good keyword search in an Internet search engine, such as Google. Be specific—including the type of record and a location produces a better result. Searching for *Lutheran church records* on Google yields 87,300 hits. Obviously, the search must be narrowed. A search on *"baptism records" Lutheran Armstrong County Pennsylvania* provides thirty-nine hits, including that of the Baptismal Record, Forks-Zion Lutheran Church 1838–1883 *(www.pa-roots.com/~armstrong/church/zionforks/zion.html)*.

When searching for Jewish ancestors, you must visit JewishGen *(www.jewishgen.org)*, a site with something for everyone. If you are just beginning your Jewish research, the JewishGen FAQ file has several articles to help you get started. JewishGen's Web pages and databases are extensive, containing thousands of records. Because information on some JewishGen pages is text-based and other information remains in separate databases, do several searches to find all the records about your ancestor available on JewishGen.

Search the text records through the search engine at *www.jewishgen.org/JewishGen/ Search.htm*, which you reach by clicking Search This Web Site on the main page. To search the databases, go to *www.jewishgen.org/databases/* and select the location of interest. The databases represent locations from around the world; in fact, most locations have multiple databases—Poland, for example, has eleven. The JewishGen Family Finder allows you to find others researching the same surnames in a given town.

The Family Tree of the Jewish People (FTJP) *(www.jewishgen.org/gedcom/)* is a cooperative effort of JewishGen, Inc., the International Association of Jewish Genealogical Societies, and the Nahum Goldmann Museum of the Jewish Diaspora (Beit Hatefutsot). It is a linked database of family data, built from GEDCOM files that people have submitted to the project. To search FTJP or to submit your GEDCOM file, you must first submit your surnames and towns of interest to the JewishGen Family Finder.

Finding the Right Pew

Since not all religious records are online, in the course of your research you may need to contact individual churches and religious archives to determine what records they may have available and to find out more about the religious organization. The Internet can be very useful. In Chapter 4, you learned about online telephone directories. You can use these not only to look up people, but also places, such as churches. Keep in mind, however, that the listings in online telephone directories are for churches currently in existence. Your ancestor's church may have closed or merged with another church. City directories from the time of your ancestors often have a section on churches and synagogues in the area, listing each facility, its address, and even the name of the minister, priest, or rabbi at that time.

Learning Church History

To get the most from church records, you need to learn the history of both the denomination and the specific church. Learning about the denomination helps you understand what types of records are available. For example, there's no sense looking for infant baptismal records if the church didn't follow that practice. When you learn the history of a particular church, you can gain valuable research clues. Often, churches were founded by people who had migrated together from another area. Researching these people may lead you to your ancestor's origins. Also, many churches had ethnic affiliations. A town of only one thousand people may have had two Catholic churches—one for Germans and one for Irish. Learning such details can make your research more effective.

When you are looking for the churches in a county, USGenWeb sites are excellent places to start. My Ramsey ancestors were Presbyterians who migrated from Adams County, Pennsylvania, to Perry County, Ohio. To find Presbyterian churches in Adams County, my first stop was the Adams County GenWeb site (*www.rootsweb.com/~paadams/adams.htm*). The site has a page for county churches with their locations. Some listings, including the Lower Marsh Creek Presbyterian Church, have links to that church's Web site. This GenWeb site was a very convenient way to find the churches in the county. Besides USGenWeb sites, you can often find church information from the Web sites of local genealogical and historical societies and city and county visitors bureaus.

Church Web sites are as varied as the churches themselves. While almost all of them list the address, phone number, and schedule of services, some sites also give the history of that church, biographies of early members, and photographs (both current and historic).

The Family History Library has many church records available on microfilm. You can look at its catalog at *www.familysearch.org*. Some church records have been transferred to archives, both religious and secular, many of which have online catalogs. You will learn more about the Family History Library and other types of online catalogs in Chapter 13.

Finding your ancestor at work and at worship is a rich and rewarding experience. The records you discover can lead you not only to earlier generations of ancestors, but also to background and historical information that can help you understand those ancestors better. And this background information can, in turn, direct your search toward many different types of records you'd not considered before.

CHAPTER 12

Finding Ancestors in Unusual Places

NOT EVERYONE DESCENDS FROM ROYALTY, FINDS ANCESTORS IN CHURCH records, or possesses an ancestor chart filled with patriots or wealthy pillars of the community. In fact, an amazing number of America's first residents were debtors or criminals who were transported from Great Britain or Ireland to the colonies for such crimes as grand larceny, theft, or being a vagabond. To learn about this colorful phase of history, read Sherry Irvine's article "Saving Their Necks: The Origins of Transportation to America," published in the *Ancestry Daily News* and available online at *www.ancestry.com/library/view/news/articles/5045.asp.*

In this chapter, we explore sources that are not the usual run-of-the-mill records, from those that document the poor, the orphaned, or the insane; to evidence of civil cases when individuals sued one another; to records of downright criminal activities. Keep an open mind and consider that you *might* find evidence of your ancestors in these types of records. If so, you might not like the facts that you find, but as a genealogist, you'll be thrilled with the details. And do not judge your ancestors too harshly until you know the circumstances surrounding why they did what they did.

The Poor, the Orphaned, and the Insane

Not every immigrant with hopes of finding wealth in a new country succeeds. Poverty is evident throughout the world's history, and it is possible to find records that document it. Children were often the victims of poverty, especially when they became

189

orphans. One solution in the United States was to place orphaned children, or even children whose parents could not care for them, on trains and send them west to be taken in by families. These "orphan trains" sometimes caused broken links in families that make them difficult to piece together even today.

Today, government social service programs offer assistance to the indigent, to children with so-called deadbeat dads or moms, or to troubled families. Medicaid and Medicare provide services for the mentally ill with no means of obtaining their own care, and Social Security offers retirement benefits to the elderly. But were there such safety nets in the past? The federal government may not have provided these services, but most communities did take care of their citizens.

New Deal Programs

Franklin D. Roosevelt's New Deal programs, such as the Works Progress Administration (WPA) and the Civilian Conservation Corps (CCC), provided work opportunities for countless Depression-era Americans and created lasting results still useful today. To find actual records from the WPA projects, search the online catalogs of state libraries or archives or use WorldCat to look for original records in manuscript collections across the United States.

To find informative articles or photographs of these agencies in the area you're researching, try searching on the Internet for something similar to *WPA projects + New Mexico*. Here is a sampling of some of the many online sources of information from this era:

- American Life Histories—Manuscripts from the Federal Writers Project, 1936–1940 (Library of Congress) *(memory.loc.gov/ammem/wpaintro/wpahome.html)*

- University of Georgia, Hargrett Rare Book and Manuscript Library—WPA projects in Georgia *(www.libs.uga.edu/hargrett/selections/wpa/index.html)*

- WPA and CCC Projects (National New Deal Preservation Association) *(www.newdeallegacy.org/wpa_ccc.html)*

- WPA Photograph Collection—Louisiana Division, New Orleans Public Library *(nutrias.org/photos/wpa/wpaphotos.htm)*

- WPA Poster Collection and Fine Prints by Federal Art Project Artists (Library of Congress) *(www.loc.gov/spcoll/265.html)*

In the 1930s and 1940s, President Franklin Roosevelt's New Deal programs, such as the Works Progress Administration (WPA), made jobs for millions of unemployed Americans. It was this era that produced WPA-sponsored writers' projects, such as county histories, slave narratives, and state tour guides. A great deal of our infrastructure was created by Civilian Conservation Corps (CCC) workers—roads, bridges, dams, and shelters like those in the Great Smoky Mountains National Park. Public buildings still in use today were built in this period—schools, courthouses, museums, community auditoriums. And don't forget the beautiful artwork in post offices and public universities that resulted from the Federal Art Project. Think of all the records that must exist from this flurry of activity.

Alleviating Poverty

In the early twentieth century, old age pensions meted out by some states helped elderly persons who had no means of support. A report from the Committee on Economic Security was transmitted to President Roosevelt in January 1935. It contained a table setting forth information about 1934 old age pension laws in effect in the United States. This table provided a list of the states that had such laws, whether the law was optional or mandatory, the numbers of people eligible, the numbers of pensioners, and the amount of pension in each state. To see whether old age pensions were available in the state you're researching, you can view a digitized image of this report on the Social Security Administration's Web site (*www.ssa.gov/history/reports/ces/ces16.html*).

If you determine that a state did provide old age pensions, you should scour that state's archives or library and search online for possible sources of old age pension records. A Google search of *old age pension* turns up a link to the Colorado State Archives Old Age Pension Records Index (*www.archives.state.co.us/oapl*). Clicking a link to El Paso County Pension Records 1933–1936 and then clicking on the letter A displays the results shown in Figure 12.1. The index provides a pensioner's name, pension number, and the year it was paid. The main index page offers instructions for obtaining a copy of the actual record by e-mailing or writing to Colorado State Archives volunteers.

Before the twentieth century, how did local communities or states take care of their less fortunate citizens? Sometimes laws were enacted in the state legislature to provide relief, such as an 1800s Kentucky Act that provided a widow and her children an area of land because her husband had burned to death in the home, leaving the family with no means of support. State libraries or law libraries at a local university may own published

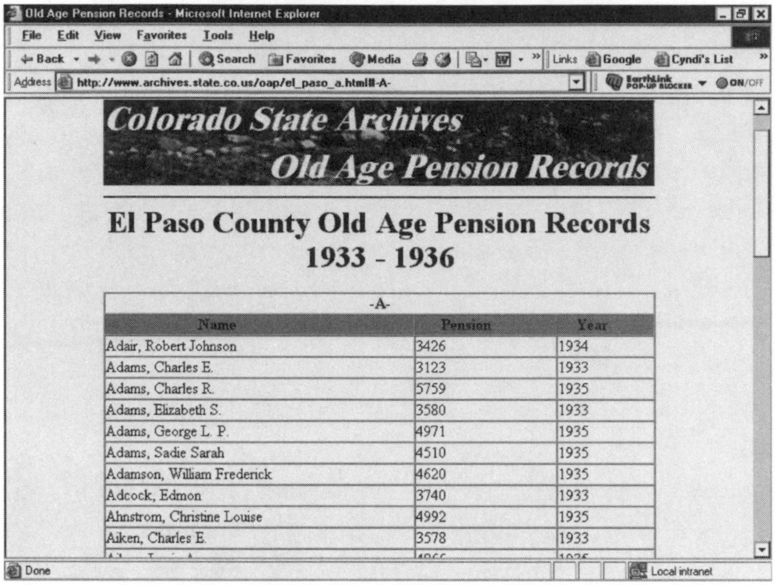

Figure 12.1 Colorado State Archives Old Age Pension Records

early Acts of the Legislature for various states; you can search these sources for mention of your ancestors.

Cities or counties operated poorhouses or poor farms where indigent people could live and work. The Poorhouse Story Web site *(www.poorhousestory.com)* acts as a clearinghouse for information about nineteenth-century American poorhouses. Not only does the Webmaster collect records, but she includes tips for finding poorhouse records and a digitized 1904 government report about laws governing poor relief in the United States.

What might you learn from records of poorhouses or poor farms? One source, the U.S. census, enumerates people living on the poor farm (calling them "inmates") and lists all the same information as for anyone else in the census. The 1930 census example in Figure 12.2 illustrates that out of ten residents at the poor farm, eight were over the age of seventy. Institutions, whether called poorhouses, almshouses, or county farms, were included in census enumerations. Often the person running the facility is listed first, with his family members next, followed by a listing of all the inmates or residents. The institution name might be recorded in the column for inmates' relationship to head of household, or it might be written in the left portion of the census where a street name usually appears.

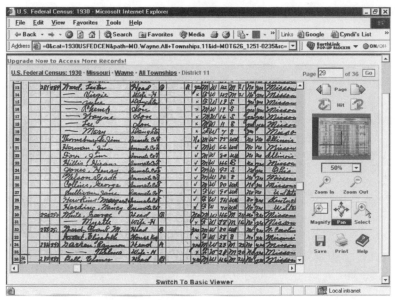

Figure 12.2 Census enumeration of poor farm residents

Other poorhouse records can provide the name of next of kin, reasons the person resided at the facility, where he or she went upon release, immigration and naturalization information, and other pertinent facts for curious genealogists. To find online records relating to institutions for the indigent, try a Web search using a phrase like *poorhouse records Rensselaer County*. Resulting Web sites often provide indexes of poorhouse records and instructions for finding or ordering copies of records.

Orphaned Children

In the 1850s, the Children's Aid Society relocated poor and homeless children primarily from New York to new homes in the rural Midwest. Some of the children sent west on the so-called orphan trains were neglected children, but not necessarily orphans. From 1854 to 1929, more than one hundred thousand children were relocated from eastern cities to America's expanding farmlands to the west. Some were adopted into welcoming families; others were little more than a source of free labor. Many were separated from siblings or parents they never saw again. To learn more about the orphan trains, visit the Web site of the television show *American Experience (www.pbs.org/wgbh/amex/orphan/)*. The Orphan Train Heritage Society of America *(www.orphantrainriders.com)* offers information about publications and beginning

Finding Orphan Train Records

If you or someone you knew were one of the thousands of children relocated from eastern cities to the farmlands of the Midwest on orphan trains from the mid-1800s up to the 1920s, you'll be glad to know that numerous resources are available to help with your research. Web sites exist for most of the states where children were received. To locate information, try an Internet search of a phrase similar to *orphan train Missouri*. Here are a few general links:

- Index of Children Who Rode the Orphan Trains to Kansas (*www.kancoll.org/articles/orphans/or_child.htm*)
- Indiana Orphan Trains Project (*home.att.net/~sharcraig/otr.htm*)
- Orphan Train Heritage Society of America (*www.orphantrainriders.com*)
- Orphan Train Riders to Iowa (*iagenweb.org/iaorphans*)
- Orphan Trains of America Links (*www.geocities.com/Heartland/Bluffs/7446/orphantrains.html*)
- Orphan Trains of Kansas (*www.kancoll.org/articles/orphans/index.html*)
- Orphan Trains of Nebraska (*www.rootsweb.com/~neadoptn/Orphan.htm*)
- Orphan Trains to Missouri (a publication) (*www.system.missouri.edu/upress/spring1997/patrick.htm*)

the search for an orphan train rider, a list of professional researchers, a schedule of nationwide reunions and conferences, and a host of other resources for those interested in orphan trains.

Finding records of children who lived in orphanages depends on a number of factors. You must identify a specific orphanage to be able to research its records. If you do not know the name of an orphanage, narrow down the possibilities by location, affiliation, years of operation, and other factors.

For example, if your great-grandmother was placed in an orphanage in New York about 1885, you might look for her in the 1880 census with her family to determine exactly where in New York she lived. If the family lived in Brooklyn and your great-grandmother was Jewish, you might narrow your search to Brooklyn orphanages in existence in 1885 that were sponsored by Jewish organizations.

Then try a Google search for *Brooklyn orphanage Jewish*. This search nets results for quite a few helpful sites, including the Jewish Orphanages, Societies, Social Services and Orphan Train Destinations Web site *(shell4.bayarea.net/~elias/hnoh/USJORPH6C.html)* shown in Figure 12.3. There, you learn that the Brooklyn Hebrew Orphan Asylum began operation in 1878, so it is a possible source for your research. Another Google search for *Brooklyn Hebrew Orphan Asylum* yields links to information where you learn that some children from this home were placed on orphan trains to Kansas. An online article entitled "Family History Research at the American Jewish Historical Society" *(www.cjh.org/family/pdf/AJHS.pdf)* states that this society holds partially indexed admission applications and unindexed discharge records for certain periods in the nineteenth and twentieth centuries. There is contact information for the society in the article, so you can call or write to see whether they have any record of your great-grandmother.

If you're fortunate enough to locate relevant orphanage records, you may find rich details about your orphaned ancestor's other family members, her ancestry, family illnesses, the circumstances of her placement in the orphanage, and where she went from there.

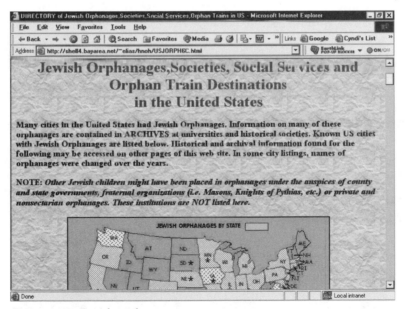

Figure 12.3 Jewish orphanages

The Mentally Ill

The mentally ill generally did not fare well in the past, often being confined to institutions then known as insane asylums, lunatic asylums, or at best, state hospitals to live out their illnesses or lives with little treatment. You may find records of those committed to institutions at the town or county level. Often, a local county had to pay fees to the state facility for lodging its citizens there. When adults were committed to state hospitals, a guardian was likely appointed by the local court of jurisdiction to oversee the ill person's business affairs or estate. Look for commitment papers and guardian orders in the local county court records. These records may provide insight into your ancestor's illness or the circumstances surrounding his or her commitment.

Try to determine the mental institution nearest your ancestor's home, and seek medical records there. It's important to know the details of the illness for your own family health history. Bear in mind that in the past, people were committed for maladies that would not bring such drastic measures today—menopausal symptoms in females, what we now recognize as Alzheimer's disease in older people, or mania (now known as depression), for example.

Often, whispers are heard in a family about the mental illness of an ancestor. These bear investigating, for often family rumors have a basis in fact. Records from an institution may reveal details about an ancestor's life and family history or about the circumstances of the illness. If the person received a military pension, be sure to carefully read all the physicians' reports in the file for any clue to mental or physical illness.

Identifying Mental Hospitals

To find the mental hospital where an ancestor may have been confined, search the Internet for a phrase similar to *insane asylum Missouri* or *lunatic asylum records Kentucky*. The Historic Asylums Web site *(darkspire.org/asylums)* provides photographs (postcards) and some histories of state hospitals founded in the latter half of the nineteenth century. Although the focus of this site is building preservation, you can learn whether an old hospital is still in operation and see how it looked.

Civil Cases of the Divorced or the Dissatisfied

If you think frivolous lawsuits are a novelty of modern times, think again. You might be surprised at how often our ancestors showed up in court to file suit against a neighbor or a family member over a seemingly trivial matter. In a family where most members could not even write their names, I found a lawsuit among siblings over a small piece of land that dragged on for several years in the early twentieth century. This event allowed me to fill in a lot of blanks in my family tree since the proceedings recorded in the county court books detailed the names and relationships of all the siblings, their parents, their spouses, and most of their children. It also indicated which daughter had cared for the mother in her old age. Another lawsuit in the same family clued me in to the fact that a great-great-grandfather had a second wife about whom I knew nothing.

Juicy Tidbits from Divorce Cases

What can you hope to learn from divorce suits? The husband in one late-nineteenth-century divorce among my collateral relatives provided in his petition a laundry list of complaints, stating that his wife refused to cook his meals or wash his clothes for months at a time, she told him she loved other men better, she tried to turn their children against him, and she even left with all his property—five head of cattle, five horses, ten hogs, all the household and kitchen furniture, a two-horse wagon, all his farm implements, and about five hundred bushels of corn. These rich details provide telling facts about the family's economic status and occupation, as well as the husband's version of their troubles.

Divorce is not unique to our times, either. It's common to run across early divorce petitions in the acts of the state legislature. Can you imagine how traumatic it must have been to go before the governing body of the entire state to ask for a divorce? Beginning with the nineteenth century, most divorce cases and resulting records occur in a local court of jurisdiction, whether a county, circuit, probate, district, or other kind of court. To find a divorce record, you have to determine the appropriate court for the state where it occurred. Refer to Chapter 6, "Acquiring Vital Records," for information about online divorce indexes.

A divorce case is a lawsuit brought by a plaintiff against a defendant, and it usually lists the reasons for dissolution of the marriage. For genealogists, the treasure lies in the details in a case file. You can learn when and where the marriage occurred, the names and ages of minor children, and the value of personal property and real estate.

Criminal Records at Every Level of Government

In my genealogical presentation "Rogues and Rascals," I discuss the possibility that anyone may have ancestors who engaged in questionable activities that landed them on the wrong side of the law. I use my own ancestors as examples, and audiences laugh out loud as I describe my chagrin and shock at finding a great-grandfather who was arrested and jailed by the county sheriff for playing cards (gambling) and who then graduated to the state penitentiary for making and selling moonshine whiskey. They roll in the aisles when I describe going on to find that while Great-grandpa was still in prison, his son and a crony were arrested and sent to prison for breaking *into* the county jail to steal from the evidence vault—you guessed it— moonshine whiskey. Oddly enough, no one recounts similar stories about their families during the audience participation time at the end of the presentation. However, there is *always* a long line of people waiting until after the lecture to confide to me individually (and confidentially) what unlawful act their ancestor committed.

If you come from a long line of extremely religious, moral, upstanding citizens— good for you! But you should consider the possibility that somewhere along the line, someone in your family tree may have run afoul of the law. If they did, and you find evidence of it, as a genealogist you'll be pleased at the information you can learn.

Read the Case Files

To find the nitty-gritty details in divorce cases, civil suits, or criminal cases, be sure to read the actual case file, not just the summary of the case in the court docket or proceedings. The case file often contains statements or depositions of parties to the lawsuit, subpoenas of witnesses, investigative reports, and sometimes even transcripts or abstracts of court proceedings. Case files are usually kept separate from proceedings and docket books, so you may have to dig a little harder to find them—but they're often worth it.

Look for indexes to criminal cases that lead to the actual case files. Depending on the seriousness of the offense, the law governing it, and the court system in the area, a criminal case may be handled by a municipal, county, district, chancery, state, or federal court. Don't be afraid to do a little Internet research to look at a few state statutes (laws) and figure out just where you might find the record of that horse thief rumored to be on the "other side" of the family. Try a search phrase similar to *livestock theft laws + Kentucky*. Many states' modern statutes are available online today, but you may have to go to a law library to read the laws in effect at the time of the offense in the geographic area you are researching.

Don't forget to check out penitentiary or prison sources. Many indexes to state penitentiary records are online today and can be found with a search similar to *Tennessee penitentiary records*. With the facts you obtain from an index like the one shown for Tennessee in Figure 12.4, you can contact the state archives or agency holding the records for more information about the person you are researching.

What kinds of information are in prison or penitentiary logs or records? Of course, they disclose the crime and sentence, but they may also provide a detailed physical description of the person, down to the exact length of his foot, color of his eyes, height, weight, hair color, and complexion. In the past prisons did not have

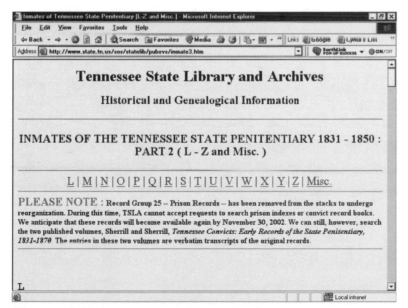

Figure 12.4 Tennessee penitentiary records index

economical access to photography, so these detailed descriptions of prisoners often had to suffice. You'll probably find the person's next of kin and an address, too.

Most researchers eventually run across "shady" ancestors with problems of their own making or ancestors who are simply the victims of circumstances such as poverty or ill health. The Internet provides an array of information about criminal and social institutions, as well as tools for finding individuals within these systems.

Finding Prison Records

To find a prison record, you have to know the kind of case involved. Was the person arrested for disorderly conduct? If so, he was probably hauled into the local county or city jail. Did she assault someone in a bar fight? That was more serious; you might consider looking at state prison records. Did a relative in a collateral line commit a murder while robbing a stage? That may have been a felony, so you might look at federal prison records. Search on the Internet for indexes to prisoners or prison records, using phrases similar to *prison records + Missouri* or *federal penitentiary records*. Don't forget to search NUCMC for older prison records in manuscript collections or RootsWeb and GenWeb for abstracts or transcriptions of prison records.

Here are some of the types of records or finding aids that can be found on the Internet:

- An Inventory of Records Relating to the Penitentiary at the Texas State Archives, 1846–1921 (finding aid) *(www.lib.utexas.edu/taro/tslac/20053/20053.html)*

- Colorado State Penitentiary Index of Inmates, 1871–1973 *(www.archives.state.co.us/pen/index.htm)*

- Crimetime.com (links to nationwide databases of prisoners, criminal and civil case court dockets, and more) *(www.crimetime.com/bbocrim.htm)*

- Inmates of the Tennessee State Penitentiary, 1831–1850 *(www.state.tn.us/sos/statelib/pubsvs/inmate1.htm)*

- Missouri State Penitentiary, 1837–1933 *(www.sos.state.mo.us/archives/pubs/archweb/pen.asp)*

- State Penitentiary for the Eastern District of Pennsylvania Records, 1819–1892 (finding aid) *(www.amphilsoc.org/library/browser/s/statepen.xml)*

CHAPTER 13

Using Libraries and Archives Effectively

LITERALLY MILLIONS OF WEB SITES ARE DEVOTED TO FAMILY HISTORY and genealogical research. Millions more have information about our ancestors' lives—the places they lived, the trades they plied, the traditions they followed.

But even in these millions of sites, not everything is available on the Internet. The amount of data—textual and digital—that exists on the Internet is but a small percentage of the total amount of available data. A whole world of libraries and archives exists with materials that can help you find your ancestors. You can use the Internet to help you tap into these marvelous resources.

Hardly a library in the United States doesn't have some presence on the Internet. Some Web sites are simple, static pages with a listing of the facility's location and hours. Other sites are robust, dynamic pages containing online catalogs, finding aids, databases, and digitized documents and photographs. Whether the site is simple or robust, it has information to help make your research more effective. Use the Internet both as a virtual library and as a tool to help you find and use those marvelous offline resources.

From the Comfort of Your Home

You may never go to all the libraries and archives in all the locations that your ancestors lived. One of the great benefits of the Internet is that you can access so much information from the comfort of your own home. No matter where your ancestors lived, make use of the libraries for that area—including the local public library, state library, state archives, and local and state genealogical and historical society libraries. Their databases of source materials, digital images, and historical information may help with your research—without your ever leaving home.

Finding Libraries and Archives

Use the Internet to find libraries and archives. These Web sites will help:

- The Library of Congress State Library Web Listing *(www.loc.gov/global/library/statelib.html)* has links to all fifty state libraries.

- Libweb *(sunsite.berkeley.edu/Libweb/)* is wonderful for finding public and private libraries. Use the keyword search to find libraries that often are overlooked, such as those for religious institutions.

- The Public Libraries *(www.publiclibraries.com)* site is arranged by state—finding a public library in your area of interest is as easy as clicking on the name of the state. The libraries are arranged alphabetically. Be certain to read the whole list to pick up those libraries whose names don't contain the name of the city or county.

- State Archives Referral List *(www.sos.state.ga.us/archives/rs/sarl.htm)*, sponsored by the Georgia Secretary of State's Office, has links to the state archives around the United States, as well as their addresses and phone numbers.

Databases

The main purpose of a library is to make information available. Traditionally, this has been accomplished by keeping materials in a brick-and-mortar building. Now source materials are often also available online. The most common types of online materials are indexes and abstracts of manuscript materials that the library owns. Because manuscripts, by definition, are not published, they are often overlooked and can be hard to use. These online databases are a great way to access them.

For example, the Cleveland Public Library has placed the Cleveland Necrology File on its Web site *(www.cpl.org)*. This database contains the text of obituaries for three Cleveland newspapers—the *Cleveland Plain Dealer*, the *Cleveland Herald*, and the *Cleveland Press*—from as early as 1833 through 1975. This is a tremendous resource for people with ancestors from the Cleveland, Ohio, area. The Cleveland Public

Library is by no means the only public library that has information like this. Your ancestors might be waiting for you at another library Web site.

Background and Historical Information

Most public libraries consider a central component of their mission to be local history—collecting, preserving, and making these materials available for research. Therefore, the Web sites of many libraries, even small, rural ones, have a section about the history of their area. In fact, some of the history pages on the small library Web sites are more extensive than those for large, urban libraries.

The Public Libraries of Saginaw (Michigan) Web site *(www.saginaw.lib.mi.us)* features essays and photographs pertaining to Saginaw's history. Among the essays are "Early Hispanic Organizations in Saginaw" by Manuela (Mamie) Ontiveros and "Logging" by Anna Mae Maday.

Digital Images

The Digital Age has made sharing pictures and documents easier than ever. As a result, libraries and archives are making some of their holdings available on the Internet. You may not find a picture of your ancestor, but you may find a scanned image of an 1885 photograph of the town where he lived. Seeing these images reminds you that your ancestor was a real person and not just a name on your ancestor chart. When looking for digital images at a library or archive Web site, you typically don't find them under the heading Genealogy. Look for headings such as Digital Collection or Online Scrapbook.

The Santa Cruz (California) Public Libraries Web site *(www.santacruzpl.org)* contains more than one thousand images from the Santa Cruz area from the 1860s to the 1990s that you can browse by category or search by keyword. (You'll learn more about finding photographs in Chapter 15, "Seeing Your Ancestors—in Pictures and in Print.")

Using Your Time Wisely

There is not enough time in the day to devote to genealogy. Even if the day were longer, there would still be more research than could fill that extra time. That's why the time you spend researching has to be as efficient as possible.

Library and archives Web sites have features to help you plan your research trip to that facility and organize your research strategy so that you can hit the ground running when you arrive. All it takes is a little planning.

General Information

Not all libraries are open during the same hours and days. Even libraries within the same system may have different hours—the main library may stay open later or be open on days when some branches close. When you have traveled for several hours to do research at a particular library, the last thing you want to see when you arrive is a "closed" sign on the front door, so be sure to check the library's Web site for hours and days of operation before you go.

If you're wondering how much copies and parking cost or whether a snack bar is available, chances are that other people have wondered the same thing. Look for a FAQ (Frequently Asked Questions) page on the facility's Web site. Also look for a listing of any restrictions. You expect restrictions on food and beverages, but there may also be limitations on pens, briefcases, and electronic devices, such as laptop computers. By finding out this information before you leave home, you can plan ahead and take only those items allowed into the research room.

A growing number of library and archives Web sites show the layout of the facility; some even allow you to download an orientation video. Both the layouts and the videos help you get your bearings when you arrive.

Library Catalogs

In the days before the Internet, a good portion of research time at a library was spent standing at the card catalog and writing down the references to the books of interest. Since most genealogy collections do not circulate, you usually have to use the books in the library. This means that every minute spent looking up books is a minute spent not using the books.

Fortunately for genealogists, an online catalog is one of the most common features on library and archive Web sites. With these online catalogs, you can virtually map out your entire research plan for that facility before you leave home.

There are many different cataloging programs, but almost all of them allow searches by title, author, and subject or keyword. Unless you are looking for a specific book and you know the title or author, most of your searches are by subject or keyword.

Writing a good keyword search in a library catalog is a lot like writing a good keyword search on an Internet search engine. First, think about what words are likely to

Lending Libraries

Most genealogical collections do not circulate—but there are notable exceptions. The twenty-thousand-volume National Genealogical Society's Book Loan Collection, housed at the St. Louis County Library, is available through Interlibrary Loan. Search the collection's catalog at the NGS Web site *(www.ngsgenealogy.org)* or the St. Louis County Library Web site *(www.slcl.lib.mo.us).*

The Mid-Continent Public Library has a five-thousand-volume circulating genealogy collection. Download the catalog and supplements for this collection at *www.mcpl.lib.mo.us/ branch/ge/heartland/.* When you find a book that interests you, contact your local public library. It requests that the book be sent to your local library. Neither NGS, the St. Louis County Library, nor the Mid-Continent Public Library charges for this service, but your local library may have a nominal processing fee.

Some genealogical societies have lending libraries as an exclusive benefit of membership. Two such societies are the Ohio Genealogical Society *(www.ogs.org)* and the New England Historic Genealogical Society *(www.newenglandancestors.org).*

provide the most accurate results. Simply entering the word *genealogy* results in far too many hits, most of which are irrelevant to your research.

Think about what type of research you want to do. Are you looking for all the records for a particular county? Family histories? Information on your ancestor's Civil War unit? Once you narrow the focus of your research, you can start to put together your keyword search.

Sometimes knowing what isn't included in a resource is just as important as knowing what is included. This is certainly true for online catalogs. There may be collections or materials in the library that do not appear in the online catalog. It may be missing the newspaper collection, manuscript collections, or materials that are on microfilm or microfiche.

Always read the FAQ file when you use an online catalog. If there isn't one, contact the facility and ask if there are any collections of materials that aren't included in the online catalog.

If you are trying to find all the books and records that a facility holds for a specific

Read the Catalog Carefully

When looking at a catalog entry, be certain to note the location of the material or any restrictions on the material. If you are looking at a public library catalog, the book that interests you may be available only at a branch library. It may or may not be possible for that book to be sent to the library where you plan to do your research.

There may be restrictions on the use of certain archival materials. For example, many state libraries and archives have hospital records. Although they appear in the catalog, use of these records is often restricted to the person in the record or their legal representative. Such restrictions are usually noted in the catalog entry.

location, you could enter just the name of the location. But this may return too many irrelevant results because genealogy books aren't the only items categorized by location. You may end up with results that include items like a copy of the county dog-catcher's budget for 1973. If this happens, search again by location and the type of record you are interested in. The keyword search you type might look like this: *Dekalb County Indiana cemeteries* or *Grundy County Missouri directories.*

Some of the best things about the Internet are the links from one page to another. The same is true for many online catalogs. When you find a book that interests you, click on the full description to look for subject listings. Some catalogs even allow you to click on the subject listing to see other book titles in the same category.

Recently, I wanted to find general books on North Carolina research. I knew that Helen F. M. Leary had written one, so I searched first by author. When I found her book in the catalog, I clicked on the subject listing and found five other books about North Carolina research in the collection.

Finding Aids

The size of some archival collections can be intimidating. It can be exciting to see an entry for a group of records you're interested in, but when you see that the collection is twenty-nine cubic feet and contains 109 volumes, you may feel overwhelmed. That's where finding aids come in.

A finding aid is anything that helps you use a particular record. It might be an overview of the collection or an inventory, such as a listing of how those 109 volumes are broken down. Use the available online finding aids to determine what that group of records contains and to make the research you do onsite more efficient.

The Wisconsin Historical Society Archives Web site *(www.wisconsinhistory.org/ archives/index.html)* has a special page for finding aids, searchable by keyword. One of the online finding aids in its growing collection is the Wisconsin Senate Standing and Special Committee Reports, 1836–1945. This finding aid takes you to the 1848 report of the Claims Committee, which is in a folder in Box 2 of the collection.

Using the National Archives

The U.S. National Archives and Records Administration (NARA) is the official archives of the United States. Its Web site *(www.archives.gov)* is a gateway into this remarkable facility, and its Genealogy page *(www.archives.gov/research_room/genealogy/)* contains links to subjects such as Soundex indexing, the 1930 census, and research topics. The Research Topics page *(www.archives.gov/research_room/genealogy/research_topics.html)* contains links to in-depth articles about commonly used records held by NARA, such as African-American research, military records, and ship passenger lists. They are must-reads if you are researching any of the topics they have listed.

The Family History Library Catalog

The Family History Library (FHL) in Salt Lake City has the largest collection of genealogical materials in the world. For the catalog, go to *www.familysearch.org* and click on Search the Family History Library Catalog. As Figure 13.1 illustrates, you can search for materials by place, surname, author, subject, call number, or film/fiche number.

Let's say I want to search Decatur County, Iowa land records from the 1880s. I go to the FHL Catalog and select Place Search. In the Place field, I enter *Decatur;* in the Part Of field, I enter *Iowa.* (When searching for county records, do not enter the word *county* in the Place field.) The catalog first confirms that I am looking in the correct location. After I click Search, the catalog produces a list of places that match my query (in this case, one item). I then see a list of the subjects pertaining to that location, as shown in Figure 13.2.

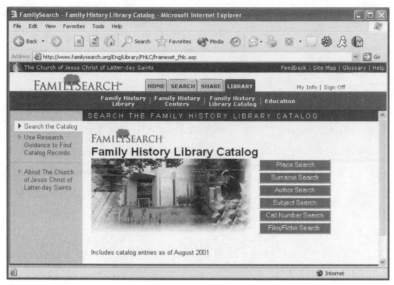

Figure 13.1 Family History Library Catalog main page

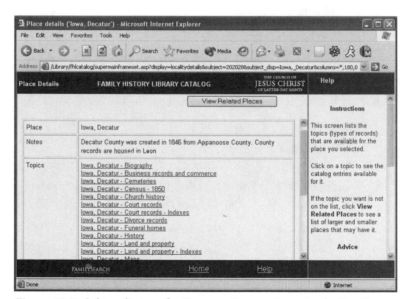

Figure 13.2 Subject listings for Decatur County, Iowa, in the Family History Library Catalog

I scroll through the subjects and click on Iowa, Decatur—Land and Property, which reveals seven items. Deeds and Mortgages, 1872–1945 seems promising, so I click on it and get a brief description of the records, as shown in Figure 13.3.

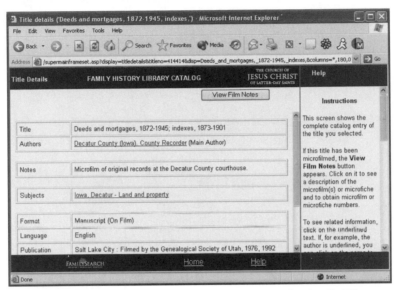

Figure 13.3 Title details for deeds and mortgages in the Family History Library Catalog

You can borrow FHL microfilm through your local Family History Center for a small fee. In the description of Deeds and Mortgages, 1872–1945, a button to View Film Notes indicates that the material is available on microfilm. Clicking on this, I find descriptions of each of the forty-four rolls of film in this collection. Now I can order only the films that I need for my research.

Carefully plan your trip to the Family History Library. When using the catalog, note the location of the materials. Some books are in the Joseph Smith Memorial Building, not the main library building. Some films are in a vault at a different location, so you must request they be brought to the library. This can take a day or more, so request them early to allow time for their arrival.

Like those of other libraries, the Family History Library's Web site includes the general information that you need to plan a trip. From the main page, click the Library tab and learn the library's hours, services, rules, floor plan, and so on. There's even a link to information specifically designed to help you plan your trip to the FHL.

Searching for the Needle in the Haystack

There are times in your research when you have to seek out hard-to-find sources. Finding a specific family history from 1893 or a collection of family letters can be difficult if you don't know where to look. A genealogist must look for every possible record—that means you have to look in as many places as possible. Two online tools are indispensable to thorough research: OCLC's WorldCat and the National Union Catalog of Manuscript Collections.

OCLC's WorldCat

You learned in Chapter 2 about the importance of evaluating source citations. There are times in your research when you want to examine the sources listed on the family group sheet or the GEDCOM file that a cousin sent you. Perhaps you want to see the source for yourself to sort out conflicting data. Perhaps you believe the cited source has additional information about a related line.

The problem is that many published sources used by genealogists are not widely available. Books of abstracted records published by genealogical and historical societies tend to have small print runs, often fewer than five hundred copies. Most of these books are sold to individual researchers; thus, there may not be many copies available to libraries. Older books are even harder to find. There may be only a few dozen copies of a particular county history published in the late 1800s.

Published family histories are perhaps the hardest to locate. Historically, they have been printed in small quantities, often just enough to go to interested family members and perhaps to one or two libraries.

For the dedicated genealogist who wants to examine these sources, the challenge is knowing where to find them. Some books lend themselves to a logical place to start looking. County histories, for example, can usually be found in the county of which they are the subject. But what about the published genealogy of a family who spread out across twenty counties in six different states?

In the case of the elusive book that might be in a library anywhere from Maine to California, you could look in every online catalog of every library you think might have the book. But an alternative is to look in a catalog that covers thousands of libraries at once—the Online Computer Library Center's WorldCat.

OCLC is a library cooperative representing libraries around the world; WorldCat is a bibliographic database of OCLC member libraries—the largest such database in the world. As of July 2002, WorldCat contained almost forty-eight million unique bibliographic records—records that describe books, magazines, electronic media, and other items owned by libraries.

Users access WorldCat through OCLC's FirstSearch program, shown in Figure 13.4, which is available for use in most public libraries in the United States. Some libraries have made arrangements with OCLC to allow their cardholders to access FirstSearch from home through the Internet.

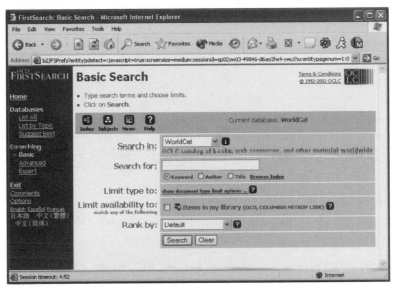

Figure 13.4 OCLC FirstSearch

You can perform a basic search in WorldCat by keyword, author, or title. The advanced search lets you perform Boolean searches on a variety of fields. From the Results screen, click on the material of interest to get a more complete description. If you want to find a copy of the material, click on Libraries That Own Item to see a list of the libraries that have the item in their collection, arranged by state.

While researching a collateral line of my own family, I found a GEDCOM file with a source citation to *Genealogy of the Athey Family in America*. I was not familiar with the book, but I wanted to see what other information it might have on the family, so I searched WorldCat by title. Since the source citation in the GEDCOM file was not clear, I was unsure whether "in America" was actually part of the title. I shortened my WorldCat search to *Genealogy of the Athey Family*, which yielded six titles, including *Genealogy of the Athey Family in America: 1642–1932*, as shown in Figure 13.5.

I clicked on the title for the full description and, from there, clicked on Libraries That Own Item. Five libraries were listed: in Ohio, Marietta College and the State Library of Ohio; in Indiana, the Allen County Public Library and the Vigo County Public Library; and in Massachusetts, the New England Historic Genealogical Society. With this information, I could do any of the following:

- Visit any of these libraries to use the book.
- Contact the libraries to see whether they allow an Interlibrary Loan.
- Find out the research or copying policies of the library.
- Hire a researcher in the area to examine the book for me.

When searching WorldCat by title, be sure to read all the results. Some entries may refer to the same book because different libraries have described the work in different ways. By looking at all the entries, you may find a book in a library closer to you or that has a more liberal research and copying policy.

Reading all the entries may also reveal related books. In the search for *Genealogy of the Athey Family in America*, one of the results was titled *Index to the Genealogy of the Athey Family in America, 1642–1932*. Before my search on WorldCat, I didn't know that a separate index to this work existed. While five libraries had a copy of the genealogy, only the Vigo County Public Library had the index. However, my options were the same: go to Vigo County myself, contact that library about the possibility of Interlibrary Loan, find out its research and copying policy, or hire a local researcher.

Of course, you don't need to look for a specific title to use WorldCat. Keyword searches are very useful. One effective way to find family histories is to search by surname with the word *family*, such as *Debolt family*. Try searching by location, such as *Monongalia County West Virginia*. You can narrow the search by adding other keywords to the location, such as *Monongalia County West Virginia history* or *Maryland immigration*.

In the next chapter, you will learn about using the Internet to put your ancestors in context. A good keyword search makes WorldCat an effective tool to help you find materials for general topics.

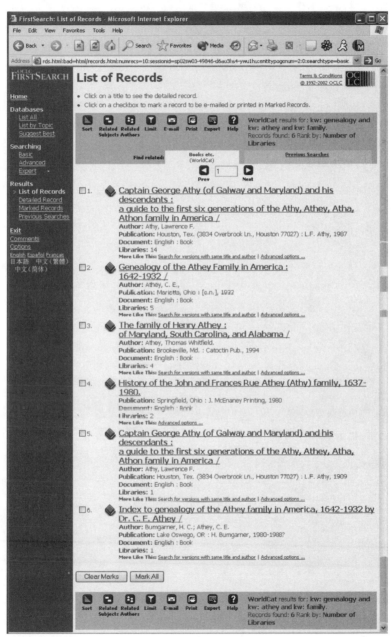

Figure 13.5 WorldCat Results

National Union Catalog of Manuscript Collections

The National Union Catalog of Manuscript Collections (NUCMC), sponsored by the Library of Congress, is similar to OCLC WorldCat in that it is a bibliographic database of many different archives (currently over seven hundred thousand entries). Go to *www.loc.gov/coll/nucmc*.

The major difference between NUCMC and WorldCat is that NUCMC lists only manuscripts—materials that have never been published. These materials are generally hard to find; not only does their one-of-a-kind nature mean that they are less known to researchers, but their subject matter does not necessarily tie them to a related facility. For example, a Bible from a family in Pennsylvania may be located in a Colorado archives because that is where the descendant who inherited the Bible lived. Because NUCMC covers libraries and archives across the United States, researchers are not bound to a specific geographic location in their searches.

From the NUCMC main page, click on Searching the NUCMC RLG Catalog. The easiest way to search NUCMC is through the Easy Search Form (word list), shown in Figure 13.6. As with WorldCat, a search like *Smith family* can be effective. When you get too many results, as happens with a common surname, narrow the search by location or record type. A search on *Skinner family* yields sixty-nine

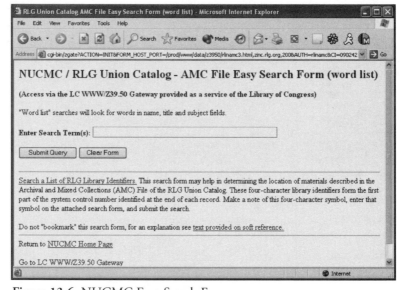

Figure 13.6 NUCMC Easy Search Form

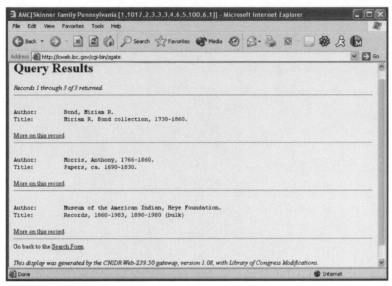

Figure 13.7 NUCMC results

results. Changing the search to *Skinner family Pennsylvania* yields three, as shown in Figure 13.7.

As you learned in Chapter 5 about finding family sources, your family history materials may be hidden under a different family name. This is certainly true in the results I received from my search on *Skinner family Pennsylvania*. None of the results have titles that include the name Skinner.

To determine which, if any, of the results may be pertinent to your research, click on the link More on This Record, which provides a full description of the materials. The Miriam R. Bond Collection is described as twenty-two items:

Deeds for tracts in Upper Makefield and one in Spring Garden, Philadelphia, Pa. (1730–1854); apprentice indentures (1785–1804) which involve the Parker, Skinner, and Strawn families; wine patent for James M. McMasters (1825); estate papers of John McMasters (1855—1860); court orders (1750—1803); and lease agreement (1815).

Every description contains the location of the materials—in this case, the Bucks County Historical Society in Doylestown, Pennsylvania.

The World Wide Web has brought a world of records to a computer near you. But even with the vast amount of data available online, an almost infinite amount isn't. Part of the joy of genealogy is finding that information, wherever it may be. Using library and archives Web sites—both for the data they contain and for their references to offline resources—is an essential step in your research.

Putting Your Ancestors in Context

HISTORY AND GEOGRAPHY ARE MORE FUN THE SECOND TIME AROUND. Some who found these subjects boring and irrelevant in school become motivated to learn more because of their interest in an ancestor from a given era and place. This chapter helps you research the areas where your ancestors lived—the lay of the land and the history—as well as property they owned. Knowing about a region's industries, crops, terrain, wars, famines, weather, and other events helps you place your ancestors in context. Learning about their property holdings allows you to understand their circumstances, to meet their neighbors, and to locate and identify your ancestors.

Exploring an Area's Geography

While researching your family history, you'll probably want to locate a town or village name, view a map, or look at migration patterns. You can do that by mining the Internet's wealth of geographical information.

Locating a Town, Village, or Area

Sometimes you run across the name of a town that you cannot locate on a modern-day map. Try to find a gazetteer that covers the area, and look for the town's description and location. Then you may be able to unearth a map of the same period and identify the town's geographic location.

217

A **gazetteer** is a book that names and describes the places in a given area, such as a county, at a specific time. Genealogists use gazetteers to find towns that do not exist in modern times.

The online Global Gazetteer *(www.calle.com/world)* is a current worldwide directory of more than 2.8 million of the world's towns and cities. To use it, click on a country name, then the applicable index entry for the town you are seeking. I used Global Gazetteer to locate Corscombe, a small farm village in Dorset, England, and learned the latitude, longitude, and altitude of the town. The results also showed a current weather forecast and, more valuable, a list of six towns near Corscombe, helpful when trying to find records of the closest church, school, or other institution. As you see in Figure 14.1, a map shows Corscombe's general location within Great Britain and links take you to other sites relevant to Corscombe.

While the online Global Gazetteer contains modern localities and information, the only way you may be able to find a place that existed in previous centuries is to locate a gazetteer for the right era. For example, I cannot find Peaked Mountain, Virginia, the birthplace in 1765 of one of my ancestors, on any modern print or online maps. A Google search for the phrase *Virginia gazetteer* leads to an index of 1835 and 1844 gazetteers of Virginia at the Library of Virginia site *(image.vtls.com/collections/GA.html)*. Looking through this index, I locate an entry for Peaked Mountain in Rockingham County, the logical place to start the research for my ancestors. With this index information, I can also write or e-mail the Library of Virginia to request a copy of the entire entry for Peaked Mountain from the publication in their holdings.

Seeing the Lay of the Land

When exploring an ancestor's habitat, pay attention to manmade and geographic features, such as nearby ports, rivers, lakes, mountains, or railroads. Was the area mountainous, or was it flat, fertile farmland near a river? Are there nearby mines? Knowing the lay of the land helps you determine an ancestor's occupation. In addition, consider what you already know. Where did your ancestor live before or after this time? Is the land similar? Tobacco farmers in Virginia did not suddenly move to Arizona and become cotton farmers; people usually moved to areas with similar soils, climate, and industries.

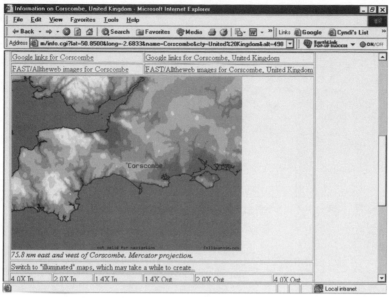

Figure 14.1 Global Gazetteer results

Determine the exact location of places mentioned in your source documents by using a modern detailed map or the Geographic Names Information System (GNIS) online *(geonames.usgs.gov/gnisform.html)*. GNIS, a service of the U.S. Geological Survey (USGS), sometimes contains information about places that no longer exist, and it details streams, churches, cemeteries, peaks, and other geographic features. For each listing, you can display several types of maps and zoom in or out, then print or save them. USGS Digital Raster Graphic (DRG) maps are digitized versions of USGS topographic maps. For some locations, Digital Orthophoto Quadrangle (DOQ) maps are available. These are black-and-white aerial photographs of an area.

I can use GNIS to locate a family cemetery and view maps of it. I access GNIS and search for Twidwell Cemetery in Wayne County, Missouri. Links to three cemeteries by the same name result; I click the link of the one I want. Next, links offer the option to view DRG or DOQ maps, so I first look at the DRG topographical map from TerraServer, shown in Figure 14.2. The shading and contours on this map represent altitude and hills. A U.S. highway and a lesser road form a V on either side of the cemetery, and I learn that another cemetery is just down the road. From this topographical map, I see that Twidwell Cemetery sits on a little hill and faces somewhat southeast.

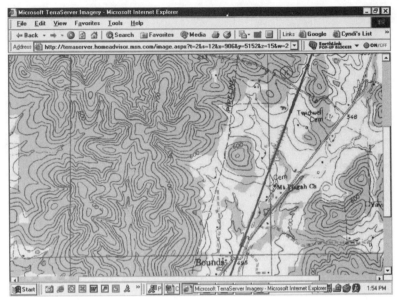

Figure 14.2 USGS topographical map

Figure 14.3 GNIS and TerraServer DOQ aerial photograph

Finding an Old Map

However helpful modern maps are, you should still find a map of the area from about the time your ancestor lived there so you can see the town or county through your forebear's eyes. Use a search engine and query for a phrase similar to *historical map + Corscombe Dorset.* You'll probably find an online reference to a library or archive that owns the map, but you may be lucky enough to find a digitized image of an old map that you can view, download, or print.

Here are some helpful online map sources:

- 1895 U.S. Atlas (maps for every county in the United States) *(www.livgenmi.com/1895)*

- British Ordnance Survey Historical Maps (click on the Historical link under the Leisure category) *(www.ordnancesurvey.co.uk/getamap)*

- David Rumsey Historical Map collection *(www.davidrumsey.com)*

- Library of Congress Map Collections: 1500–2002 *(lcweb2.loc.gov/ammem/gmdhtml/gmdhome.html)*

- Tony Campbell's Map History Web Site—Images of Early Maps on the Web *(ihr.sas.ac.uk/maps/webimages.html)*

- University of Texas at Austin, Perry-Castañeda Library Map Collection (links to historical map Web sites around the world) *(www.lib.utexas.edu/maps/map_sites/states_sites.html)*

When I move back in my browser and choose the DOQ map for the same area, a black-and-white photograph displays. As with the topographical map, clicking on a portion of the map enlarges it. I can zoom in to the maximum resolution size and view the cleared land lying just northwest of the old highway and southwest of a gravel road—there, directly across the road from my cousin Davy's house, is the family cemetery. Figure 14.3 represents the kind of map you see if you use GNIS to find a geographic feature and then view the accompanying TerraServer DOQ black-and-white aerial photo. Besides viewing maps at the USGS GNIS Web site, you can download, print, or even e-mail them. You can probably even locate an aerial photo of your own house with these tools.

Many state highway departments sell modern detailed county maps that show

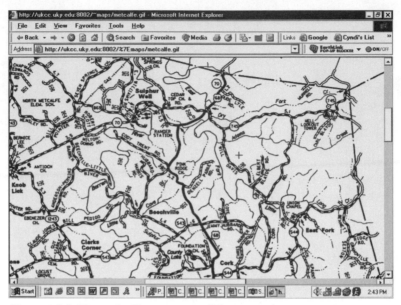

Figure 14.4 Kentucky Department of Transportation county map

watercourses, railroads, roads, and even homes, churches, schools, and cemeteries, similar to the digitized Metcalfe County, Kentucky, map in Figure 14.4. Query a search engine for a phrase such as *department transportation county maps* + *Indiana* to search for any reference to county maps for a state. You may find digitized county maps like that of Kentucky, or you may find information about ordering the actual maps from the state.

Try to find historic maps of the area you are researching by searching online catalogs of relevant libraries and manuscript collections. More and more maps are being digitized and added to online collections at the Library of Congress and other Web sites, so search on the Internet, too.

Looking for an Ancestor's Property

Be it ever so humble, there's no place like your ancestor's home. Numerous immigrants came to the United States to realize their dreams of owning property, and many continually migrated farther west as more lands opened up at affordable prices.

You've already learned from Chapter 8 how to find the right courthouse for your ancestor's records. Now, let's explore the kinds of documents that help you cobble together your ancestor's neighborhood.

Insurance Maps

Some incredibly detailed maps of cities and towns were created in the nineteenth and twentieth centuries primarily for fire insurance companies. Some of these maps even show individual buildings and combustible materials.

Charles Goad published such maps for the United Kingdom and Ontario (Canada). Visit Hugh Reekie's Web site *(members.attcanada.ca/~max-com/Goad.html)* to learn about these Goad maps and to access an index of the Canada National Map Library's collection of them.

The D. A. Sanborn Company produced similar maps for commercial, industrial, and residential areas of U.S. cities from 1867 to 1969. The Library of Congress holds a complete set of Sanborn maps for the entire United States, and many libraries own partial collections. Some are available as digitized images on the Web. For instance, the J. W. Marriott Library at the University of Utah provides a large digitized collection of Sanborn maps for cities and towns in Utah at *www.lib.utah.edu/digital/sanborn/index.html*. The Western Association of Map Libraries provides a catalog of institutions that own fire insurance maps for western states at *www.lib.berkeley.edu/EART/sanbul_libs.html*.

To find these specialty maps for your area, try a Google search of a phrase similar to *Sanborn fire insurance maps + Las Cruces*.

Who Owned the Land First?

A history of land ownership in the United States would fill an entire volume, and that's certainly true of other countries' systems, too. History and geography go hand in hand, and as a genealogist, you benefit greatly from learning a little about the history of the area you are researching. For instance, if it was once under Spanish rule, like much of the United States west of the Mississippi River, you may find evidence in your research of Spanish land grants that were later honored by the U.S. government. If the object of your research is a colonial area, such as Virginia, you may find transactions in which land patents were handed out from the Crown to an individual or in which land grants were made from the Commonwealth to an individual. (Both patents and grants required payment and were not gifts from the government.) Or your ancestors may have come later and just purchased their lands from an individual, recording the transaction at the local courthouse.

Abundant numbers of Web sites provide background information and history about land ownership in an area. For example, to learn about land acquisition and settlement

Land Records Clarified

If you don't understand the difference between state land states or public land states (also known as public domain or federal land states), or if you can't figure out metes and bounds terminology, take advantage of the Land Record Reference Web site hosted by Direct Line Software *(users.rcn.com/deeds/landref.htm)*. There you find informative articles about land acquisition in the United States, bounty lands awarded for military service, land history in several states, surveying units and terms, and links to other land sites.

Direct Line Software also hosts a data pool of deeds contributed by its users *(users.rcn.com/deeds/pool.htm)*. Deeds in the pool can be downloaded at no cost and imported into the DeedMapper program for viewing, editing, or printing. This is another fine example of how everyone benefits when genealogists share their data.

in the region around North Dakota, read about land ownership, homestead files, land laws, surveying, and speculators at the Web site of the State Historical Society of North Dakota *(www.state.nd.us/hist/infland.htm)*. Search online for your area with a phrase such as *land ownership + Oklahoma*.

State Land States

States where land was originally controlled and disbursed by the government to the first owners are known as state land states. This includes the thirteen original colonies (Virginia, New Jersey, Massachusetts, New Hampshire, Pennsylvania, New York, Maryland, Connecticut, Rhode Island, Delaware, North Carolina, South Carolina, and Georgia), states that once belonged to or were part of one of the colonies (Kentucky, Maine, Tennessee, Vermont, and West Virginia), plus Hawaii and Texas. The colonial states were administered by the British government until the Revolutionary War, Texas was administered by the Mexican government until its independence, and Hawaiian lands were disbursed by the islands' rulers before it became a U.S. territory.

Metes and Bounds Surveys

Basically, state land states and parts of Ohio use the metes and bounds system of surveying, where the boundary of a piece of land begins at a designated marker and proceeds from point to point. Descriptions of metes and bounds land often read like this early Virginia patent for land my third great-grandfather received from George III on 5 July 1774 for the sum of forty shillings:

> . . . do give, grant, and confirm unto John Westmoreland one certain tract or parcel of land containing three hundred and eighty acres lying and being in the County of Mecklenburg on the waters of Buffalo and bounded as followeth, to wit. Beginning at pointers in Taylor's line and running on his and Walls line South seventy degrees West three hundred and seventy poles to Walls corner poplar. Still on Walls and Griffins line North three degrees East one hundred and thirty poles to Griffins corner hickory . . . .

I confess that I did not travel to Virginia to obtain a copy of my ancestor's original land patent. I visited the Library of Virginia's Land Office Patents and Grants database at *eagle.vsla.edu/lonn*, searched for John Westmoreland's name, and located a two-page patent in digitized form online. The patents and grants in this database document the *first* sale of the parcel of land. When the patentee or grantee (buyer) disposed of the land, that transaction was recorded at the county courthouse or wherever deeds were handled.

When I clicked on the link to John Westmoreland's record, the information screen (shown in Figure 14.5) provided me with an abstract of the patent. Knowing that the original record itself has much more information than the abstract, I clicked on the link for Patent (to the right of Multimedia). This brought up another screen that allowed me to download and save John's patent as a .tif (graphic) file on my own computer. Then, using a .tif viewer or a graphics program, such as Paint Shop Pro, I can view the patent as you see it in Figure 14.6, zoom in to read the text better, or print a copy for my files.

Federal Land States

Lands were disbursed by the U.S. government, rather than by individual states, in the thirty federal land (or public domain) states: Alabama, Alaska, Arizona, Arkansas, California, Colorado, Florida, Idaho, Illinois, Indiana, Iowa, Kansas, Louisiana, Michigan, Minnesota, Mississippi, Missouri, Montana, Nebraska, Nevada, New Mexico, North Dakota, Ohio, Oklahoma, Oregon, South Dakota, Utah, Washington, Wisconsin, and Wyoming.

Untold numbers of records exist for federal land transactions, including private

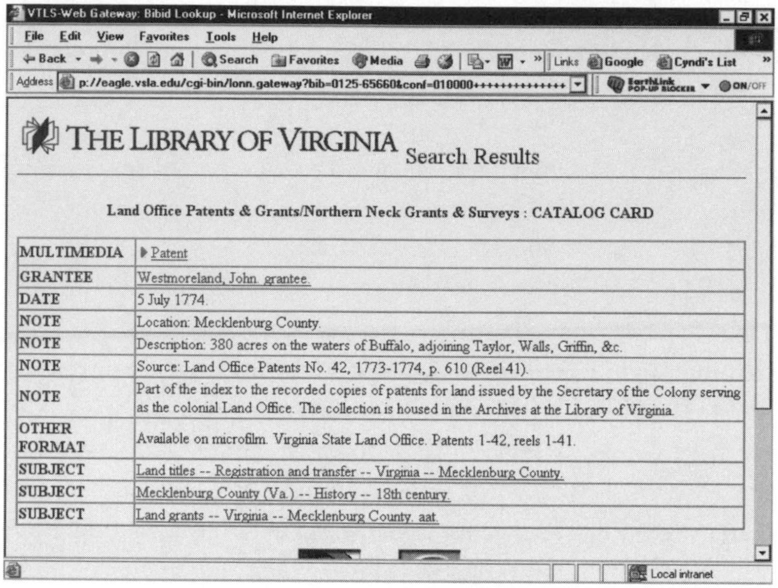

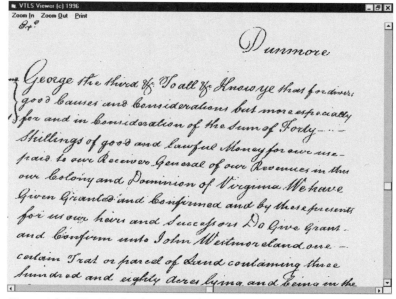

Figure 14.5 Virginia land patent information screen

Figure 14.6 Virginia land patent online image

claims to lands owned by individuals under other governments (Spain or France), bounty lands, homestead lands, and cash purchases of land. To understand more about the complicated process of land acquisition in the United States, you may want to look online for articles, such as "American Land Records" by Julia M. Case, Myra Vanderpool Gormley, CG, and Rhonda McClure at *www.rootsweb.com/~rwguide/lesson29.htm*, which also includes links to other resources.

Rectangular Grid Surveys

Public domain (federal land) states are organized along meridians—imaginary lines running from the North to the South Pole—and base lines, which run east and west. Meridian regions in the United States are divided into tracts of about twenty-four square miles, and tracts are then divided into sixteen townships of about sixteen square miles each. Each township is further divided into thirty-six one-mile squares or sections, each consisting of 640 acres. Most commercial atlases show meridian lines, townships, and ranges. If you've flown over the wide-open spaces of the American West, you've undoubtedly noticed those precise dirt roads creating perfect squares or rectangles on the ground below. Those are evidence of the rectangular survey or range/township/section system with its range line and section line roads.

One of the best places to find answers to questions about land acquisition in public

The Exception Is Ohio

For almost every rule that applies to land surveys in the United States, the state of Ohio has an exception. It's a public land state, but two states—Connecticut and Virginia—claimed lands there. It's surveyed in a rectangular survey—except for the twenty-three counties of the Virginia Military District, which are surveyed in metes and bounds. And the rule about ranges being numbered east-west? Not in the Symmes Purchase and the Between the Miamis Survey, where they're numbered from south to north.

Fortunately, the Auditor of State's Office has made two publications available online that explain Ohio's land surveys. Go to *www.auditor.state.oh.us/* and click Learning Center; then click Along the Ohio Trail. There you can download "Ohio Lands," a classic in Ohio research, or "Along the Ohio Trail," the student version. Both versions are indispensable for understanding the crazy quilt that makes up Ohio's land surveys.

domain states is the Bureau of Land Management General Land Office Records Web site *(www.glorecords.blm.gov/Visitors).* It provides information about the nine million General Land Office (GLO) records, a public lands history timeline, a section about the various kinds of land patents and the process to obtain these lands, and a detailed explanation of the rectangular survey system. At *www.glorecords.blm.gov/Visitors/StateResearch.asp,* the site also provides links to general land research sites and to resources for researching in many states.

Bureau of Land Management General Land Office Patents

The Bureau of Land Management (BLM) General Land Office (GLO) Web site *(www.glorecords.blm.gov)* offers online access to more than two million records transferring land ownership from the federal government to the first purchasers of the land. Not only can researchers read and print text descriptions about these land transactions, but they can also view, download, and print digitized images of the actual documents.

I want to determine when my ancestor, Pleasant Wilcox, might have migrated to Missouri, so I use the Basic Search feature of the BLM GLO Web site, shown in Figure 14.7, to enter the state and his name. When I click the Search button, I am excited to see two results of patents issued in 1859 to Pleasant Wilcox (see Figure 14.8).

I click on the name Pleasant Wilcox to link to land patent details (see Figure 14.9). By looking at the patent description, I learn that Pleasant Wilcox was the patentee (buyer) of forty acres of land transferred to him on 1 March 1859. He purchased the land through the Jackson, Missouri, land office by authority of the 24 April 1820 Sale—Cash Entry Statute. Clicking on the Legal Land Description tab at the top of the shaded area displays information that enables me to plot the land—the northeast quarter of the southwest quarter of section 33, township 29 north, range 5 east, along the fifth principal meridian in Wayne County, Missouri. On a map that shows sections, townships, and ranges, I can precisely locate this exact plat of land within the county.

As a good genealogist and a Missourian, I often utter the phrase "Show me," and the BLM GLO Web site delivers. I click on the Document Image tab to access a digitized image of the original patent (shown partially in Figure 14.10); now I can download and save it for use in another program, zoom in or out, and print it. This original document provides essentially the same information as the abstract in the text version of the patent and legal descriptions. But if I scroll down to the

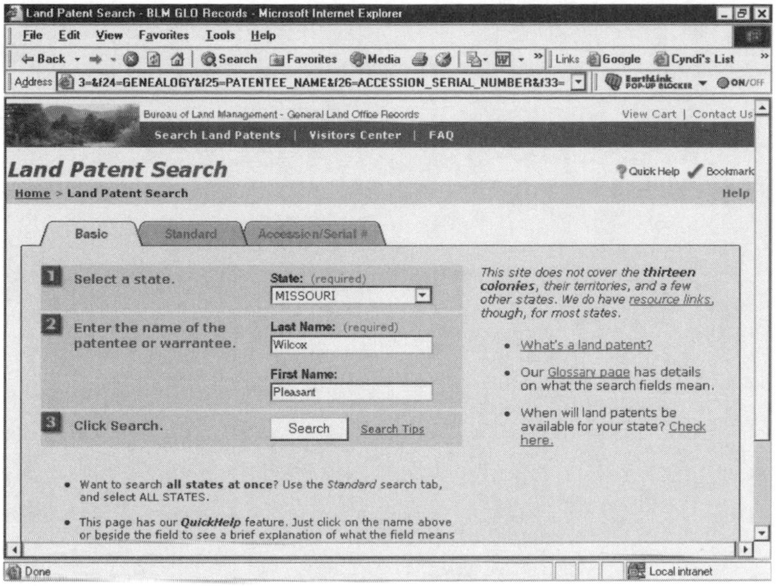

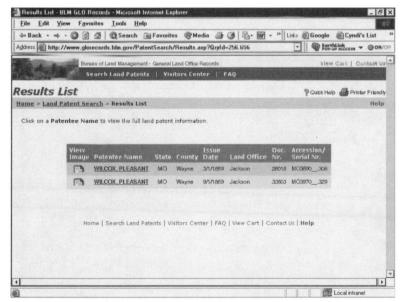

Figure 14.7 Basic Search at BLM GLO online database

Figure 14.8 Search results at BLM GLO online database

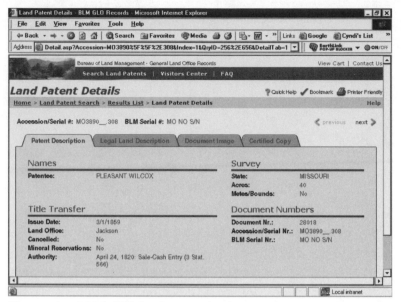

Figure 14.9 BLM GLO land patent details

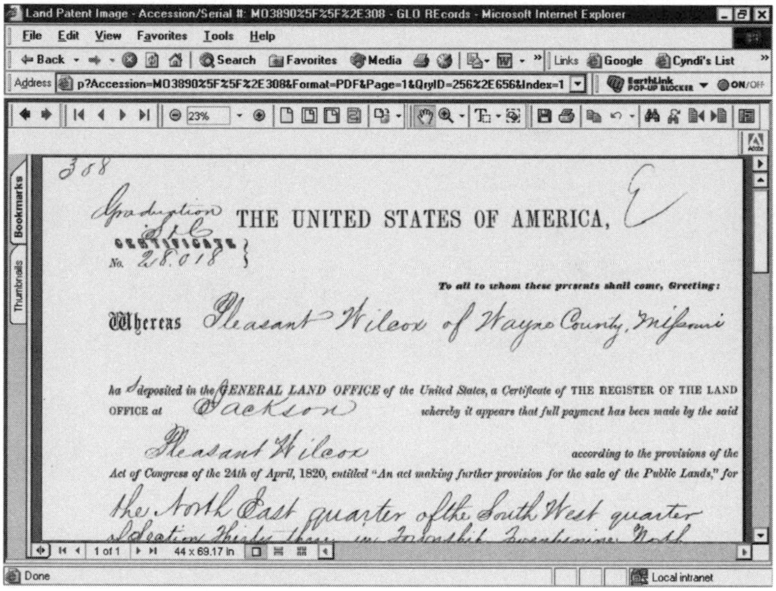

Figure 14.10 BLM GLO land patent image

bottom of the document, a signature catches my eye—that of James Buchanan, U.S. president when the patent was issued. Many individuals own original patentee copies of federal land purchases that have been passed down in their families. Does this mean they possess valuable historical documents with a president's signature? Well, yes and no. Yes, they own valuable historical papers that document their family's history of land ownership. And yes, some own patents with a president's signature—those dated before 2 March 1833. Until that date, all original patents were actually signed by the president of the United States; after that, designated officials signed on his behalf.

Adjusting for Declination

Original survey lines were referenced to magnetic north. But magnetic north today is not the same as it was two hundred years ago when colonial lands were surveyed—it is constantly, slowly changing. To place your land plats accurately, you must adjust for this compass declination, or deviation. An explanation and instructions for corrections can be found at *users.rcn.com/deeds/decl.htm* in an article entitled "Historic Values of Compass Declination."

Use the U.S. Government's National Geophysical Data Center Web site (*www.ngdc.noaa.gov/cgi-bin/seg/gmag/fldsnth1.pl*) to compute a location's magnetic declination for a date or range of dates since 1900.

Land Platting

It is possible to use a protractor and a ruler to plot a deed and draw a picture of the land's boundaries and shape. But because it has been many years since I used my geometry skills, I prefer to enter the patent information and land description in a computer program called DeedMapper, by Direct Line Software (*users.rcn.com/deeds*). DeedMapper then automatically draws the plat map and calculates the area. Because it is important to research the property surrounding an ancestor's land, good genealogists also plot surrounding lands and piece the patchwork together into a community quilt of sorts.

Learning the History of an Area

If you know nothing about the history of the areas where your ancestors lived, you are researching in a vacuum. Without understanding events surrounding lives in the past, you cannot know the kinds of records to seek out and where to look. But perhaps more importantly, you cannot truly understand and know your ancestors if you have no knowledge of the events that affected them.

The Internet is particularly wonderful for learning about history, since historical Web sites abound for all areas of the world. You can seek out an online history, read magazine articles from the 1800s, and transport yourself back in time to your ancestor's community.

What Were People Doing There?

Why do towns grow into cities? People come together in an area, and then more move in, perhaps because the community is strategically located like St. Louis (at the confluence of the Missouri and Mississippi rivers) or Chicago (strategically situated as a railroad hub). What industries and natural resources influenced the growth of an area? If your ancestors were lumbermen in the hills of east Tennessee, where did they go when the timber was gone there? They most likely moved west to another hilly, wooded area to engage in the timber industry. If your Slavic ancestors were coal miners in the old country, they probably joined fellow countrymen in a coal-mining region of the United States when they immigrated. Studying the history of your ancestor's town, county, and state can provide important clues for follow-up research.

To find a history of the state or county you're researching, search the Library of Congress online catalog *(www.loc.gov)* or the online catalog of a library in the region to see whether area histories have been published. Then try a Google search for the title of the book. You may find excerpts of county histories on the Internet, especially those no longer under copyright protection. Quite a number of regional histories were published in the mid- to late 1800s, most containing a section of local residents' biographies. Some of these have been transcribed and can be found on RootsWeb or USGenWeb sites. Be sure to take the biographies with a grain of salt, though, since their subjects paid to have their stories included.

One good way to understand your ancestors' lives is to read publications of the era, such as newspapers or magazines. The Making of America online collection at Cornell University *(cdl.library.cornell.edu/moa)* comprises digitized images of more than 267

Finding a Regional History

To determine whether a regional history has been published about an area you are researching, search the Internet for a phrase similar to *Southeast Missouri history*. If a history for an area you are researching is no longer in print, you may be able to find a copy of your own using such Web resources as these:

- Alibris Used Books *(www.alibris.com)*

- Bibliofind (now combined with Amazon.com—used books) *(www.amazon.com/exec/obidos/subst/books/misc/bibliofind.html/)*

- Book Avenue (used, antiquarian, out-of-print books) *(www.bookavenue.com)*

- BookFinder.com (new, used, or out-of-print books) *(www.bookfinder.com)*

- Brookhaven Press (on-demand publisher of out-of-print historical and genealogical titles) *(www.brookhavenpress.com)*

- eBay (antiquarian, collectible, antique, used books) *(pages.ebay.com/catindex/books.html)*

- Page One (collectible books) *(www.page1book.com/perl/antiquarian_books.pl)*

- Powell's Books (used books) *(www.powells.com/usedbooks/usedbooks.html)*

monograph volumes and 100,000 journal articles from the nineteenth century. The University of Michigan's Making of America collection *(moa.umdl.umich.edu)* contains approximately 8,500 books and 50,000 journal articles. Both these Web sites contain amazing information for any historian or genealogist. Cornell's collection includes the entire multivolume *War of the Rebellion: A Compilation of the Official Records of the Union and Confederate Armies*, sometimes known as the *Official Records of the Union and Confederate Armies* or, simply, the *OR*. If you've seen the more than fifty books making up this publication on the shelf of your local library, you'll understand how impressive it is that this important Civil War research tool is available online for researchers to read, search, copy, or print from their own homes.

It's worth your while to simply browse some of the titles, such as the *New England Magazine* (1831–1835) or *Harper's New Monthly Magazine* (1850–1899). You can

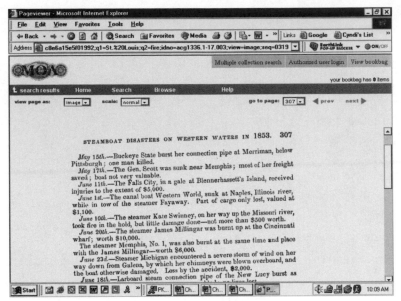

Figure 14.11 Journal article at Making of America

perform simple or advanced searches for words or phrases (including names) contained in the journals or books, and browse books or articles by title or author. Someone interested in steamboat accidents near St. Louis might search for *St. Louis near steamboat* to find the *Debow's Review, Agricultural, Commercial, Industrial Progress and Resources* journal article shown in Figure 14.11, "Steamboat Disasters on Western Waters in 1853" (a digital reproduction from the Making of America, printed by permission of the University of Michigan University Library.) This piece documents steamboat accidents by date, including the 26 July 1853 fire at the St. Louis wharf that destroyed the steamers *Dr. Franklin No. 2*, valued at $8,000; *Bluff City*, valued at $40,000; and *Highland Mary No. 1*, valued at $5,500—valuable information if you know your ancestor died 26 July 1853 on a steamboat in St. Louis.

Historical Reenactor Resources

On weekends and holidays, America's historical battlegrounds are often filled with ghostly figures in period costume fighting battles believed settled more than a century ago. On closer examination, the apparitions are found to be living history buffs who invest copious amounts of time and money to learn about and reenact important events in history. This is about as close as anyone can come to actual time travel, and genealogists can learn a lot from reenactor Web sites.

My friend, Ron Taylor, and I share an interest in history and discovered that we both had ancestors from Cumberland County, Virginia, who served during the Revolutionary War in Captain William Cunningham's Company, 1st Virginia Regiment. Thomas Fitzsimmons, Ron's fourth great-grandfather, and John Hatcher, a first cousin of my fifth great-grandmother, served together in this regiment, enlisting within two days of one another in February 1778.

Ron and I marveled that our ancestors probably knew one another, coming from the same area and serving in the same company of soldiers. Those two young men, sick and huddled around a campfire at Valley Forge that awful winter, could not possibly have known that their descendants would grow up in New Mexico, a far-away Spanish possession during their lifetimes, and meet at work some two hundred years in the future.

How did we learn details about our ancestors' service? I found the informative reenactor site of the 1st Virginia Regiment of the Revolutionary War *(www.1va.org/1va/history.html),* shown in Figure 14.12.

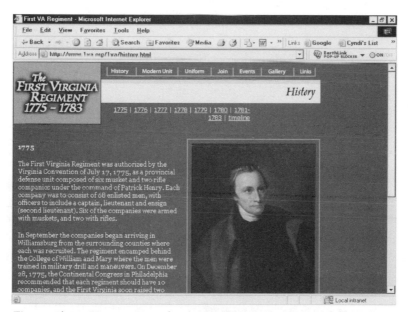

Figure 14.12 Reenactor site for the 1st Virginia Regiment of the Revolutionary War

Reenactor Web sites often provide the background surrounding the events of the era. The 1st Virginia Regiment Web site discusses the regiment's history year by year from its inception in 1775 to the soldiers' mustering out in 1783, even providing a timeline of events and published sources for further reading. It describes the exact clothing and uniforms the men wore and the arms and accoutrements they carried, with depictive photographs of the reenactors. A schedule tells where the reenactors will appear next, and links lead to other Revolutionary War sites of interest.

How Did Your Ancestors Dress?

Learn about the clothing your ancestors wore by looking at Web sites that offer historical costumes or patterns for making them. Just query a search engine for *historical clothing* or *historical patterns* to find such Web sites as these:

- Blanket Brigade (historical clothing and blankets—buckskin, leather, Civil War products, etc.) *(www.blanketbrigade.com)*

- Kannik's Korner (historic costume patterns 1750–1820) *(www.kannikskorner.com/home.htm)*

- Past Patterns (historic patterns 1830s–1940s) *(www.pastpatterns.com)*

- Sewing Central (historic patterns and fabric—Dark Ages through the Roaring Twenties) *(www.sewingcentral.com/histpat.html)*

Let's Talk about the Weather

With our nicely air-conditioned and heated twenty-first-century homes, the weather does not affect us as much as it did our ancestors. Natural and manmade disasters are a source of terrible suffering for many people, but they are often a rich source of information for genealogists. For example, on 31 May 1889, the Johnstown flood wiped out a town and killed more than two thousand people. The victims' names and an explanation of the disaster are available online from several sources. The National Park Service lists victims at *www.nps.gov/jofl/victims.htm*. This site includes a description of the events and a list of the most frequently used burial places.

The Johnstown flood Web site also contains a list of major U.S. disasters, from an 1825 forest fire in Maine to the 1964 earthquake in Alaska. Another such event was the "night of the big wind" in County Mayo, Ireland, in January 1839, which caused havoc and left hundreds homeless. Read about it at *www.mayoalive.com/MagApr23/BigWind.htm.* To find evidence of such violent weather in an area you are researching, query a search engine for a phrase similar to *tornado + southern Illinois.* That particular search turns up the story of the great tristate tornado of March 1925, which left 15,000 destroyed homes and 695 dead in its 219-mile wake across Missouri, Illinois, and Indiana.

The Aviation Weather Center in Kansas City provides a calendar of historical weather facts for the entire United States at *www.awc-kc.noaa.gov/wxfact.html.* According to this site, on 15 September 1752, a "hurricane produced a tide along the South Carolina coast which nearly inundated downtown Charleston. However, just before the tide reached the city, a shift in the wind caused the water level to drop five feet in ten minutes." Wouldn't this exciting information liven up a dry written family history?

Learning about the geography, property transactions, and history of your ancestors creates a whole new understanding of their lives. When you have explored enough to discover the economic situation of your ancestral family based on its property holdings, visualized the terrain of an area based on maps and photographs, and come to understand the hardships and the rewards of living in a particular community, then you may feel as if you have actually walked in your ancestors' footsteps.

CHAPTER 15

Seeing Your Ancestors— in Pictures and in Print

HAVEN'T YOU COME TO KNOW PEOPLE BY TALKING TO THEM ON THE phone or e-mailing them, without ever having seen them? Most people form a visual image of how someone looks. When we actually meet that person, we're often surprised to see that he or she looks nothing like the image we carried in our imagination. We've all heard comments like "He had very little gray hair even in his seventies—that's those Westmoreland genes, you know" or "She's got those long Twidwell legs." Family photographs can reveal similarities in appearance that bind us to our families, and they certainly satisfy the longing to see what an ancestor actually looked like.

A Picture Is Worth a Thousand Words

If your house caught fire, what possessions would you first try to save? For many, it would be family photographs, irreplaceable reminders of our places in time. Photographs arouse memories of our own childhoods and allow a glimpse into those of our parents or grandparents. Many genealogists have described the emotional, often tearful, moment they finally laid eyes on a picture of an ancestor about whom they knew many details but whom they had never seen. What if only a few photographs—or none at all—of your ancestors and their surroundings survive in your family?

239

Finding Photos in the Family

Think creatively in your quest for more family portraits. Sometimes family members recall a detail that leads to a treasure hunt. My mother offhandedly mentioned one day that a portrait of her grandfather, Joel Westmoreland, who had died in 1912, had hung on her grandmother's living room wall as long as she could remember. Although I had sought out every bit of minutiae I could find about him from his Civil War pension file, I had never seen or heard of a picture of my great-grandfather until that day. I had to find that picture; I had to know what he looked like.

Since none of Joel's children were still living, I asked my mother's first cousins, his other grandchildren, if they knew anything about the portrait's location—no one did. Knowing that his widow had lived with my grandfather and his second family just before she died, I asked both my step-uncles and their wives about any photos. They recalled from their childhoods seeing a picture of Joel, but a search of their inherited family photos did not turn up one. My aunt provided an important clue, however: before moving in with her son, Joel's widow had lived with her grandson and his family, and they might know something about a photo. I located the grandson's widow by using an Internet telephone directory and called her to ask if she had ever seen a picture of her husband's grandfather. To my surprise and delight, she replied, "Sure—I have one of him with his wife and family." At a pre-arranged meeting with this relative, she provided a copy of a circa-1903 photograph of my great-grandparents, their nephews, and two of their sons, including my grandfather as an infant.

Searching the Internet for Family Photographs

If you have talked to or corresponded with every family member you know and you still haven't unearthed the photograph you want, it's time to turn to the Internet. There's no telling how many millions of pictures appear on the World Wide Web. Even if you cannot find a portrait of your ancestor, chances are very good that you will locate a few digitized photos or drawings of something relevant to this ancestor— his church, school, business, courthouse, community, or even his tombstone.

Google is a good starting place for image searches on the Internet. When you access *www.google.com*, click the Image tab just above the search field and type in the search phrase. Use the same kind of phrases that you use to search Google for Web sites. Figure 15.1 shows the image search results for the query *"Daniel Boone,"* which includes about 1,680 portraits, photos of statues, and miscellaneous images somehow related to Daniel Boone—even a map of a hunting area named for Daniel Boone in Missouri. Of course, you probably won't find this many images by searching for your ancestor's name unless he or she was equally prominent, but it's worth a try.

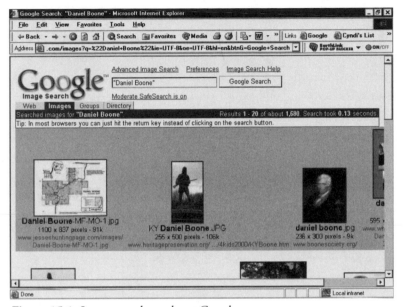

Figure 15.1 Image search results at Google

Searching for images of the community where an ancestor lived can reap great rewards—photos, maps, scanned newspaper articles, and more. A search of Google images for *"Powhatan County"* + *Virginia* brings up forty-four results, including these:

- 1895 Powhatan County map from the 1895 Atlas on the Livingston County, Michigan GenWeb page *(www.livgenmi.com/powhatanVA.htm)*

- Portrait on the Alabama State Archives Web site of Napoleon Lockett, born in Powhatan County 24 February 1813, who became a prominent attorney in Marion, Alabama *(www.archives.state.al.us/marschall/N_Lockett.html)*

- Photograph of a young John Singleton Mosby, born in Powhatan, who became the leader of Mosby's Rangers in the Civil War *(www.mosbysrangers.com/bio/bio1.htm)*

- Several photographs of modern homes or farms for sale in Powhatan County

An 1895 map of an ancestor's county could be a boon to research, and knowing that the famous Colonel John Mosby hailed from the area adds to an understanding of the area's history. If you are researching the Lockett family, you might feel incredibly lucky to find a portrait of a family member who moved off from Powhatan County and managed to get his portrait in the Alabama State Archives collection. Even the modern images are helpful to a researcher's understanding of an ancestor's community since they show a hilly and wooded terrain with lakes and streams.

Going back a little further in history and "jumping the pond," I locate the Images of England Web site *(www.imagesofengland.org.uk/search/basicsrch.asp),* where the Images of England project is building a digital library of some 370,000 listed English Heritage properties (similar to the U.S. Registered Historical Landmarks). These include public buildings, churches, even tombs. St. Mary's Church in Corscombe, Dorset, is shown in Figure 15.2.

Figure 15.2 Church photo at Images of England

Genealogists are usually generous people, willing to share information and finds, including photographs. The AncientFaces site *(www.ancientfaces.com)* shows the results of successful sharing of family and military photos. It also offers a section devoted to mystery photos of unidentified people whom the owners wish to identify.

Search the AncientFaces database for names or keywords, or just browse the photos by surname or category (Civil War, weddings and anniversaries, etc.).

AncientFaces is a great place to share or find military photographs of comrades in arms, such as the Vietnam-era search results in Figure 15.3. If everyone posted photos like the unidentified World War II Navy group photos my father left me, thousands of people could help identify the subjects.

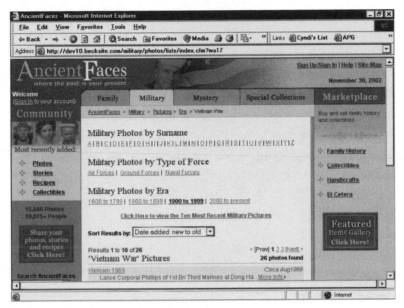

Figure 15.3 Photo results at AncientFaces

Identifying Ancestral Photographs

Most people inherit photos that include some people they do not recognize or know. My cousin showed up at my house one day with a box of old pictures that he inherited upon our grandfather's death. We sat cross-legged on the floor and waded through photos that had postcard backs on them, pictures of women in long dresses, images of men with handlebar mustaches—none of whom we knew. I suspected that they had belonged to our great-grandmother, Naomi, and that they might be pictures of her children or her brothers' and sisters' families, but I needed help.

If you, too, need help figuring out who those mysterious strangers in your photo album are, try a simple Google search like *identifying old photographs*. The results lead

Finding Photographs on the Internet

Historic photographs abound, in collections from the Library of Congress to the National Archives to private institutions. You can use the Internet to locate photographs, but you may have to order copies the old-fashioned way—through the mail.

As more and more digital collections are placed on the Web, you'll be able to find the actual photos you want. Here are a few sites that can help, either with finding aids, still photographs, or digitized images:

- eBay (look at the Collectibles category for images) *(www.ebay.com)*
- Library of Congress American Memory Collection *(memory.loc.gov/ammem/amhome.html)*
- NARA—Guide to the Holdings of the Still Picture Branch *(www.archives.gov/research_room/media_formats/still_pictures_guide.html)*
- U.S. Army Military History Center at Carlisle Barracks (searchable database of Civil War photographs that can be ordered) *(carlisle-www.army.mil/usamhi/PhotoDB.html)*

you to Web sites that offer advice and techniques for pinning down the date a photo was made. Knowing a time helps narrow down your possible subjects. The City Gallery site *(www.city-gallery.com)* offers downloadable forms to help identify and date old photographs. An article by Diane VanSkiver Gagel, "Historic Photography: Identification and Preservation," details various photographic processes and the years they were used. Originally published in *Ancestry's* November/December 1997 issue, the article is now available online at *www.ancestry.com/library/view/ancmag/759.asp.*

Scrapbooking and Preservation

Photographs are precious heirlooms that we hope last well beyond our lifetimes. Their longevity depends on how you handle and care for them. Be careful not to touch the images since your hands can leave harmful oils on them. Instead, handle the photos by their edges. Don't buy so-called bargain photo albums and risk the acid in their leaves destroying your images. Pay a little more for acid-free or archival-quality albums that will preserve your keepsakes.

With the recent boom in scrapbooking, it is easy to find good storage albums and

Help Among the Collaterals

Many new hobbyists say, "I don't care about those other people; I'm interested in tracing only my direct family line." Of course, we are more interested in our own great-grandparents than in their siblings and the descendants of their siblings—those other relatives known as *collateral lines*. But especially when looking for family papers or memorabilia, it is essential that you fan out and search among all descendants of an ancestor. You never know which child may have inherited the Bible or the old Revolutionary War rifle from your third great-grandfather back in Virginia—and to whom it was passed on.

Some years ago, I was given a photograph of a large family obviously dressed for a solemn event in the early 1900s, with a few handwritten names on the back—enough for me to surmise that it was a picture of my Tibbs great-great-grandparents and their children's families in Metcalfe County, Kentucky. I despaired of ever knowing the exact circumstances of the photo or the identities of everyone in it. A few years later, while researching my great-grandmother's collateral lines, I contacted her sister's great-great-granddaughter in California. My newfound third cousin, once removed, had a copy of the same photograph, and hers identified it as having been taken on the funeral day of the family's patriarch, Henry Tibbs. Furthermore, her copy identified people in the photo that mine did not; between us, we were able to identify almost every person in the family portrait. If I had foregone researching collateral lines, I would not have discovered this new information, verified a hunch, or come to know a distant relative who has become a close friend.

decorations to enhance your albums and scrapbooks. In fact, a Google search for *scrapbooking* yields more than two hundred thousand results, and *archival supplies* yields about seventy-nine thousand, so you should have no trouble finding ideas and supplies.

The National Archives and Records Administration is tasked with preserving our nation's history, so it is a natural place to turn for information about preservation. The NARA Caring for Your Family Archives Web page *(www.archives.gov/preservation/caring_for_your_family_archives.html)* answers questions about preserving family papers, choosing a good album, attaching photos or memorabilia to album or scrapbook pages, removing photos that have already been improperly placed in black-paper or self-stick albums, and digitizing photo collections.

Read All about It!

In the days before radio and television, our ancestors read newspapers for current events coverage, entertainment, and local news. Newspapers are still a good way to keep abreast of the happenings in an old hometown or the deaths of distant relatives throughout the country. Many newspapers today have a Web site with recent stories, obituaries, nostalgia or history articles, and advertisements. Most feature a search mechanism for the paper's online archives, although sometimes a paid subscription is required to access an article in a newspaper's archives.

Browsing Current Newspapers

To find modern newspapers, use a springboard such as Online Newspapers.com *(www.onlinenewspapers.com)*, which links to newspapers in all fifty states and many countries of the world. Newspaper Links *(www.newspaperlinks.com)* is a springboard to U.S. daily and weekly newspapers, Canadian and international newspapers, and college newspapers around the world. It also links to newspaper archives on the Web, newspaper groups like Pulitzer Inc. or Community Newspapers Inc., state press associations, and media organizations such as Associated Press or the Freedom Forum. The Internet Public Library *(www.ipl.org/div/news)* offers extensive links to newspapers from Algeria to Wyoming.

Newspapers such as the *New York Times* or the *Washington Post* often present material of interest to a much broader audience than just regional readers. For instance, poignant obituaries and stories about victims of the 11 September 2001 terror attacks on New York and Washington appeared regularly in these publications during 2001 and 2002. Read and search the *New York Times* online version at *www.nytimes.com* free of charge. But only articles from the last seven days and reviews back to 1996 are free; other "premium archive" articles back to 1996 can be purchased online. The *Washington Post* online archives date back to 1977; payment is required to access articles older than two weeks.

Locating Old Newspapers

Genealogists are usually more interested in newspapers that reflect the era in which their ancestors lived. The Internet does not disappoint in this realm, either. Researchers can find actual scanned images of old newspaper articles on specialty sites and at USGenWeb and RootsWeb. At the very least, you can find online newspaper indexes, which lead you to the original newspapers in collections across the country or around the world.

To find an online index, try a Google search using a phrase similar to *historical newspaper index + CCC* or *historical newspaper index + Arkansas*. Resulting hits provide links that lead you on a merry exploration of Internet resources, some free and some requiring paid membership or access through a library or institution. Be sure to check with your local library or university to see whether they offer access to any online historical newspapers or indexes.

Many newspapers of the past, some from as long ago as the eighteenth century, have been microfilmed and can be viewed at your public library, Family History Center, or even the newspaper office itself. To locate regional collections, query a search engine for a phrase similar to *historical newspaper + Missouri*. That particular search reveals an article at the State Historical Society of Missouri Web site *(www.system.missouri.edu/shs/newscardfiles.html)* giving details of its own collection of microfilmed Missouri newspapers as early as 1808 and links to the St. Louis Mercantile Library *(www.umsl.edu/mercantile),* custodian of the clippings file of the now-defunct *St. Louis Globe-Democrat*. Similar results for the area you are researching can lead you to newspaper resources of the past that will aid in your research.

The Fairfax County (Virginia) Library provides an article at *www.co.fairfax.va.us/library/virginia/varoom/newsindx/using.htm#form* about its online index of eight local historical newspapers, explaining how newspapers are indexed and how searchable newspaper index databases are built.

Reading Old Newspapers Online

The race is on to digitize newspapers of the past and make them available to researchers and interested readers. Every day, more images of historical newspapers appear on the Internet, making it easier for genealogists to do armchair research at home.

The British Columbia Digital Library *(bcdlib.tc.ca/links-subjects-newspapers.html)* describes and provides links for current and historical digitized newspaper collections around the world.

The NewspaperArchive.com site *(www.newspaperarchive.com)* provides a free searchable database of scanned newspapers, currently at least one newspaper in fifteen states and one Canadian province. You can search by keyword, and narrow the search by newspaper, date range, or exact date. Clicking on any search result link brings up a thumbnail image of the text with a miniature image of the entire page (see Figure 15.4). You

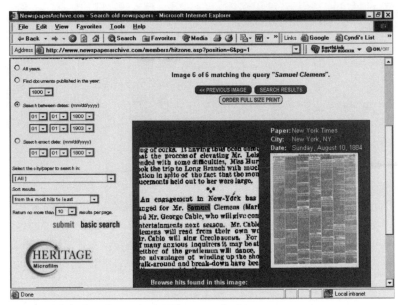

Figure 15.4 Search result at NewspaperArchive

can pay to receive a full-sized acid-free paper image of the entire page, or you can pay to subscribe as a full member to receive online access to all newspapers at this site.

TheOldenTimes.com *(theoldentimes.com)* is a unique free Web site with scanned images of newspaper obituaries, marriage notices, hotel guest lists, old advertisements or cartoons, and other items of interest. It partially covers areas of the United States, Australia, England, Scotland, and Ireland from 1788 to 1920.

One helpful feature of the TheOldenTimes.com site is that it categorizes a news item under the state it was about or from. For example, the item shown in Figure 15.5 was originally published in the *Denison (Texas) Daily News*, but it describes an incident in Santa Fe, New Mexico, that occurred in April 1880 when one William Robinson shot a policeman named Sunday, knocking off two of his fingers, whereby Sunday returned fire, killing Robinson (who was intoxicated). A researcher might not think to look in Texas for information about this incident that occurred in New Mexico, but it was easy to find in TheOldenTimes.com New Mexico news section.

One of Ancestry.com's recent additions is a series of fully searchable digitized historical newspapers from across America. You can search this database free of charge at *www.ancestry.com/search/rectype/periodicals/news*, but you cannot view the search

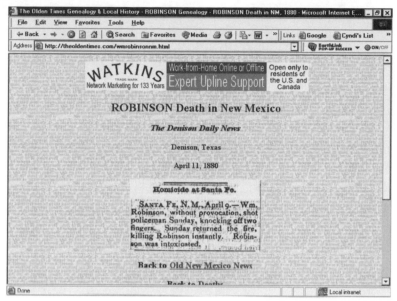

Figure 15.5 Death item at TheOldenTimes.com

results at home unless you have a paid subscription for this service. Check to see whether your local library has a subscription to the service so you can access it free at the library.

Viewing Online Obituaries

One of the best genealogical uses of newspapers is finding obituaries. Chapter 6 covers vital records, including death records. Obituaries are published records of deaths, usually giving the deceased's name, date and place of birth, date and place of death, and burial place. Often, modern obituaries also provide information about the person's spouse and children, listing the names of survivors and those already deceased. Obituaries of the past were not as informative; sometimes they were no more than a terse paragraph informing readers of the death of the person and little else. Still, to a genealogist, any record is better than none. Obituary transcription or indexing projects abound on the Internet.

The Rutherford B. Hayes Presidential Center obituary index *(index.rbhayes.org)* is an example of an easy-to-use index that provides clear instructions on how to obtain copies of obituaries. It catalogs obituaries and death notices, mostly from the Northwest Ohio region, from the 1830s to the present. A search of the surname Hennessey results in nine

Some Obituary Links

Try some of these Web sites to find online published obituaries:

- Legacy.com (links to online U.S. newspaper obituaries) (*www.legacy.com/LegacySubPage1.asp?Page=SelectNewspapers*)

- Legacy.com (links to online Canadian newspaper obituaries) (*www.legacy.com/LegacySubPage1.asp?Page=SelectNewspapersCanada*)

- National Obituary Archive (*www.arrangeonline.com*)

- Obits.com, the Internet Obituary Network (*www.obituary.com*)

- Obituary Central (numerous links to all kinds of obituary resources) (*www.obitcentral.com*)

hits, as shown in Figure 15.6. Clicking on the details link beside Mary Hennessey's name brings up the particulars of the obituary items available for her (see Figure 15.7). To see the source newspaper for the obituary, I click on the source link and learn that item one was obtained from the *Fremont Journal.* The obituary can be ordered online from the Hayes Presidential Center by charging the fee to a credit card, or it can be ordered by mailing a check and details to the Hayes Presidential Center.

The Obituary Daily Times *(www.rootsweb.com/~obituary)* is a free daily index of published obituaries. For a list of the many U.S. publications indexed in the Obituary Daily Times database, see *www.rootsweb.com/~obituary/publications.html.* You can subscribe to the Obituary Daily Times's mail list to receive daily distribution or you can search its database at *obits.rootsweb.com/cgi-bin/obit.cgi.*

I want more information about my husband's aunt, who we heard had passed away in Michigan. We know only that her maiden name was Ruth Porter and that she had lived somewhere near Muskegon, Michigan. Taking a chance, I search the Obituary Daily Times for *Ruth Porter MI* (the index uses the postal abbreviation MI for Michigan). The search results, shown in Figure 15.8, provide this listing:

DEGROAT, Ruth Marie (PORTER); 70; Twin Lake MI; Muskegon Chron; 1997-1-15; carolann

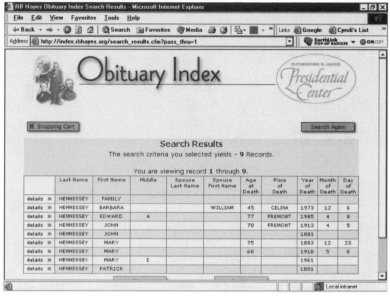

Figure 15.6 Search results at Rutherford B. Hayes Presidential Center obituary index

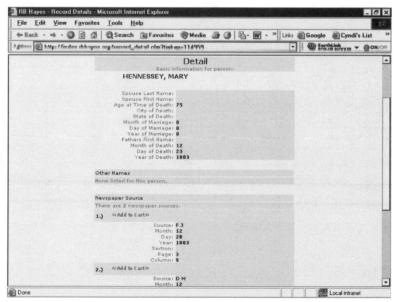

Figure 15.7 Obituary index details for Mary Hennessey

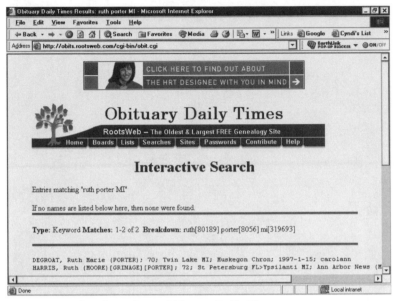

Figure 15.8 Search results at Obituary Daily Times

That is, an obituary for Ruth Marie (Porter) DeGroat, age seventy, of Twin Lake, Michigan, appeared in the *Muskegon Chronicle*'s 15 January 1997 issue, and this index item had been submitted by a volunteer known as "carolann."

The Obituary Daily Times does not have copies of the many obituaries indexed at its site—it simply provides the one- or two-line index entry. The rest is up to you. I am thrilled to learn the newspaper and date of Ruth's obituary. Now I can contact a library or genealogical society in Muskegon to request a copy of the actual obituary.

Getting to know your ancestors is not just about gathering their vital facts. Finding photographs of family members, old home places, or businesses round out your family's history, and newspapers of their era provide rich details about lives that were more than dates on a tombstone. Even browsing contemporary newspapers holds rewards for genealogists, allowing instant access to obituaries of distantly related kin.

CHAPTER 16

Sharing with Others

TO PARAPHRASE A FAMOUS QUOTE, "NO GENEALOGIST IS AN ISLAND."
When you consider that the number of your ancestors doubles with each generation—that is, you have two parents, four grandparents, eight great-grandparents, sixteen great-greats, and so on—odds are good that you are related within some degree
to someone else looking for the same ancestors. Once you've gathered everything you
can from relatives and sources near you, turn to the Internet for further clues.

Joining a Genealogy Mailing List

You can learn a lot by joining a mailing list for the surname, topic, or geographic area
you are researching; thousands of lists are available for genealogists. List participants
send e-mail messages that everyone else on the list receives. Subscribing is as simple as
sending a message to the list administrator—and it is free. You can subscribe in list
mode and receive individual messages as other subscribers post them. But on a busy
list, this can become overwhelming, so you may want to subscribe in digest mode and
receive all the messages in one digest message periodically (usually once a day).

How do you know which lists relate to your interests? I am researching the
Westmoreland and Tibbs families during the Civil War in Metcalfe County,
Kentucky. To learn about those topics, I subscribe to Westmoreland and Tibbs sur-
name lists, a South-Central Kentucky mailing list that covers Metcalfe County, a
Kentucky Civil War list, and several others that relate to my research.

How can I use these lists? I have little information about my great-great-grandfather, Henry Tibbs, before his 1858 Barren County, Kentucky marriage to Arminta Smith and his service in the Civil War from Metcalfe County. Some evidence suggests that Henry's father was actually a man named Nathaniel Parrish and that Henry's stepmother was Nancy Tibbs Parrish. Posting a message to the mailing list for South-Central Kentucky, which covers both Metcalfe and Barren counties, reaches a large audience that may have answers to some of my questions about the Tibbs or Parrish families.

I can also post a message about Henry's Civil War regiment and company to the Kentucky Civil War list, in hopes of contacting other people researching the same unit. We may be able to pool our resources and share our ancestors' records to learn new facts.

Mailing lists aren't just about asking for something; they're also about giving back to the community. If I recently reviewed Henry's Civil War pension file and found supporting statements from his comrades or medical reports from area physicians, I can post this to several mailing lists: to the Tibbs surname list because it is directly relevant to Tibbs research, to the South-Central Kentucky list because it relates to other people who lived in the community during Henry's time, and to the Kentucky Civil War list because it concerns military service during the Civil War. The same message can be e-mailed to all three lists at the same time, sharing some potentially helpful information with several hundred other genealogists.

Searching or browsing a list's archives is a good way to acquaint yourself with the kinds of questions and answers other subscribers are sharing. (You'll learn more about that later in this chapter.) Feel free to lurk quietly in the background when you first join the list, until you understand how it works.

Finding a Mailing List

Ready to jump in? To find a genealogy mailing list for an area or topic, try searching for a phrase similar to *"Wayne County Missouri" "genealogy mailing list."* Some of the following sources should help you find the lists that are right for you.

Genealogy Resources on the Internet
Chris Gaunt's and John Fuller's Genealogy Resources on the Internet Web page *(www.rootsweb.com/~jfuller/internet.html)* explains mailing lists and Usenet newsgroups and provides an inventory of many available genealogy mailing lists. The

Standards for Sharing Information with Others
Recommended by the National Genealogical Society

Conscious of the fact that sharing information or data with others, whether through speech, documents or electronic media, is essential to family history research and that it needs continuing support and encouragement, responsible family historians consistently:

- Respect the restrictions on sharing information that arise from the rights of another as an author, originator or compiler; as a living private person; or as a party to a mutual agreement

- Observe meticulously the legal rights of copyright owners, copying or distributing any part of their works only with their permission, or to the limited extent specifically allowed under the law's "fair use" exceptions

- Identify the sources for all ideas, information, and data from others, and the form in which they were received, recognizing that the unattributed use of another's intellectual work is plagiarism

- Respect the authorship rights of senders of letters, electronic mail, and data files, forwarding or disseminating them further only with the sender's permission

- Inform people who provide information about their families as to the ways it may be used, observing any conditions they impose and respecting any reservations they may express regarding the use of particular items

- Require some evidence of consent before assuming that living people are agreeable to further sharing of information about themselves

- Convey personal identifying information about living people—like age, home address, occupation, or activities—only in ways that those concerned have expressly agreed to

- Recognize that legal rights of privacy may limit the extent to which information from publicly available sources may be further used, disseminated, or published

- Communicate no information to others that is known to be false, or without making reasonable efforts to determine its truth, particularly information that may be derogatory

- Are sensitive to the hurt that revelations of criminal, immoral, bizarre, or irresponsible behavior may bring to family members

site briefly describes the purpose of each mailing list and provides instructions for subscribing.

RootsWeb Mailing Lists

The oldest and largest free genealogy site on the Web, RootsWeb *(www.rootsweb.com)* offers more than twenty-four thousand genealogy mailing lists—from surnames to places to topics such as immigration, fraternal organizations, the military, or religion. Go to the RootsWeb Mailing Lists page *(lists.rootsweb.com)* for an inventory of all available lists; then click on a list name to view details about it, to subscribe to it (or unsubscribe from it if you change your mind later), or to search or browse the list's archives of past messages.

Searching RootsWeb Mailing List Archives

To search the archives of past messages for any RootsWeb mailing list, access *searches2.rootsweb.com/cgi-bin/listsearch.pl.* Family historians around the world have sent millions of messages to genealogy mailing lists seeking or sharing information about their surnames and ancestors. Most mailing lists have online archives of all past messages, and you can search these for a name, place, or topic. For example, I am researching the Hatcher surname in Cumberland County, Virginia, so I search the VACUMBER (Cumberland County) mailing list archives on RootsWeb. I find the surname Hatcher and some relevant information in several messages on that list.

Figure 16.1 shows the typical search screen for any RootsWeb mailing list archive. This search of the Hatcher surname mailing list archive for my ancestor Drury Hatcher turns up four e-mails mentioning him in 2002 alone (see Figure 16.2). One of these provides a Web site URL for a Hatcher Families Resource Center where I can search for more information. Of course, this convinces me to subscribe and contact others on the Hatcher surname mailing list. Be sure to search the archives of relevant mailing lists when you begin your genealogical search—or any time you begin work on a new family or area.

CataList Catalog of LISTSERV Lists

Some genealogy mailing lists are hosted by public LISTSERV sites on the Internet. To find a list of interest, access the online CataList catalog at *www.lsoft.com/catalist.html* and enter the word *genealogy* as a search term. You then see an inventory of all

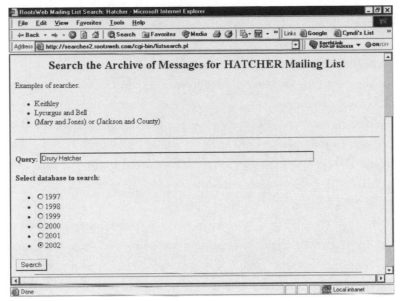

Figure 16.1 Mailing list search for Hatcher surname

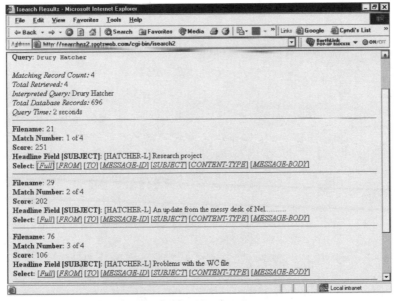

Figure 16.2 Mailing list results for Hatcher surname

LISTSERV mailing lists with *genealogy* in the list name or list title. Click on a list name to see a description and instructions for subscribing.

FamilySearch Internet Collaboration E-mail Lists

The FamilySearch Web site also offers free surname and subject mailing lists at *www.familysearch.org/Eng/Share/Collaborate/frameset_share.asp*. The first time you access this feature, you have to create a unique user name and password to identify yourself. Then you may search all the mailing lists by keyword to find one for your surname or topic. You can also create a new list if you don't find what you're looking for.

The AfriGeneas Community

This site devoted to African-American genealogy *(www.afrigeneas.com/community)* features a Community section with mailing lists relating to general African-ancestored research; to African-American genealogy in several states; and to special topics, such as slave research or black Smoky Mountain families in eastern Tennessee or western North Carolina. Click on the AfriGeneas mailing list link to move to a page on Mississippi State University's Majordomo Web site with instructions for subscribing to the list. Because the AfriGeneas special-interest mailing lists are available through Yahoo! Groups, you have to provide a unique user name and password and create a profile the first time you subscribe to one.

Learning Computer Terminology

If you don't know what *smileys* or *emoticons* are and computer terminology stumps you, use an online Internet dictionary, such as NetLingo *(www.netlingo.com)* or the Free Online Dictionary of Computing (FOLDOC) *(foldoc.doc.ic.ac.uk/foldoc/index.html)*.

Using Genealogy Message Boards or Bulletin Boards

You've probably seen the bulletin board in your local grocery store where people tack up notices—"missing Labrador Retriever," "want to buy 1965 Ford Mustang," or "need babysitting services." They're hoping to find someone with information or services that they need. A genealogy message board, sometimes called a bulletin board or forum, is simply an online community gathering place where you can post a message, respond to someone's request for information, or learn more about a topic.

Message boards are different from mailing lists because messages stay posted on a bulletin board for everyone to see and because you have to remember to go to the message board to find new messages. Most boards, however, will forward an e-mail with responses to your posting or will at least notify you that a response has been posted. You can follow a posting thread to read the original message and all responses to it.

A **thread** is a chain of postings about a particular topic, usually linked by the subject line of the message. You can follow a thread by moving from one posted message to the next.

Improve the odds that someone will respond to your posting on a message board by making sure that your message subject is clear and descriptive. *Smith family* probably won't get as many results as *Allen Smith family, 1830s, Barren County, Kentucky.* Make it easy for someone to see at a glance what information you seek.

For example, when I search the Parks Family Genealogy Forum at GenForum for *Thomas Jefferson Parks*, I get thirty-three matches. One message, from 6 December 1999 (shown in Figure 16.3), shows the Thomas Jefferson Parks I am seeking in a family with siblings, parents, and grandparents. This information was provided by a descendant who was requesting information about the grandparents. Two other descendants responded to this message. While this information is not documented, it at least presents a possible family for T. J. Parks, and it's worth a follow-up message to the other three descendants working on this same family line.

Free bulletin boards abound on the Internet, from large ones such as GenConnect to smaller ones sponsored by individuals on their Web pages. Some Internet and e-mail service providers, such as America Online, Prodigy, and CompuServe, offer genealogy bulletin boards for their customers. Consult your provider's online help for information about its bulletin boards. To find a message board on a particular topic, try a Google search for a phrase similar to *Wilcox message board* or *"Mexican*

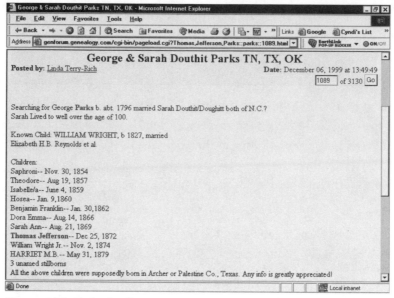

Figure 16.3 Parks family message at GenForum

War" message board. Here are a few of the larger genealogy message boards to get you started.

GenForum

Sponsored by Genealogy.com, GenForum *(www.genforum.genealogy.com)* provides message boards, also called forums, for surnames, regional, and general topics. When you enter a forum, messages are arranged by date, with the most recent ones appearing first. You can browse all the messages, search for messages that contain a specified name or phrase, post a new or follow-up message, or print any message.

RootsWeb Message Boards

The site at *boards.ancestry.com*, hosted by Ancestry.com, combines RootsWeb's former GenConnect message boards with Ancestry.com's message boards. There are message boards for various surnames, localities, or topics. Many messages posted to RootsWeb message boards are also gatewayed (forwarded) to the corresponding RootsWeb mailing lists. For example, if you subscribe to the Smith mailing list and someone posts a query on the Smith message board, you may receive an e-mail from the Smith mailing list with the message board posting.

Finding Your Family Tree on the Web

Perhaps you've heard that everyone's family tree is out on the Web, on a CD-ROM, or in some library. That's just not so! Still, as millions of people become involved in tracing their family trees and sharing the information they gather, great numbers of family tree files *are* available on the Internet. Chances are good that you'll find at least some portion of your family's information at one of the many family tree sites on the Web.

But you must heed two warnings when seeking information about your ancestors and family: (1) not everything printed in a book is a fact and (2) just because someone placed your family tree on the Internet doesn't mean all the information is verified and true. Many genealogists are conscientious researchers who take care to ensure that their information is backed by factual sources. But I'd be wealthy if I had a dime for every time I've heard someone say, "I don't need to cite sources and verify facts—this information is just for my family, and no one else will ever see it anyway." Then a niece or cousin submits those files to a family tree Web site, and suddenly those unverified tidbits become hardcore facts to people who view them.

You will undoubtedly find many valuable clues in family files on the Internet; just be sure to check the facts and verify the sources before you tell everyone you're descended from George Washington. (George and Martha left no joint descendants.)

On the other hand, even though there are drawbacks to believing everything you see in a family tree on the Web, there are also numerous benefits to sifting through the information. You may be fortunate enough to find a well-documented family file that takes one line of your family back many generations. All you have to do is tie into that line, and you have a good deal of your ancestry chart completed. Perhaps you are one of the many Americans related to a U.S. president or a founding father or a patriot who served in the Revolutionary War. Your family history efforts are made easier by the already-completed work of others—work you can use in your own family tree. Even when you find questionable or undocumented genealogies online, you can use the clues in them to find solid information that verifies or disclaims the results.

So go ahead and look. On most free sites, you can view family trees, then print them or download them as GEDCOM files for importing into your own genealogy program. Fee-based sites provide instructions for accessing or purchasing the file, CD, or publication that contains the information you find.

Family tree Web sites appear all over the Web. Thousands of Internet users have personal Web pages where they've posted their family trees. Try searching for a phrase like

GEDCOM stands for **GEnealogical Data COMmunication,** and is simply a file format that allows users to share genealogical data between programs. Most genealogy database programs today are GEDCOM-compatible, meaning that other genealogy programs can read their files and vice-versa.

Taylor family tree, and then follow the links that result. Narrow the search further by adding a locale—*Taylor family tree "Jefferson County" Alabama.* The following handy tools help you search several Web sites to find family trees that may include your ancestors.

GENDEX

The GENDEX site *(www.gendex.com/gendex)* provides an index to thousands of Internet family tree databases, from large databases like Ancestry World Tree to a single family on a personal Web page. Use GENDEX to find and view those of interest to you. You can access this service as an unregistered (free) user, but more search and display options and a faster response time are available to registered (paid) users.

FamilyTreeSearcher.com

FamilyTreeSearcher.com *(www.familytreesearcher.com)* is a free search tool that helps you search from one location for some of the biggest family tree Web sites. You enter an ancestor's name and identifying information and then search several paid and free family tree sites, all from within FamilyTreeSearcher's site.

Geneanet

Geneanet genealogical database *(www.Geneanet.org)* intends to set up a universal register of the world's genealogical resources, both paid and free. Results for name searches include individual family Web pages, commercial sites, and databases around the world.

How Do Family Tree Sites Work?

The Internet offers huge numbers of family tree sites. There just isn't room in this one book to show you how each individual site works, but most are similar. They allow

Genealogy Numbering Systems

Ahnantafel translates from German as *ancestor table* and consists of an easy way to number a list of your ancestors. The number 1 is assigned to you, your father is 2, your mother is 3, your paternal grandfather is 4, paternal grandmother 5, maternal grandfather 6, maternal grandmother 7, and so on. Notice that except for the first person, all male ancestors are assigned even numbers and female ancestors are assigned odd numbers.

The **register system** is a method of recording a descending genealogy originated by the New England Historic Genealogical Society. It uses three numbers—a generation number, a birth-order number, and an identifying number. But no identifying number is given to a person whose line is not subsequently carried on in the genealogy.

The **NGS Quarterly System** (sometimes referred to as the **Modified Register System**) also uses three numbers and provides an identifying number whether or not the person's line is subsequently carried on. A plus mark in front of the number denotes a continuation of that line later in the report.

A **pedigree** or **ancestor report** is a list or chart of ancestors that may resemble a tree. It begins with an individual, moving upward or backward to two parents, four grandparents, eight great-grandparents, and so on. A pedigree or ancestor chart can go from the bottom upward on a page or from left to right.

For more information and examples of numbering systems for genealogy, refer to Helm's Genealogy Toolbox *(www.genealogytoolbox.com/numberingsystems.html)* or to *Numbering Your Genealogy: Basic Systems, Complex Families, and International Kin* by Joan Ferris Curran, CG; Madilyn Coen Crane; and John H. Wray, Ph.D., CG (Arlington, Virginia: National Genealogical Society, 1999); available from the NGS Bookstore *(www.ngsgenealogy.org/BookStore)*.

you to view, print, and download a family file and to contact the submitter of the file. Here are a few of the larger family tree Web sites.

Ancestry World Tree/RootsWeb WorldConnect

Recently combined with Ancestry World Tree *(www.ancestry.com/trees/awt)*, RootsWeb's WorldConnect project *(worldconnect.rootsweb.com)* now claims more than 200 million names and more than 2.5 million surnames in family trees submitted by users of these sites. Once you locate a family file of interest, you can view an index of all its names; view individual, descendancy, register, pedigree, or Ahnantafel reports; download a GEDCOM version of as much of the file as you want; or send an e-mail to the person who submitted the file.

Ancestry.com also offers a free genealogy program, Ancestry Family Tree, that you can download from the site *(aft.ancestry.com)*. This program simplifies your searches for ancestors in the Ancestry World Tree files. When you are connected to the Internet, the genealogy program automatically searches the Ancestry.com site for any matches to the persons in your family file. If you are an Ancestry.com subscriber, you can then access the family tree files and records and add them to your database in just a few steps.

Everton's Bureau of Missing Ancestors Database

Everton's Bureau of Missing Ancestors *(www.everton.com/search/advanced.php)* combines Everton databases (formerly, the Root Cellar, Family File, and Pedigree File) from research submissions over the past forty years. You must be a paying member of Everton's service to see details of family trees at this site.

FamilySearch Resources

The Church of Jesus Christ of Latter-day Saints (LDS) FamilySearch Web site *(www.familysearch.org)* provides two types of family tree files—Ancestral File and Pedigree Resource File. Ancestral File contributions were made in the past by submitting family files on disks to the LDS. Use Ancestral File to find pedigrees, family group sheets, and contact information for the submitter. You can view, print, or download a GEDCOM file of the data. Figure 16.4 shows a typical Ancestral File. To download it, click on the Download GEDCOM link just under the title Family Group Record.

FamilySearch Pedigree Resource File is a lineage-linked database of files submitted by individuals through FamilySearch. The online version allows you to search and display information from these records. The CD version includes more details, notes, and sources that were submitted with the files, and allows you to print charts and reports or to download the files to your genealogy program. The CD version can be used without charge at most LDS Family History Centers or can be purchased.

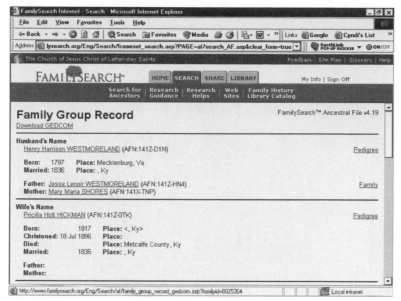

Figure 16.4 FamilySearch—Ancestral File Family Group Record

Genealogy.com Resources

Genealogy.com, maker of FamilyTreeMaker software, provides a variety of free and paid services. Here are two ways to obtain family tree files from this Web site:

- **Genealogy.com Family Home Pages:** Users of the site create free family home pages hosted on the Genealogy.com Web site. These family pages may contain a family tree, photographs, or other items. Access the Genealogy.com Family Home Page Search feature at *www.genealogy.com/users/index.html.* A search for a surname provides a listing of first names. Selecting a first name brings up a summary of search results for that name. Click on the link for Matches in Family Home Pages; then select any of the Genealogy.com Family Home Pages that appear in the list.

- **Genealogy.com World Family Tree:** FamilyTreeMaker and Genealogy.com have gathered submitters' family trees into their World Family Tree collection. When you search for a name in Genealogy.com's Family Finder *(www.genealogy.com/allsearch.html),* the summary of results shows matches in

World Family Tree. These family files, which include contact information for the contributors, are available online with a monthly or annual paid subscription, or for purchase on CD-ROMs.

Global Tree GenCircles

GenCircles *(www.gencircles.com)* offers unique SmartMatching technology. If an individual appears to be the same as someone in another GenCircles file, you can display the information side-by-side for comparison. Site users can also post messages on individuals in a file. This site is free, and so is registration. Registered users can upload their genealogy files, post messages in the clubs section, and use advanced features.

MyTrees.com

This Kindred Konnections paid subscription service *(www.kindredkonnections.com/index.html)* provides search capability for its pedigree-linked archive of member-submitted files. You can earn subscription services by sharing your own family tree.

Uploading and Downloading

When you find a family tree file that you want to add to your own genealogy program, you have to move it from that great big company's computer in Utah or California to your own little PC or Mac. The process of transferring data from another computer to yours over a communication link—such as your telephone modem or high-speed cable connection—is called **downloading.** There's nothing mysterious or scary about this process. You have control over the file that is copied from the other computer to yours, and you determine which directory on your hard drive it is copied into.

You may want to share your research by **uploading** it to one of the family tree projects on the Internet. Uploading is the opposite of downloading; you are copying a file from your computer to that big computer in another location over your Internet connection. The Web site you are sending the file to provides instructions for uploading or submitting a family tree file or a GEDCOM file. Just read the instructions on the Web site and follow the steps.

Sharing Your Research

Sharing is a big part of successful genealogical research. Our work would be very difficult if no one had indexed all those deed books or marriage records and published them to share with everyone. Likewise, many genealogists benefit from the sharing of family information. Many family tree Web sites encourage you to upload a GEDCOM version of your family history research for posting on the site. Be sure you remove information about living persons before you share your files on the World Wide Web for the entire world to see. You can use a utility program such as GEDClean *(www.raynorshyn.com/gedclean)* to remove information about living individuals from your GEDCOM files before submitting them.

Separating the Wheat from the Chaff

Most family researchers quickly become overwhelmed with the information available on the Internet. How do you judge which family tree is valid or whose research about your family is good? Before you believe every tidbit in that family tree back to Moses, let's talk a little about the *right* way to trace your family's history and to share the information you find.

Judging Your Sources

How do you know that the sixteen-generation tree you find on someone's Web site is accurate? Where did that person get the information, anyway? You often find varying names or dates on family trees available on the Internet, so you must learn to be a doubting Thomas. When two sources offer conflicting information, you have to decide which is more likely to be correct, based on whether the data came from a credible witness or source.

Let's evaluate the content of some family trees downloaded from the Internet. A search for Henry Westmoreland, born about 1797 in Virginia, son of Jesse Westmoreland, turns up several files online. Reports from RootsWeb's WorldConnect project, FamilySearch Ancestral File, and two FamilySearch Pedigree Resource Files submitted by different individuals are summarized in Figure 16.5.

Several similarities and differences jump out at us in this table. Three of the family trees provide Henry's middle name as Harrison, and three list his father as Jesse *Lenoir* Westmoreland and his mother as Mary Maria Shores. All concur with Henry's

Item	FamilySearch Ancestral File	FamilySearch Pedigree Resource File 1	FamilySearch Pedigree Resource File 2	RootsWeb WorldConnect
Last Name	Westmoreland	Westmoreland	Westmoreland	Westmoreland
Given Names	Henry Harrison	Henry	Henry Harrison	Henry Harrison
Father	Jesse Lenoir Westmoreland	Jesse Westmoreland	Jesse Lenoir Westmoreland	Jesse Lenoir Westmoreland
Mother	Mary Maria Shores	Maria (Molly) (Mary)	Mary Maria Shores	Mary Maria Shores
Birth Date	1797	1797	1797	1797
Birthplace	Mecklenburg, Va.		Mecklenburg Co., Va.	Mecklenburg, Va.
Death Date			1860	
Death Place			Albany, Clinton Co., Kentucky	
Wife 1	Priscilla Holt Hickman b. 1817 <Ky.> Christened 18 Jul 1896 Died Metcalfe County, Ky.	Priscilla Holt b. 1817 d. Feb 1880 Other husband: Martin Hickman	Priscilla Holt Hickman	Priscilla Holt Hickman b. 1817 in Kentucky d. 18 Jul 1896 in Metcalfe Co., Kentucky
Marriage Date 1	1836		1836	1836
Marriage Place 1	Ky.		Kentucky	Kentucky
Children of Marriage 1	1. Polly b. 1829 2. Mahalah b. 1841 3. Jesse M. b. 1845 4. Telitha b. 1849 5. Clementine b. 1850 6. Sarah b. 1839 7. Joel b. 1844 8. Hannah Hickman b. 1836 9. William Harrison b. 1843	1. Sarah b. 1839 2. Mahalah b. 1841 3. William Harrison b. 1843 4. Joel b. 1846 (44) 5. Jesse M. b. 1846 6. Telitha b. 1849 7. Clementine b. 18??		1. Sarah b. 1839 2. Polly b. 1836 3. Mahalah b. 1841 4. William Harrison b. 1843 5. Joel b. 1844 6. Jesse M. b. 1845 7. Telitha b. 1849 8. Clementine b. 1850

Figure 16.5 Summary of family tree Internet sources

Item	FamilySearch Ancestral File	FamilySearch Pedigree Resource File 1	FamilySearch Pedigree Resource File 2	RootsWeb WorldConnect
Wife 2	Sarah (b. abt 1801, Va.)		Sahah	
Marriage Date 2				
Marriage Place 2				
Children of Marriage 2			1. Telitha b. 1849 2. Sarah b. 1839 3. Mahala Jane b. 1841 4. William Harrison b. 1843 5. Joel b. 1844 6. Jesse N. b. 1846 7. Mary Clementine b. 1854	
Sources or Notes				1850 Fentress Co., Tennessee, District 1 Census, page 423, Roll Number 877. **Text:** Henry age 53, farmer. Pricie age 37. **Children:** Polly age 21 Hannah age 15 Sarah age 10 Mahalah age 9 Garrison age 7 Joel age 6 Jessi age 5 Tabitha age 1 Dwelling 641–641

Figure 16.5 Summary of family tree Internet sources *(continued)*

birth year of 1797, and three list the place as Mecklenburg or Mecklenburg County, Virginia. Three of the files provide information about only one marriage for Henry—to Priscilla Holt or Priscilla Holt Hickman. Only one mentions that Priscilla had another husband, Martin Hickman, while two report that Henry had another wife, Sarah or Sahah [*sic*]. One file lists nine children for Henry and Priscilla, one lists seven, and one lists eight. The children appear in varying order, though most submitters agreed about the children's birth years. However, one file lists at least seven of these children for Henry and Sahah [*sic*], rather than for Henry and Priscilla. Who is right? Who is wrong? What is true? What's a descendant to do?

We can probably contact the people who submitted these files—at least an e-mail address was available for each one. They may be able to tell us where they obtained the information they submitted, and they are probably distant cousins if they're researching our ancestors. But only one submitter included any sources or notes with the file. Perhaps it would be better to try to verify some of the alleged facts with a little research of our own.

Let's start with that 1850 census mentioned as a source in one of the files we downloaded. We can quickly view a digitized version of census records on the Internet if we have access to a paid subscription service offering the census. Or we may be able to use the subscription at a local library, free of charge. Using an online subscription, we do find an enumeration for Henry Westmoreland on page 423 of the 1850 U.S. census of Fentress County, Tennessee. However, there are discrepancies between the actual census image and the notes included in the WorldConnect family file we downloaded. Henry is actually listed in District 7 (not 1) and dwelling 640, family 640 (not 641). Figure 16.6 is an abstract of the census data for Henry Westmoreland's household, with extrapolated birth years based on the ages given on the date of the census, 2 October 1850.

The 1850 census was the first to list the name of every person in a family, but it does not provide relationships. This listing is not conclusive evidence that the persons listed on lines 18–25 are children of Henry and Priscilla. Because Prisci would have been only twelve or thirteen at Polly's birth, it's more likely that Polly is Henry's daughter by an earlier marriage. Prisci is a more reasonable age to be Hannah's mother, yet Hannah's surname is recorded as "ditto"—assuming Westmoreland. This does not support the Ancestral File tree that gives Hannah's surname as Hickman or the assumption that she is Prisci's daughter by a previous husband by the name of Hickman. Also, notice that Henry's birthplace is listed on the census as Tennessee.

Line Number	First Name	Last Name	Age	[Birth Year]	Sex	Occupation	Place of Birth	Persons over 20, Cannot Read or Write
16	Henry	Westmoreland	53	[1796–97]	M	Farmer	Tenn.	1
17	Prisci	Westmoreland	34	[1815–16]	F		Va.	1
18	Polly	Westmoreland	21	[1828–29]	F		Tenn.	
19	Hannah	Westmoreland	15	[1834–35]	F		Tenn.	
20	Sarah	Westmoreland	10	[1839–40]	F		Tenn.	
21	Mahalah	Westmoreland	9	[1840–41]	F		Tenn.	
22	Harrison	Westmoreland	7	[1842–43]	M		Tenn.	
23	Joel	Westmoreland	6	[1843–44]	M		Tenn.	
24	Jesse	Westmoreland	5	[1844–45]	M		Ky.	
25	Telitha	Westmoreland	1	[1848–49]	F		Ky.	

Figure 16.6 1850 census data for Henry Westmoreland household

Yes, the four files we downloaded can provide a jumpstart to our research on this family. But we must carefully sort the wheat from the chaff to judge the reliability of our sources. By all means, try to find and interpret the original source for yourself. In this case, our best evidence points to Tennessee as Henry's birthplace even though three of the four downloaded files list it as Virginia. Why? No documentation or sources back up the Virginia birthplace, but an image of the original census record clearly shows it as Tennessee. You may do further research and find that in other censuses or records, Henry's birthplace is listed as Virginia. But with just the evidence we currently have, Tennessee is the only reasonable judgment.

Citing Your Sources

Yes, you've already read in Chapter 2 about citing your sources. But some important points bear repeating. One common mistake that most beginning genealogists make is neglecting to record where they obtained information. We all have family group sheets or unidentified letters in our old files whose origins we simply don't remember now. Good researchers note a source for every date, every name, and every relationship they record. This needn't be long-winded or scientific—it should simply inform anyone else looking at the information how the researcher knows this fact and where someone else might find the same information.

Going back to the family tree files that we downloaded, we see the need for citing sources so others know where we got our information. Only one submitter of the files I found cited any sources, so for all we know, one person simply made up this information and passed it on to others until it spread all over the Internet and became set in stone. How much more valuable those downloaded family files would be if the sources were clearly defined as census records, mortality schedules, individual death certificates, cemetery transcription books, family Bible pages, tax lists, or simply as

Interview with Mary Wilcox (1471 Sproule Ave., St. Louis, MO 63139), by Pamela Boyer Porter, 3 August 1990. Transcript held in 1996 by Porter (1282 Whispering Pines Dr., St. Louis, MO 63146). Mrs. Wilcox is deceased.

How do you determine the source of a fact? That's easy—where did you get the information? The source of each family tree we downloaded for Henry Westmoreland is simply the person who supplied that family file.

Now, let's say that we combine the four family tree files we downloaded and the new facts we got from the online census image into one new file in our genealogy program. We'll then have five sources for the information in the new file—one citing each contributor of the four downloaded family trees, and a fifth citing the 1850 online census that we looked at ourselves. Ideally, each name, date, or fact you add to your files or database will have one or more sources. After all, you found that information *somewhere*, didn't you?

Being Considerate of Family Members

Just because you *can* easily print a photograph or report from someone's Web page doesn't mean you *should*. The golden rule certainly applies to genealogical research and sharing the results. Distant cousins can make much greater progress by working together on a given family's research. But in your enthusiasm for your newfound avocation, remember to be considerate of other family members.

Don't post or share names and birth dates of living people with commercial or free family tree sites. You would feel terrible if an unscrupulous person found your relative's maiden name and birth date on your Web site and used the information for criminal purposes. In an era when parents are advised not to display their child's name on a garment for safety reasons, is it safe to post a minor child's name, parents' names, and birth date on the Web?

Don't take a file given to you by a fellow researcher and share it with the entire world without at least asking permission. Yes, those names, dates, and facts may be public records available to anyone. But long-time researchers may have spent years of hard work ferreting out those items, carefully citing a source for each one, analyzing the dry facts to reach valid conclusions, and wrapping their own words around the dry data. It isn't right for anyone else to take that unique collection of family history and pass it on without even acknowledging its creator.

Along these same lines, don't take work from another's Web site or file, dump it into your database, and then represent it as your own work. Give credit where credit is due. Several years ago, I shared my entire paternal research database with a distant cousin with the intent of filling in our line in a print book he planned to publish. I have since seen several Web sites displaying this very family information, living members and all. How do I know this is the same information I provided? In addition to some unique identifying information in the files, they all have a glaring omission: two cousins and I were "pruned" from our own family because we were adopted by our stepfathers.

It's a heart-pounding experience when a family tree Web site search turns up a whole new tree of relatives and ancestors or a distantly related cousin living in the same town as you. Go ahead and be excited about adding to your extended family. But when you calm down a bit, remember to carefully evaluate what you have found before adding these folks to your family tree.

CHAPTER **17**

Now That You're Hooked . . .

IF YOU'VE READ THIS BOOK AND HAVE STARTED TO GATHER INFORMATION about your ancestors, you may want to know about a few other resources that can help you. If you've been researching your family for some years and have file cabinets full of interesting facts about your ancestors, now's the time to write that family history. Even if you have only a passing interest in genealogy, getting together with distant cousins can be fun—so organize a family reunion. This chapter will help you explore some activities related to your new obsession—er, hobby—a little more.

Take an Online Genealogy Course

Most people begin a new pursuit or hobby by taking a class or private lessons or by learning from a more experienced friend. Genealogy is no different. While it may be tempting to dive right in and look for your entire genealogy on the Internet, you may quickly become overwhelmed and confused. You won't know a census record from a deed. Better to start with an online course to learn the basics of genealogy.

Self-paced genealogy courses are available on the Internet, and prices vary from free to several hundred dollars. Enter a phrase like *online genealogy class* in an Internet search engine to find current courses about family history. Browse the Education category on Cyndi's List *(www.cyndislist.com/educate.htm)* or the guide to online genealogy lessons at About.com *(genealogy.about.com/cs/beginnerlessons)*. Here are a few sites that can help you get started.

275

Guidelines for Genealogical Self-Improvement and Growth
Recommended by the National Genealogical Society

Faced with ever-growing expectations for genealogical accuracy and reliability, family historians concerned with improving their abilities will on a regular basis

- Study comprehensive texts and narrower-focus articles and recordings covering genealogical methods in general and the historical background and sources available for areas of particular research interest, or to which their research findings have led them

- Interact with other genealogists and historians in person or electronically, mentoring or learning as appropriate to their relative experience levels, and through the shared experience contributing to the genealogical growth of all concerned

- Subscribe to and read regularly at least two genealogical journals that list a number of contributing or consulting editors, or editorial board or committee members, and that require their authors to respond to a critical review of each article before it is published

- Participate in workshops, discussion groups, institutes, conferences, and other structured learning opportunities whenever possible

- Recognize their limitations, undertaking research in new areas or using new technology only after they master any additional knowledge and skill needed and understand how to apply it to the new subject matter or technology

- Analyze critically at least quarterly the reported research findings of another family historian, for whatever lessons may be gleaned through the process

- Join and participate actively in genealogical societies covering countries, localities, and topics where they have research interests, as well as the localities where they reside, increasing the resources available both to themselves and to future researchers

- Review recently published basic texts to renew their understanding of genealogical fundamentals as currently expressed and applied

- Examine and revise their own earlier research in the light of what they have learned through self-improvement activities, as a means for applying their new-found knowledge and for improving the quality of their work-product

National Genealogical Society (NGS)

The National Genealogical Society *(www.ngsgenealogy.org)* offers several online courses, including an Introduction to Genealogy course that covers the basics, family and published sources, and vital records (births, deaths, marriages). Another of its popular online offerings is Using Census Records. Course fees are reasonable, and NGS offers a discount to its members.

In NGS's acclaimed, in-depth home-study course, American Genealogy: A Basic Course, you learn about census records, military sources, immigration and naturalization records, and much more. As with its online courses, NGS offers a discount to its members.

You might also benefit from the informative NGS Virtual Lecture Series *(www. ngsgenealogy.org/edu_virtuallectures.htm)* which is hosted at the About.com Web site *(genealogy.about.com/hobbies/genealogy)*. On scheduled dates and times, anyone who wants to participate can drop by the online chat room to read a presentation posted by an expert genealogist about a specific topic. The session then opens up for visitor questions and participation. For a list of upcoming topics, to read transcripts of past lectures, or to sign up for a newsletter, go to *genealogy.about.com/library/blngsgenealogy.htm*.

RootsWeb's Guide to Tracing Family Trees

RootsWeb, the oldest and largest free genealogy site on the Web, offers free guides *(rwguide.rootsweb.com)* by experts in the genealogical field on topics ranging from "Where to Begin?" to researching records of various ethnic or religious groups, military service, naturalization, courts, adoption, or orphans. Each guide provides detailed information about its topic, including links to more sources of information on the Web or in printed publications.

Genealogy.About.com's Introduction to Genealogy

About.com's genealogy guide *(genealogy.about.com/library/lessons/blintro.htm)* makes available a beginning genealogy course with self-grading quizzes, an interactive classroom where you can post comments and questions or interact with classmates, and some beginner resources, all free.

Genealogy.com Courses

Genealogy.com *(www.genealogy.com/university.html)* provides free courses on beginning genealogy, Internet genealogy, and tracing immigrant origins. Other lessons on this site explore the resources at Genealogy.com. These online classes are free, but since Genealogy.com is a commercial site, you may have to pay to access some of the resources that are described.

MyFamily.com Courses

MyFamily.com, parent company of Ancestry.com, provides four weeks of online independent study lessons and a thirty-day subscription to Ancestry.com databases. Check the MyFamily.com *(www.myfamily.com)* or Ancestry.com *(www.ancestry.com)* Web sites for current class topics and fees.

Union Institute and University, Vermont College

Learn family history online and earn undergraduate college credits or continuing education units with Vermont College's ten-week online classes at *www.tui.edu/ vermontcollege/templates/online_learning.php?article_id=32.* Topics range from Introduction to Family History, to Using Land Records in Your Research, to Understanding the British Isles in the 1600s. There is a fee for these classes.

Brigham Young University Independent Study

Brigham Young University's Independent Study division *(ce.byu.edu/is/site)* provides some free online courses as a starting point in family history and offers several low-fee personal enrichment classes in family history/genealogy. You can also enroll in an online college credit Certificate Program in Family History at BYU. Check the Web site for tuition costs.

National Institute for Genealogical Studies

In association with the Faculty of Information Studies at the University of Toronto, the National Institute for Genealogical Studies *(www.genealogicalstudies.com/eng/ gstudies.html)* offers a wide variety of fee-based online courses in American, Canadian, and other countries' records.

Genealogy Spot's Genealogy for Children

The Genealogy Spot site *(www.genealogyspot.com/features/kids.htm)* is one of many links to children's guides to genealogy, resources for children, and activities to aid in teaching genealogy to young students.

Join a Genealogical or Historical Society

If you're new to searching for your roots, you may not know that thousands of genealogical societies all over the world can help. Do yourself a favor: join one in your local area—even if none of your family or ancestors lived there. You'll meet some nice volunteers willing to share their expertise, and you'll learn about seminars, conferences, and events in your area just for genealogists. Consider, too, joining a society in the locale you are researching even if you can't attend events there. You'll receive the society's publications and learn about the surnames, history, and geography of the area, which is all part of finding your ancestors and filling in the details of their lives. Here are some sites to help you find a society you can join.

Genealogy Events

You know that wonderful feeling you get when you're around people who enjoy doing the same things that you do? You feel energized and are excited about doing more. You can get that feeling—and so much more—when you attend genealogy events. Most genealogical societies offer programs, seminars, or conferences lasting from an evening to several days. They feature lectures, workshops, vendors, and lots of camaraderie with fellow genealogists. On any given day, there's a genealogical society offering an educational opportunity. Look for the ones in your area. Several major national conferences take place every year, including ones sponsored by the National Genealogical Society (held in the spring), the NGS GENTECH Division (held in the winter), and the Federation of Genealogical Societies (held in the late summer or early fall). Attend these events, learn about genealogy, and get recharged from being around people who share your passion for family history—it's a great combination.

National Genealogical Society

Anyone can become a member of the nationwide genealogical community by joining the National Genealogical Society *(www.ngsgenealogy.org)*. Membership entitles you to receive NGS's topnotch publications—the *National Genealogical Society Quarterly* and the *NGS Newsmagazine*—and discounts on educational opportunities, events, and products.

Federation of Genealogical Societies (FGS) and Ancestry.com Society Hall

The Federation of Genealogical Societies *(www.fgs.org)* is an umbrella organization—a society made up of societies—that serves the needs of member organizations all over the United States. FGS and Ancestry.com developed a site called Society Hall *(www.familyhistory.com/societyhall/main.asp)* to provide an online comprehensive directory of genealogical and historical societies. Here you can search by keyword, city, state, or zip code to find a genealogical or historical society of interest, then read about its application process, membership fees and benefits, periodicals and publications, library, and meeting dates.

Cyndi's List—Societies and Groups

Cyndi's List always includes links to a wide variety of resources. To find a genealogical or historical society, fraternal organization, or other type of association, visit *www.cyndislist.com* and click the name of the state or country. Then click the Societies and Groups category to access a list of links to those organizations, similar to the resources shown for Ireland in Figure 17.1.

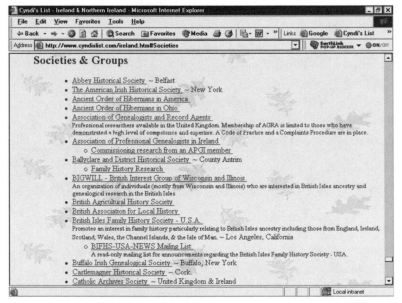

Figure 17.1 Cyndi's List—Societies and Groups

Write Your Family History

When you've been to countless archives, visited numerous old cemeteries to photograph tombstones, interviewed dozens of cousins, and gathered many of the details of your ancestors' lives, it's time to do something with all those papers. After all, someday your spouse will want to reclaim the dining room table that has been covered with three-foot-tall stacks of files ever since you started this ancestral quest. It's time to write your family history so that all your hard work isn't lost when you pass on.

First, decide how big a project you want. Will your book be a small monograph that you reproduce at the copy store or a multivolume hard-bound set that is typeset and printed by a professional printer? The answer often depends on your budget.

Gauge the response to your book so you know how many copies to print. The rule of thumb in printing is that the more copies you print, the less expensive each one is. But if you sell only two hundred copies and you paid an enormous sum to have five hundred printed, ordering the larger quantity was not a good decision.

Sometimes just planning a book is the hardest part of getting started. How many generations will you cover? Who is your intended audience (who will buy your book)? Will you start with an ancestral couple and document all their descendants or work backward up your own direct lines?

The Internet offers a wide range of resources to help in your authoring and publishing venture. Try looking at the PBS television *Ancestors* series lesson, Writing a Family History, at *broadcasting.byu.edu/ancestors/records/familyhistory/intro2.html*. A search of Google for the phrase *"writing family history"* results in 612 hits. Try your own search, and browse some of the resulting Web sites to get ideas and find guidelines for your project.

Most family histories or genealogies are paid for by the author, so decide early in the process how you want to print your book. Talk to several printers and get at least two or three cost estimates. Once you make your choice, work with that printer from the beginning. The printer can help you format your work correctly so that it can be printed directly from your computer disk or from camera-ready copy that you provide. If you're looking for publishers or printers that specialize in family histories or genealogies, go to Cyndi's List—Books category *(www.cyndislist.com/books.htm#Publishers)* for Family History Publishers links. You can also search the Internet using a phrase like *"genealogy book printer"*. These printers will be aware of the importance of acid-free paper to guarantee the longevity of your book. They will also be accustomed to working with genealogists, who often know a lot about history and families, but less about desktop publishing and the printing process.

Organize a Family Reunion

My husband often accuses me of spending more time with my dead relatives than with the living, and there's some truth to his observation. But nothing is more energizing or inspiring to a genealogist than attending a gathering of relatives and sharing old family stories and memorabilia. Family reunions are a great opportunity to find answers to burning questions, such as "Whatever happened to that big framed picture of Grandpa's twin brother, Loy, that used to hang in Great-grandma's house?" "Oh, Cousin Ruby has it! I'll get a copy from her."

Reunions are also a place to connect with your own roots and to feel a sense of belonging that runs deep in everyone, but particularly in genealogists. You'll look around the crowd and see an exaggerated common physical characteristic, or you'll listen to the jokes that define your family's sense of humor. Perhaps you'll hear stories from long ago and learn new details about your ancestor that suddenly make him dance in your mind's eye. You'll even find yourself telling your children or nieces and nephews about grandparents or great-grandparents gone long before they were born.

The next time someone invites you to a family gathering—go. There are always more ancestors to hunt down, but it would be a shame to miss seeing a favorite great-aunt at this year's reunion, especially if she passes on before the next one. If no one starts a family reunion, do it yourself. As a genealogist, you're the one who knows when the family migrated west and where the old farm was located. You can locate the living descendants of that pioneer couple who set out over the mountains back in the mid-1800s and gather them in one location for a good visit. There's even a book to help you—*A Family Affair: How to Plan and Direct the Best Family Reunion Ever*, by Sandra MacLean Clunies, CG, another in this NGS series.

Congratulations! You have become interested in genealogy, and when your family knows this, you will soon become the family historian, a designation you should accept with great pride and honor. In your hands will be all the intimate details of everyone, living and dead. In your care will be the debt of honor that you and your family owe to your ancestors. Whether you publish the family history (leaving out *some* of those intimate details, of course), start a family newsletter, or organize a family reunion, you are hooked on that most personal of pursuits—your family history. Enjoy the experience.

APPENDIX

National Genealogical Society Standards and Guidelines

THE NATIONAL GENEALOGICAL SOCIETY HAS WRITTEN A SERIES OF genealogical standards and guidelines, designed to help you in your family history research. NGS developed these as a concise way to evaluate resources and skills, and to serve as a reminder of the importance of reliable methods of gathering information and sharing it with others.

All of the NGS Standards and Guidelines appear in this book. They also appear online at *www.ngsgenealogy.org/comstandards.htm.*

- Standards for Sound Genealogical Research (page 34)
- Guidelines for Using Records, Repositories, and Libraries (Appendix, page 284)
- Standards for Use of Technology in Genealogical Research (page 25)
- Standards for Sharing Information with Others (page 255)
- Guidelines for Publishing Web Pages on the Internet (Appendix, page 285)
- Guidelines for Genealogical Self-Improvement and Growth (page 276)

283

Guidelines for Using Records, Repositories, and Libraries
Recommended by the National Genealogical Society

Recognizing that how they use unique original records and fragile publications will affect other users, both current and future, family history researchers habitually

- Are courteous to research facility personnel and other researchers, and respect the staff's other daily tasks, not expecting the records custodian to listen to their family histories nor provide constant or immediate attention

- Dress appropriately, converse with others in a low voice, and supervise children appropriately

- Do their homework in advance, know what is available and what they need, and avoid ever asking for "everything" on their ancestors

- Use only designated workspace areas and equipment, like readers and computers intended for patron use; respect off-limits areas; and ask for assistance if needed

- Treat original records at all times with great respect and work with only a few records at a time, recognizing that they are irreplaceable and that each user must help preserve them for future use

- Treat books with care, never forcing their spines, and handle photographs properly, preferably wearing archival gloves

- Never mark, mutilate, rearrange, relocate, or remove from the repository any original, printed, microform, or electronic document or artifact

- Use only procedures prescribed by the repository for noting corrections to any errors or omissions found in published works, never marking the work itself

- Keep note-taking paper or other objects from covering records or books, and avoid placing any pressure upon them, particularly with a pencil or pen

- Use only the method specifically designated for identifying records for duplication, avoiding use of paper clips, adhesive notes, or other means not approved by the facility

- Return volumes and files only to locations designated for that purpose

- Before departure, thank the records custodians for their courtesy in making the materials available

- Follow the rules of the records repository without protest, even if they have changed since a previous visit or differ from those of another facility

Guidelines for Publishing Web Pages on the Internet
Recommended by the National Genealogical Society

Appreciating that publishing information through Internet Web sites and Web pages shares many similarities with print publishing, considerate family historians

- Apply a title identifying both the entire Web site and the particular group of related pages, similar to a book-and-chapter designation, placing it both at the top of each Web browser window using the <TITLE> HTML tag, and in the body of the document, on the opening home or title page, and on any index pages

- Explain the purposes and objectives of their Web sites, placing the explanation near the top of the title page or including a link from that page to a special page about the reason for the site

- Display a footer at the bottom of each Web page that contains the Web site title, page title, author's name, author's contact information, date of last revision, and a copyright statement

- Provide complete contact information, including at a minimum a name and e-mail address, and preferably some means for long-term contact, like a postal address

- Assist visitors by providing on each page navigational links that lead visitors to other important pages on the Web site, or return them to the home page

- Adhere to the NGS "Standards for Sharing Information with Others" (see page 255) regarding copyright, attribution, privacy, and the sharing of sensitive information

- Include unambiguous source citations for the research data provided on the site, and if not complete descriptions, offering full citations upon request

- Label photographic and scanned images within the graphic itself, with fuller explanation if required in text adjacent to the graphic

- Identify transcribed, extracted, or abstracted data as such, and provide appropriate source citations

- Include identifying dates and locations when providing information about specific surnames or individuals

- Respect the rights of others who do not wish information about themselves to be published, referenced, or linked on a Web site

- Provide Web site access to all potential visitors by avoiding enhanced technical capabilities that may not be available to all users, remembering that not all computers are created equal

- Avoid using features that distract from the productive use of the Web site, like ones that reduce legibility, strain the eyes, dazzle the vision, or otherwise detract from the visitor's ability to easily read, study, comprehend, or print the online publication

- Maintain their online publications at frequent intervals, changing the content to keep the information current, the links valid, and the Web site in good working order

- Preserve and archive for future researchers their online publications and communications that have lasting value, using both electronic and paper duplication

Glossary

Abstract: A statement that summarizes the essential facts in a record.

Adoption: The process of legally taking a child of other parents as one's own.

AFIHC: See **American Family Immigration History Center.**

AfriGeneas: A Web site that features numerous articles on African-American genealogy, along with discussion groups and abstracts of records.

Agricultural schedule: A special schedule of the U.S. census that provides details about farms in an enumeration district.

Ahnantafel: A table of one's ancestors in which each ancestor is assigned a unique number.

Alien: A noncitizen.

Allen County Public Library: A library in Fort Wayne, Indiana, with a large genealogical collection.

American Family Immigration History Center (AFIHC): A Web site that provides search capability for the Ellis Island Archives database, which contains more than twenty million records of passengers and crew members who entered the United States through Ellis Island and the Port of New York from 1892 to1924.

Ancestor: A person from whom you are descended.

Ancestor chart: A list or chart of ancestors that may resemble a tree. It begins with an individual, moving upward or backward to two parents, four grandparents, eight great-grandparents, and so on. An ancestor chart (also called a *pedigree chart*) can go from the bottom upward on a page or from left to right.

Ancestor report: A report that includes all known ancestors of an individual—parents, grandparents, great-grandparents, and so on.

Ancestral File: A large collection of lineage-based family tree files submitted by individuals to the Church of Jesus Christ of Latter-day Saints.

Ancestry World Tree: An Ancestry.com project, recently combined with RootsWeb WorldConnect, consisting of family trees submitted by users of these sites.

Ancestry.com: A company and Web site (owned by MyFamily.com) that provides free information and fee-based subscription services for genealogical information.

Annulment: A legal pronouncement that declares a marriage invalid.

Archives: A repository in which records or documents are preserved.

Audio interview: A tape-recorded conversation in which a researcher obtains information from a subject.

Birth certificate: An official record that documents an individual's parents and date and place of birth.

BLM: See Bureau of Land Management.

Boolean logic: A system of combining logical operators (*and, or, not*) between terms when looking for a topic on an Internet search engine.

Bounty land warrant: A document that authorized free land to the holder, given to veterans or their survivors for wartime service through 1855.

Browser: Programs that allow computer users to access and view Web pages, such as Internet Explorer or Netscape Navigator.

Bulletin board: An online community gathering place where users can post a message, respond to someone's request for information, or learn more about a topic; also known as a *message board* or a *forum*.

Bureau of Land Management (BLM): A U.S. government agency that administers America's public lands, including the General Land Office (GLO) federal land conveyance records for the public land states.

Cached link: A snapshot, or saved version, of a Web page as it looked when Google originally indexed the page.

CanadaGenWeb: Nonprofit all-volunteer organization dedicated to assisting researchers in locating Canadian genealogical information available on the Internet.

Case sensitive: If a search distinguishes uppercase (capital) letters from lowercase letters, it is case sensitive.

CD-ROM: Compact Disk Read-Only Memory; a compact disk, used with a computer, that contains a large amount of digital information.

Census: An official enumeration of a population.

Certificate of Citizenship: A document proving citizenship, issued to persons who have been naturalized and become U.S. citizens.

Certified Genealogical Instructor (CGI): An associate of the Board for Certification of Genealogists who presents an integrated series of classes that teach students to begin and continue their own genealogical studies. [Definition from Board for Certification of Genealogists, *The BCG Application Guide* (Washington, D.C.: Board for Certification of Genealogists, 2001), p. 15.]

Certified Genealogical Lecturer (CGL): An associate of the Board for Certification of Genealogists who delivers oral presentations that address genealogical sources, methods, and standards. [Definition from Board for Certification of Genealogists, *The BCG Application Guide* (Washington, D.C.: Board for Certification of Genealogists, 2001), p. 15.]

Certified Genealogical Records Specialist (CGRS): Associates of the Board for Certification of Genealogists who share common research and analytical expertise, demonstrating through their findings and written reports sound knowledge of the records within their specific geographic, ethnic, subject, or time-period areas of interest and experience. [Definition from Board for Certification of Genealogists, *The BCG Application Guide* (Washington, D.C.: Board for Certification of Genealogists, 2001), p. 2.]

Certified Genealogist (CG): Associates of the Board for Certification of Genealogists whose work extends to broadly based genealogical projects whose goal is finding the evidence, assembling the proof, and compiling a coherent historical account of the identities and relationships of *all the descendants* of a particular ancestor or ancestral couple. [Definition from Board for Certification of Genealogists, *The BCG Application Guide* (Washington, D.C.: Board for Certification of Genealogists, 2001), p. 2.]

CG: See **Certified Genealogist.**

CGI: See **Certified Genealogical Instructor.**

CGL: See **Certified Genealogical Lecturer.**

CGRS: See **Certified Genealogical Records Specialist.**

Church of Jesus Christ of Latter-day Saints: A Christian religion, also known as the *Mormon Church* or *LDS*, whose members gather genealogical records from all over the world. These records are available at the LDS Family History Library in Salt Lake City, Utah, and at LDS Family History Centers throughout the world.

Citation: An authoritative source of information.

City directory: A book containing a listing of names, addresses, and other information for residents of a city or county. City or county directories also contain listings for businesses, schools, organizations, cemeteries, hospitals, and newspapers in a classified business section. Some include a crisscross or reverse directory of streets, allowing users to look up an address and determine the resident or business at that address.

Civil registration: The act of officially recording an event, usually a birth, marriage, or death, with a local or state government agency.

Civil War Soldiers and Sailors System (CWSS): An index of some 5.4 million entries of Union and Confederate Civil War soldiers and sailors created by a cooperative effort among the National Parks Service, the Federation of Genealogical Societies, the Genealogical Society of Utah, and numerous other volunteer organizations across the United States.

Collateral line or **collateral relatives:** Persons with an ancestor in common, but who descend from different lines.

Compiled service record: Information extracted from original muster rolls, post returns, medical files, prison registers, and other records that may show a soldier's name, age at enlistment, place of enlistment, place of birth, rank, military organization, term of service, presence or absence on a particular date, or other information.

County directory: See **City directory.**

Crisscross directory: See **City directory.**

Customs: A governmental agency authorized to collect duties or taxes on imported goods or to track the arrival of ships' passengers in the United States.

Customs passenger list: See **Passenger list.**

CWSS: See **Civil War Soldiers and Sailors System.**

Cyndi's List of Genealogy Sites on the Internet: A springboard to more than 150,000 genealogy-related Web sites.

DAR: See **National Society Daughters of the Revolution.**

DAR library: The library of the Daughters of the American Revolution, located in Washington, D.C.

Database: A structured collection of records in an automated form.

Daughters of the American Revolution: See **National Society Daughters of the American Revolution.**

Death certificate: An official record that documents an individual's date and place of death and other details.

Declaration of intent: A document filed with a court of record by a noncitizen in which he or she declares the intent to become a citizen of the United States, also known as *first papers*.

Declination: The variation between magnetic north and true north.

Deed: A document conveying property.

Delayed birth certificate: An official record, filed after the fact, that documents an individual's date and place of birth and parents. Often a delayed birth certificate is filed to verify birth of an individual born before official state registration was required.

Derivative source: Any source that is not original; one in which the information was derived—copied, compiled, abstracted, transcribed, etc.—from another source.

Descendant: A person whose descent can be traced from a particular ancestor.

Descendant chart: A list or chart of descendants that may resemble a tree. It begins with an individual or couple, moving downward to children, grandchildren, great-grandchildren, and so on.

Descendant report: A report that includes information about all descendants of an individual or a couple.

Digital Orthophoto Quadrangle (DOQ) map: A scanned image of an aerial photograph.

Digital Raster Graphic (DRG) map: A scanned image of a U.S. Geological Survey (USGS) standard series topographic map, showing geographic features for an area.

Digitized image: An electronic image represented as binary data, which can be used to create a computerized version of a photo.

Dissolution: Annulment or termination of a legal contract, usually a marriage.

Divorce: The legal dissolution of a marriage.

Dogpile: A metasearch Internet tool that looks within other search engines and provides results from several sources.

DOQ map: See **Digital Orthophoto Quadrangle map.**

Download: Transferring data from one computer to another, usually from a larger mainframe to a personal computer.

DRG map: See **Digital Raster Graphic map.**

Ellis Island database: See **American Family Immigration History Center.**

E-mail: Electronic mail or messages passed from one computer user to another.

Emigration: Leaving one country to settle in another.

Enumeration: A listing or count, as in a census.

Executor: The person designated by a testator to execute, or carry out the terms of, a will.

Extant: Still in existence; not destroyed or lost.

Extract: A portion of information exactly recorded from a document or record.

Family group sheet: A form that contains information such as names, dates, and places of births, marriages, and deaths for a single family—a husband, a wife, and their children.

Family History Centers: LDS genealogy research centers located around the world. Microfilmed records from the Family History Library can be ordered and viewed at any Family History Center.

Family History Library: The largest genealogical library in the world, run by the Church of Jesus Christ of Latter-day Saints (LDS or Mormons) in Salt Lake City, Utah.

Family tree: A chart showing members of a family; it can include ancestors and all collateral lines or only certain branches of a family.

Family Tree of the Jewish People (FTJP): A cooperative project among JewishGen, Inc.; the International Association of Jewish Genealogical Societies (IAJGS); and the Nahum Goldmann Museum of the Jewish Diaspora (Beit Hatefutsot) to disseminate user-contributed family files on CD-ROM, on-site at the Beit Hatefutsot facility in Tel Aviv, and as a searchable database at the JewishGen Web site.

FamilySearch Internet: An Internet service sponsored by the Church of Jesus Christ of Latter-day Saints to help people find and share family history information.

FAQs: Frequently Asked Questions; a document or Web page that provides answers to questions that new readers might ask.

FASG: Fellow of the American Society of Genealogists; membership in this honorary society is limited to fifty life-time members.

Federal land states: States in which lands were disbursed by the U.S. government, rather than by individual states.

Federation of East European Family History Societies (FEEFHS): An umbrella genealogical organization—a society made up of societies—that covers all of Europe (and Russian Asia/Siberia) except England, France, the Benelux countries, the Iberian peninsula, Italy, and Norway.

Federation of Genealogical Societies (FGS): An umbrella organization—a society made up of societies—that serves the needs of member organizations all over the United States.

FEEFHS: See **Federation of East European Family History Societies.**

FGS: See **Federation of Genealogical Societies.**

FHL: See **Family History Library.**

File Transfer Protocol (FTP): A set of formal rules that enables a user on one computer to transfer files to and from another computer over a TCP/IP (Transmission Control Protocol over Internet Protocol) network.

Finding aid: An explanation or document that helps a user locate specific material within a collection or group of records.

First papers: See **Declaration of intent.**

FirstSearch: Online Computer Library Center's reference service, available only through libraries, which accesses databases, electronic collections, online articles, links to the World Wide Web, union lists of periodicals, and many other resources.

FNGS: Fellow, National Genealogical Society.

Forum: See **Bulletin board.**

Freedmen's Bureau: Formally, the Bureau of Refugees, Freedmen, and Abandoned Lands, a federal agency set up at the close of the Civil War to supervise relief efforts in the former Confederate and border states, the District of Columbia, and the Indian Territory.

FTJP: See **Family Tree of the Jewish People.**

FTP: See **File Transfer Protocol.**

FUGA: Fellow, Utah Genealogical Association.

Funeral home records: Business documents from a mortuary relating to an individual's funeral or burial.

Gateway: A process whereby postings to a forum or message board are also sent to that topic's mailing list subscribers and vice versa, by choice of the board admistrator.

Gazetteer: A geographic dictionary listing place names and locations.

GEDCOM: GEnealogical Data COMmunication, a file format that allows users to share genealogical data between genealogy database programs.

GENDEX: A Web site that provides an index to thousands of Internet family tree databases.

Genealogy: The study or investigation of ancestry and family history.

Genealogy database or **genealogy program:** A software program that enables users to enter, save, and export or print genealogical information about individuals and families. Popular programs include Brother's Keeper, Family Tree Maker, Family Origins, PAF, and Reunion.

Genealogy.com: A subsidiary of A&E Television Networks that provides tools, resources, and an online community for genealogists, as well as Family Tree Maker software.

General Land Office (GLO): A government organization within the Bureau of Land Management that maintains and protects the official copies of land patent documents for public lands, some dating from the late 1700s.

GENUKI: A United Kingdom and Ireland Web site that contains a large collection of genealogical information for England, Ireland, Scotland, Wales, the Isle of Man, and the Channel Islands.

Geographic Names Information System (GNIS): A database of information about physical features in the United States identifying the feature type, location, county and state, latitude and longitude, elevation, and USGS topographic map on which it is located.

GLO: See **General Land Office.**

Global Positioning System (GPS) device: A machine that sends and receives signals to and from a system of satellites that orbit the earth in an effort to determine a current position.

GNIS: See **Geographic Names Information System.**

Google: A powerful search engine that helps you find topics, names, images, or other information on the World Wide Web by searching for keywords.

GPS: See **Global Positioning System device.**

Guardian: A person who is legally responsible for a minor or an incompetent person.

Head of household: The head of a family.

HeritageQuest: A company, owned by ProQuest Company, that provides genealogical data, publications, reference books, and periodicals to genealogists.

Hits: Search results.

ILL: Interlibrary loan.

Immigrant Ships Transcribers Guild (ISTG): An all-volunteer group that has transcribed the lists for almost five thousand ships, representing thousands of passengers.

Immigration: Moving to a country of which one is not a native.

Immigration passenger list: See **Passenger list.**

Industry and manufacturing schedule: A special schedule of the census enumerating businesses and industries.

Informant: A person who provides information.

Internet: The World Wide Web.

ISTG: See **Immigrant Ships Transcribers Guild.**

JewishGen: An Internet source with the goal of connecting researchers of Jewish genealogy worldwide.

JPG (or JPEG): A graphics file extension for a compressed storage format developed by the Joint Photographic Experts Group.

Keyword: A word used in an Internet search for finding other words or phrases.

Land deed: See **Deed.**

Land grant: Transfer of land from a government to a private owner.

Land patent: Title for the transfer of land from a government to a private owner.

Land warrant: See **Bounty land warrant.**

LDS: Latter-day Saints; see **Church of Jesus Christ of Latter-day Saints.**

Library of Congress: The largest library in the world, with the mission of making its resources available to the American people and the Congress.

Lineage: One's ancestry or line of descent.

Link: A phrase or graphic with a cross-reference to another Web site.

LISTSERV: An automatic mailing list server.

Lycos: A World Wide Web search engine that indexes phrases from document titles, headings, links, and keywords.

Mailing list: An electronic mail discussion list to which users subscribe online.

Manifest: A list of passengers on a ship.

Manuscript: An original handwritten document, book, diary, etc.

Manuscript collection: A group of original handwritten documents, books, diaries, personal papers, etc.

Marriage bond: A legal affirmation promising payment of a defined sum of money if a reason existed that a legal marriage between a bride and groom could not take place.

Marriage license: A legal document issued by a governmental representative authorizing the marriage of a couple.

Marriage return or **marriage record:** A document that contains information about the marriage of a couple, possibly including their names, the date and place of marriage, and the official who married them.

Message board: See **Bulletin board.**

Metasearch tools: A search engine that looks within other search engines and provide results from several sources.

Metes and bounds: A land survey system where the boundary of a piece of land begins at a designated marker and proceeds from point to point.

Microfilm: A film on which images of printed materials are photographed at a reduced size.

Migration: The movement of a group of people from one area to another.

Miracode: An index for the census similar to the Soundex, but providing county, volume, enumeration district, and the family number assigned by the census taker.

Mormon: See **Church of Jesus Christ of Latter-day Saints.**

Mortality schedule: A special enumeration of the census listing individuals who had died within a certain period.

Mother tongue: One's native language.

MyFamily.com, Inc: An Internet company that includes Ancestry.com, MyFamily.com, FamilyHistory.com, and RootsWeb.com.

NARA: See **National Archives and Records Administration.**

National Archives and Records Administration (NARA): The U.S. governmental agency tasked with preserving the records of government.

National Genealogical Society (NGS): A service organization that leads and educates the national genealogical community.

National Society Daughters of the American Revolution: An organization composed of descendants of Revolutionary Patriots.

National Union Catalog of Manuscript Collections (NUCMC): A searchable database that catalogs manuscript materials in repositories throughout the United States.

Naturalization: The process of becoming a legal citizen of a land other than where you were born.

NGS: See **National Genealogical Society.**

NSDAR: See **National Society Daughters of the American Revolution.**

NUCMC: See **National Union Catalog of Manuscript Collections.**

Obituary: A published death notice that sometimes includes a biography or personal details of the deceased.

OCLC: The Online Computer Library Center; a library cooperative representing libraries around the world, which makes its reference service available through libraries.

OCLC FirstSearch: See **FirstSearch.**

OCLC WorldCat: See **WorldCat.**

Oral history: Historical information obtained from interviews of people with firsthand knowledge, often written down, audiotaped, or videotaped.

Original source: The first or earliest source that presents particular items of information.

Orphan train: A train that carried orphaned children or those whose parents could not care for them in eastern U.S. cities to families in the Midwest or West.

Parent county: An original county contributing land to a newly formed county.

Passenger list: A list of persons arriving by ship in U.S. ports, completed by ship personnel and presented to U.S. Customs.

Patent: See **Land patent.**

Pedigree chart: See **Ancestor chart.**

Pedigree Resource File: A lineage-linked database of family tree files submitted by individuals through FamilySearch Internet.

Pension: Money paid regularly to a recipient, based on disability or service.

Periodical Source Index (PERSI): An index of genealogical and historical periodical articles created and updated regularly by the Allen County Public Library in Fort Wayne, Indiana.

PERSI: See **Periodical Source Index.**

Personal history: See **Oral history.**

Personal papers: Diaries, letters, or other documents of a personal nature.

Petition for citizenship: A document filed by a noncitizen in which he or she requests U.S. citizenship.

Population schedule: The portion of the census that enumerates people and facts about them, such as relationship to head of household, education, marital status, sex, and race.

Primary information: Information provided by someone with knowledge of an event.

Probate: The process of legally establishing the validity of a will or appointing someone to administer the estate of a person who died intestate (without a will).

Public land states: See **Federal land states.**

Query: An inquiry or a search.

Rectangular grid surveys: A land survey system in which public domain (federal land) states are organized along meridians and base lines, and are divided into tracts, townships, and sections.

Regimental history: A report documenting the activities of a military regiment during a given time.

Repository: A place where documents, books, or other items are kept or preserved.

Research log: A document that records sources a researcher has checked and the results of any searches.

Reverse directory: See **City directory.**

RootsWeb.com: The oldest and largest free online community for genealogists, with extensive guides and resources for tracing family histories.

Scanned image: A picture created by using an electronic scanner to digitize the image.

Search engine: A Web site where users enter a query and the search engine scours the Internet to find documents, URLs, or text that contains the search term. Users can then click on any of the links to view the information found.

Secondary information: Information given by someone who doesn't have personal knowledge of an event.

Ship manifest: See **Manifest** or **Passenger list.**

Sibling: An individual's brother or sister.

Slave schedule: A special schedule of the census enumerating slaves in the United States.

Social Security Death Index (SSDI): A searchable database containing information about deceased people who had a Social Security number and may have received Social Security benefits.

Soundex: A coded index based on the way a surname sounds, which groups similar names together regardless of spelling.

Source: A document that supplies information.

Source citation: See **Citation.**

Special Interest Group (SIG): A group of people that meets online or in person to discuss a common interest, such as a Computer Genealogy Special Interest Group.

Special schedule: Census lists beyond the regular population schedules that enumerate special statistics such as mortality, veterans, and slaves.

Springboard: A Web site that provides links to online sources of information about a particular topic. Cyndi's List is a springboard to genealogy sites on the Internet.

State archives: A facility within a state charged with preserving and making available documents relating to the state's government and history.

State land states: States where land was originally controlled and disbursed by the government to the first owners.

Subject line: A brief summary of the topic of an e-mail message.

Subscription service: An agreement, usually for a fee, to receive access to electronic information via the Internet. For example, Genealogy.com and Ancestry.com offer subscription services to their online genealogy databases.

Tax list: A list of taxpayers in an area, often a county, that may include information about land, livestock, slaves, or personal property owned by residents.

TIF: Tagged Image File; a file name extension describing a type of graphic file.

Topographic map: A graphic representation of a place or region that pictures the surface features, their relative positions, and area elevations.

Transcription: An exact handwritten or typed duplication of an entire record, including headings, insertions, notes, capitalization, and cross-outs. "A transcription of the Jones deed will have to suffice; I was not allowed to make a photocopy of it."

Unit history: Description of a particular military unit, usually listing the battles or campaigns in which it was involved.

United States Geological Survey (USGS): A government agency that provides information about the earth and mapping.

Upload: Transferring data from one computer to another, usually from a personal computer to a larger, remote mainframe computer.

URL: Uniform Resource Locator; an Internet address that consists of the access protocol, a domain name, and an optional path to a specific file. An example is *http://www.NGSgenealogy.org/conf.htm*, which uses the access protocol *http*, the domain name *www.NGSgenealogy.org*, and the file *conf.htm*, resulting in a user accessing a Web page of information about NGS conferences. (URLs provided in this book omit the rarely necessary *http://*.)

Usenet: A computer messaging system that transfers messages about a particular thematic group. An example is the soc.genealogy.Hispanic Usenet discussion forum.

USGenWeb: A nonprofit all-volunteer organization dedicated to providing genealogical research Web sites for every county and state in the United States.

USGS: See **United States Geological Survey.**

Veterans schedule: A special 1890 census listing of those who served in the armed forces, providing the branch of service, regiment and company, rank, and dates of service.

Virtual cemetery: A real cemetery that is represented by information on a Web site.

Vital records: Birth, marriage, divorce, and death documents that record these important life events.

Warrant: See **Bounty land warrant.**

Web: See **World Wide Web.**

Wildcard search: Using a symbol in place of one or more characters when searching for a name or term. For example, the wildcard search *Sm*th* would find both *Smith* and *Smyth.*

Works Progress Administration (WPA): An agency of the federal government during the Depression of the 1930s.

World Family Tree: A collection of family trees submitted by individuals and available for sale or by subscription access from FamilyTreeMaker and Genealogy.com.

World Wide Web: A part of the Internet; sometimes used as a synonym for the Internet.

WorldCat: A bibliographic database of the Online Computer Library Center's member libraries, which contains records that describe books, magazines, electronic media, and other items owned by libraries. WorldCat is accessed through OCLC's FirstSearch program.

WorldConnect: A RootsWeb project, recently combined with Ancestry World Tree, consisting of family trees submitted by users of these sites.

WorldGenWeb: A nonprofit organization composed of volunteers who provide free genealogical information on Web sites around the world for specific countries and regions, including country- or county-specific free e-mail lists.

WPA: See **Works Progress Administration.**

Yahoo: An Internet search engine that, based on query terms, looks for Web sites, news stories and photos, audio/video, and the *New York Times.*

Index

National Genealogical Society

. . . . the national society for generations past, present, and future

What Is the National Genealogical Society?

FOUNDED IN 1903, THE NATIONAL GENEALOGICAL SOCIETY IS A dynamic and growing association of individuals and other groups from all over the country—and the world—that share a love of genealogy. Whether you're a beginner, a professional, or somewhere in between, NGS can assist you in your research into the past.

The United States is a rich melting pot of ethnic diversity that includes countless personal histories just waiting to be discovered. NGS can be your portal to this pursuit with its premier annual conference and its ever-growing selection of how-to materials, books and publications, educational offerings, and member services.

NGS has something for everyone—we invite you to join us. Your membership in NGS will help you gain more enjoyment from your hobby or professional pursuits, and will place you within a long-established group of genealogists that came together a hundred years ago to promote excellence in genealogy.

To learn more about the society, visit us online at *www.ngsgenealogy.org.*

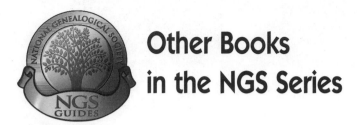

Other Books in the NGS Series

Genealogy 101
How to Trace Your Family's History and Heritage
Barbara Renick

A guide to basic principles of family research, this is a book the uninitiated can understand and the experienced will appreciate.

$19.99
ISBN 1-4016-0019-0

A Family Affair
How to Plan and Direct the Best Family Reunion Ever
Sandra MacLean Clunies, CG

Family reunions can create memories and celebrate a common heritage. Here's how to do it with a minimum of fuss and maximum of good times.

$19.99
ISBN 1-4016-0020-4

Planting Your Family Tree Online
How to Create Your Own Family History Web Site
Cyndi Howells, creator of Cyndi's List

A guide to creating your own family history Web site, sharing information, and meeting others who are part of your family's history and heritage.

$19.99
ISBN 1-4016-0022-0

The Organized Family Historian
How to File, Manage, and Protect Your Genealogical Research and Heirlooms
Ann Carter Fleming, CG, CGL

A guide to the best way to file, label, and catalog the wide variety of material and information related to a family history.

$19.99
ISBN 1-4016-0129-4
Coming Soon

Unlocking Your Genetic History
A Step-by-Step Guide to Discovering Your Family's Medical and Genetic Heritage
Thomas H. Shawker, M.D.

An informative guide to completing a meaningful family health and genetic history. Includes the basics of genetics for the non-scientist.

$19.99
ISBN 1-4016-0144-8
Coming Soon